MW00622850

Praise for
Straight Acting

'A scholarly romp through the rich complexities of Shakespeare's queer life, work and culture. Engrossing, enlightening and hugely entertaining'
Sarah Waters, author of *Fingersmith*

'At once magisterial and saucy, *Straight Acting* gets to the heart of Shakespeare's queer literary formation. Will Tosh writes with clarity and cheek, drawing on forgotten contemporaries, reminding us of the cultural status of ancient Greek texts and their sexual mores, and remapping a homoerotic geography of Elizabethan London . . . This fresh account kickstarts the queer canon of English literature: Shakespeare won't go back in the closet again'
Emma Smith, author of *This is Shakespeare*

'Brilliant – so vivid and so sharp, fantastically clever and consistently fascinating. It will change the way people think about Shakespeare, in rich and valuable ways'
Katherine Rundell, author of *Super-Infinite*

'Will Tosh's tour through the spaces of Shakespeare's childhood, youth and early years as a dramatist is utterly captivating. Marshalling his deep knowledge of the period and of Shakespeare and his contemporaries, he convinces us of the queerness of these times . . . he pushes us to question how a sense of queerness weaves through our present and how it should figure in the ways we think about, stage and represent Shakespeare and his astonishing work now'
Professor Matt Cook, Jonathan Cooper Chair of the History of Sexuality, University of Oxford

'A remarkable work of scholarship. Will Tosh brings Shakespeare's world to life, revealing the queer connections between his life and works in an amusing and accessible manner'
Paul Baker, author of *Camp!*

'As well as a deep analysis of one man's life, *Straight Acting* is a treasure trove of queerness from the Elizabethan era as a whole. I loved it, and it is required reading for anyone who thinks they know Shakespeare'
Sacha Coward, author of *Queer as Folklore*

STRAIGHT
ACTING

THE HIDDEN QUEER LIVES OF
WILLIAM SHAKESPEARE

WILL
TOSH

SEAL PRESS

Copyright © 2024 by Will Tosh

Cover design by Chin-Yee Lai
Cover image © duncan1890 / DigitalVision Vectors via Getty Images
Cover copyright © 2024 by Hachette Book Group, Inc.

Hachette Book Group supports the right to free expression and the value of copyright.
The purpose of copyright is to encourage writers and artists to produce the creative
works that enrich our culture.

The scanning, uploading, and distribution of this book without permission is a theft of
the author's intellectual property. If you would like permission to use material from the book
(other than for review purposes), please contact permissions@hbgusa.com. Thank you for
your support of the author's rights.

Seal Press
Hachette Book Group
1290 Avenue of the Americas, New York, NY 10104
www.sealpress.com
@sealpress

Printed in the United States of America
Originally published in 2024 by Sceptre in Great Britain

First U.S. Edition: September 2024

Published by Seal Press, an imprint of Hachette Book Group, Inc. The Seal Press name and
logo is a registered trademark of the Hachette Book Group.

The Hachette Speakers Bureau provides a wide range of authors for speaking events.
To find out more, go to hachettespeakersbureau.com or email HachetteSpeakers@hbgusa.com.

Seal books may be purchased in bulk for business, educational, or promotional use.
For more information, please contact your local bookseller or the Hachette Book Group
Special Markets Department at special.markets@hbgusa.com.

The publisher is not responsible for websites (or their content) that are not owned by the publisher.

Typeset in Dante by Hewer Text UK Ltd, Edinburgh

Library of Congress Cataloging-in-Publication Data has been applied for.

ISBNs: 9781541602670 (hardcover), 9781541602687 (ebook)

LSC-C

Printing 1, 2024

For Piers

Contents

Prologue

Was He or Wasn't He?

You can buy a pastel wool blanket on Etsy with William Shakespeare's Sonnet 116 engraved on a leather patch. You know the one: 'Let me not to the marriage of true minds / Admit impediments' (116.1–2). You've probably heard it at a church wedding: love is an 'ever-fixed mark' (5), says the sonnet, never bending nor buckling, but holding out 'even to the edge of doom' (12). It's a sweetly delusional sentiment to deliver from the pulpit, and it goes rather well with the bit in the marriage service when the priest demands if the bride or groom 'know any impediment, why ye may not be lawfully joined together in matrimony.' The manufacturer recommends the blanket as an anniversary present.

Lots of people don't know that Sonnet 116 sits in the portion of *Shakespeare's Sonnets* (1609) addressed to a young man. Most of the 154 love poems in his collection have a 'thou' or 'thy' as well as an 'I', and in 126 of them the addressee is, or is implied to be, male. The speaker's desire for the youth is many things – erotic, chivalric, metaphysical, quasi-religious, self-abasing, teasing, sometimes coarse – but perhaps the first thing one notices on flicking through a copy is that the sonnets to the 'fair youth' take up a lot of space. Judged by the quantity of sonnets alone, Shakespeare is one of our most prolific poets of queer love. The twenty-eight sonnets in the sequence that are addressed to a woman aren't often heard at wedding ceremonies, mostly because the caustic verses about the poet's mistress don't make heterosexual love sound like much fun; who'd feel confident ascending the pulpit to read out the opening lines of Sonnet 129, 'Th'expense of spirit in a waste of shame / Is lust in action'? Nowadays, when the cry goes out for a classy poem to dignify the marriage day, the 'fair youth' sonnets are dusted off, de-queered and put to safely straight use (Sonnet 18, 'Shall I compare thee to a summer's day?' That's to him, too).

Such is the destiny of queer literature. And it's not just the sonnets that have suffered un-gaying. How many of us, reading Shakespeare at school, were given the chance to explore the queer relationships of Sebastian and Antonio (*Twelfth Night*), Bassanio and Antonio (*The Merchant of Venice*) or Orlando and 'Ganymede' (*As You Like It*) on their own terms? How often were we encouraged – even allowed – to think about the queer dynamics between Romeo and Mercutio, or Hamlet and Horatio, or Helena and Hermia (*A Midsummer Night's Dream*)? I still go to productions of Shakespeare's plays that seem determined to scrub away any signs of homoeroticism, a bowdlerisation that arises either out of old-school homophobia or a misguided sense that queer readings of classic texts are some sort of modern imposition. When the screenwriter Russell T. Davies added a lesbian kiss between Titania and Hippolyta to his 2016 BBC adaptation of *A Midsummer Night's Dream*, the conservative press took great pleasure in magnifying the social media outrage of viewers who claimed to hear Shakespeare 'turning in his grave'.

But that tut-tutting seems of another innocent age compared to the treatment meted out to Shakespeare in the culture-war-blasted 2020s. The artistic director of Shakespeare's Globe in London, where I work, maintains an inglorious file of correspondence from audience members who are driven to letter-writing by the shocking sex and gender transgressions they see in our theatres: male characters played by women actors, even while other female parts are *also* taken by women; men attired in clothing 'which seemed to be a cross-over from modern *female* fashion', and – worst of all – a presentation of Shakespeare's work in accordance with 'the young people's own sexual preferences' (as one vigilante-moralist put it in response to a production of *As You Like It* in summer 2023). His plays have even fallen foul of Florida's 2022 'Parental Rights in Education Act', the homophobic legislation known as the 'don't say gay' law because it prohibits discussion of sexuality or gender identity in schools. The law makes instantly problematic plays such as *Twelfth Night* and *As You Like It*, with their gender nonconformity and queer desire, but it ensnares stories built around straight desire, too: *Romeo and Juliet* and *Macbeth* must now, fear teachers, be studied only in excerpts, lest students stumble upon sexually explicit material. It seems some gatekeepers can't decide what's worse: all the gay and trans people stomping over plays which were serenely straight before the queers got their hands on them; or the original texts, with their dubious passions and hard-to-fathom identities. In today's addled cultural landscape, Shakespeare's work manages to attract suspicion both for its susceptibility to appropriation by queer theatre-makers, and for being unwholesome in and of itself.

Enough! Enough with the ignorant misrepresentation of Shakespeare's time as an era innocent of queer sexuality. Enough with the homophobic suspicion that queer emotion is unwelcome or inappropriate. Enough with the weirdly self-contradictory stance that enables people to hold both views simultaneously! There is evidently a good deal of confusion and misapprehension surrounding the topic of queer Shakespeare. His queer lives – his own, and those he created for his plays and poems – remain little understood.

Little understood outside of the scholarly community, I should say. In academic circles, one can't move for queer Shakespeareans (of whom I am one). Historians of sexuality, literary critics and queer theorists have transformed the study of Shakespeare over the past half-century, and what follows relies on their work for every chapter – you'll find the foundations in the bibliographic essay at the end of the book. But for a long time, those intrepid and innovative scholars worked in an environment that was hostile to their conclusions. The pioneers of the field began their careers when queer people in the United Kingdom and North America enjoyed no civil rights at all beyond the flimsiest decriminalisation of certain sexual acts. Major leaps forward in queer readings of Shakespeare's work, and in the understanding of early modern sexuality, took place amid the devastation of the HIV/AIDS epidemic in the 1980s and 1990s, and the slow and unfinished progress towards equality (for some queer people in the West) in the first decades of the twenty-first century. Trans scholars who are expanding the subject today understand very well what it means to work in a world that tries to delegitimise their field and deny their experiences (the opponents of queer scholarship in the 1980s haven't gone away; they've just turned their ire on a different community). Queer Shakespeare developed as an intellectual movement at the same time as queer political organisation as a concept was coming of age; little wonder there wasn't an immediate transfer of ideas from the seminar room to the conversation at large. Views like those expressed in the correspondence received by the Globe's artistic director reflect a widespread confusion about the history of sexuality and the place of queer desire in literature and culture. Shakespeare has been made to act straight for centuries; as far as I can establish, this is the first full-length book about Shakespeare's queer world that isn't intended primarily for scholars and university students (although I hope they read it).

That's because the main question on most people's lips has always just been, 'Was he or wasn't he?', and it doesn't take a whole book to say, 'Probably.' But treating Shakespeare's sexuality like some kind of cold case awaiting investigation misses the point. Sodomy between men was technically a capital crime in early modern England (although prosecution was very rare), but same-sex desire was also articulated and sustained by institutions across the land. What we now call queerness wasn't just – or even mostly – a matter of criminal law in Shakespeare's time. As we'll see, questions of identity aren't the be-all and end-all when it comes to uncovering Shakespeare's queer lives. This book reveals Shakespeare the queer artist – one of the greatest artists of same-sex desire in the English language. And, just as importantly, it celebrates a queer Renaissance society that has long been overlooked. In the following chapters, I'll take you on a tour through queer culture as Shakespeare lived it: the Stratford schoolroom where he learned about Roman homoerotic passion while reciting Latin declensions; the bustling London bookstalls where he discovered Greek love between men, and the smoky taverns where he discussed it with his literary friends; the privileged law colleges at the Inns of Court, the chief market for decidedly not-straight erotic verse; and above all, the London playhouses, ground zero for gender nonconformity and queer goings-on. These places – and, more importantly, the people in them – left a deep mark on the way he thought about desire, sex and queer emotion. It's high time we paid attention to Shakespeare's queer lives – not least so we can put straight those who want him to remain an unblemished icon of heterosexuality.

The un-gaying of Shakespeare has a long history. For more than four centuries those passionate sonnets, filled with first-person queer ardour, have put editors and critics on the back foot. As far back as 1640, the publisher John Benson released a rearranged edition of Shakespeare's sonnets with some tactical de-queering: here a pronoun switch, there a transformation of 'sweet boy' to 'sweet love', and the occasional misleading header to create the impression they were more traditionally hetero than they really are. It wasn't a thorough sanitisation, although it set a trend. When Shakespeare's poems were republished in 1711, they were announced as 'One hundred and fifty-four sonnets, all of them in praise of his mistress' – and one assumes the editor had to resist the temptation to underline 'all' and set it in bold capital letters.

The sonnets continued to cause difficulty as Shakespeare assumed his status of national icon in the eighteenth and nineteenth centuries. The poet Samuel Taylor Coleridge couldn't shake the feeling that the sonnets revealed something worrying about his hero's 'disposition', but he consoled himself by thinking 'how impossible it was for Shakespeare not to have been in his heart's heart chaste.' His fellow Romantic Percy Bysshe Shelley likewise insisted that while Shakespeare had hymned the virtues of 'a certain sentimental attachment towards persons of the same sex [. . .] we cannot question [it] was wholly divested of any unworthy alloy.' Other readers found such self-delusion more challenging: 'it is impossible not to wish Shakespeare had never written [the sonnets],' lamented the historian Henry Hallam – whose own son Arthur was to be the subject of Alfred Tennyson's magnificent queer elegy, *In Memoriam* (1850).

For rigid Victorians, the sonnets carried an unmistakeable whiff of unhealthy eroticism, even if critics tried to interpret them according to the terms of sexless manly friendship. Oscar Wilde adored the sonnets precisely because they captured the truth of romantic and sexual passion between men, but his championing of them became a point of contention during his lawsuit for libel against the Marquess of Queensberry, the father of his lover Lord Alfred Douglas. Queensberry's barrister, Edward Carson, confronted Wilde with his short story 'The Portrait of Mr W. H.' (1889), in which Wilde put forward the theory that many of the sonnets were addressed to a beautiful young actor beloved by Shakespeare:

CARSON: I believe you have written an article to show that Shakespeare's sonnets were suggestive of unnatural vice?
WILDE: On the contrary, I have written an article to show that they were not. I objected to such a perversion being put upon Shakespeare.

Wilde hoped to win the suit and prove that Queensberry's description of him as a 'sodomite' was libellous (Queensberry had actually written on a visiting card that Wilde was a 'posing Somdomite' [sic]). Wilde wanted the court to believe that, when he vaunted same-sex love, and used ardent romantic language in his published works and private correspondence, he meant it in the same idealised, non-sexual way that polite Victorian society chose to interpret Shakespeare's sonnets to the young man. But even as Wilde needed the court to see his queer desire as sexless, he wanted to push back against the idea that sex between men was a perversion or 'unnatural vice'. He hoped Shakespeare offered multi-modal protection: to be like Shakespeare meant Wilde was literary and not deviant; but if the court was determined to see deviancy in him, then it had better be prepared to see deviancy in Shakespeare, too – a conclusion that might challenge the very idea of 'natural' or 'unnatural' sexuality.

His approach, for all that it failed to save him from conviction and cruel punishment in the subsequent criminal trial, chimed with campaigning psychological and cultural research. By the 1890s, 'unnatural vice' was being studied in some quarters with more sympathy as 'Uranism' or 'homosexuality' – then a new term – and part of the project of the early pioneers of queer civil rights was the reclamation of people from the past with the same 'condition'. Magnus Hirschfeld, the German sexologist, deplored

Wilde's imprisonment for 'a passion he shares with Socrates, Michelangelo and Shakespeare.' Queer thinkers were beginning to conclude that Shakespeare's plays and poems gave every indication that the man himself had been a homosexual – an identity that now had the dignity of a definition, a historical hinterland, and a glittering list of alumni.

For some, this was a damaging devaluation of Brand Shakespeare. 'Homosexualists have done their utmost to annex Shakespeare and use him as an advertisement of their own peculiarity,' complained the biographer Hesketh Pearson in 1942. Even the queer poet W. H. Auden wrote with disapproval of the attempt 'to secure our Top-Bard as a patron saint of the Homintern' – an imagined international cabal of homosexuals inspired by the Soviet Union's Comintern. This was in 1964, three years before the partial decriminalisation of gay sex between men in the UK, and Auden was being disingenuous; in private, he conceded that the time wasn't right 'just yet' to publicly acknowledge Shakespeare's queerness. But gayness was no guarantee of a fair hearing: the discreetly gay historian A. L. Rowse took care to remind his readers on five occasions in his 1977 account of 'homosexuals in history' that Shakespeare was 'even more than normally heterosexual'.

Most mid-century editors and critics had a powerful attack of coyness when contemplating the idea that Shakespeare might have been queer. The literary critic G. Wilson Knight allowed for the presence of 'homosexual idealism' in his work – by which he meant totally non-carnal homoeroticism – but he insisted that Shakespeare had no thought of physical consummation in the sonnets or in any of the plays' powerful same-sex relationships. Homophobic prudishness has a long half-life. The Riverside collected works, the edition of Shakespeare that sits on my bookshelf, maintained in its revised second edition of 1997 the claim that the sonnets addressed to the young man express 'not at all a sexual passion', unlike the 'frankly lustful' poems about the female addressee. Shakespeare's modern biographers remain on the whole committed to the idea that while there may be a 'hint of homosexual passion' in the sonnets and elsewhere in his work, we mustn't assume that the man himself was more than an occasional non-participatory tourist into the strange terrain of queer desire.

Ironically, the vibrant field of queer theory was partly responsible for allowing straight Shakespeareans to separate him from any association with homosexuality. Late twentieth-century queer scholars began to look again at those categories of sexual identity that had been laid down by nineteenth-century psychologists, and wondered whether 'the homosexual' as a type of person was a legitimate classification when applied to people in past societies. These scholars were inspired by the French cultural theorist Michel Foucault, who argued that the connection between what one does in bed and who one is as a person was a creation of modern psychiatry – and part of the bourgeois urge to classify, control and bring to heel the transformed populations of industrial Europe. Overenthusiastic followers of Foucault took his theories to mean that modern-day same-sex-attracted people didn't have a cultural history that pre-dated the last decades of the nineteenth century. The implication of this shift was stark: theorists were suggesting that what most of us now recognise – and lots of us now celebrate – as an aspect of human-ity was, until the modern age, simply a repertoire of erotic acts that anyone might find themselves performing.

The spread of Foucault's ideas interrupted what had been a buoyant field of gay and lesbian history in which the main endeavour had been to find evidence of homosexual lives in the classical, medieval and early modern pasts. The 1980s and 1990s saw academic civil war break out between scholars who argued that people with recognisable queer identities had always existed, and those who saw sexuality as a product of culture, and post-eighteenth-century culture at that.

Shakespeare was always going to be contested ground. When historians and queer theorists re-examined his world, they found an unfamiliar sexual landscape. Early modern terms denoting queer nonconformity – 'catamite' and 'ingle' for men, 'tribade' for women – weren't precise predecessors for labels of identity such as gay, bisexual or lesbian. Even a seemingly unambiguous word like 'sodomy' glistened with extra meaning: the King James Bible uses 'sodomitess' as a synonym for prostitute. Major works by the British historian Alan Bray and the American critical theorist Eve Kosofsky Sedgwick transformed the study of sexuality in the Renaissance by suggesting that male same-sex desire was a constituent aspect of patriarchy. Early modern English society was certainly virulently homophobic, in that brutal punishments existed for men convicted of sodomy. But it was also a culture in which sex between men, or between men and boys, could be wholly unremarkable: among teachers and pupils at school, masters and servants at home, sex workers and clients on the streets, and in the male-dominated world of the theatre (female homoeroticism wasn't understood to exist in the same institutional contexts). Sedgwick saw these 'homosocial' environments as a vital means by which male power renewed itself; she wrote of 'ideological homosexuality' as a glue that kept hierarchical, misogynist societies like Shakespeare's together. In the developed world today, a potent 'bro' culture in single-sex environments like prisons, the military and boarding schools keeps queer desire constantly within reach but always unacknowledged. We could imagine a similar cognitive dissonance at work in Shakespeare's world: lots of patriarchal sexual domination; not so much gay pride.

Yet there were celebrated aspects of queer desire in Shakespeare's culture. His lifetime saw a rich flowering of homoerotic literature – in which he was an enthusiastic participant. Passionate friendship, based on the model of Roman *amicitia perfecta*, could be expressed in giddily excessive terms of affection. Youngsters were often devoted to their same-sex bedfellows. Some ardently religious men experienced very powerful yearnings for the body of Christ. That these queer articulations were generally held to be non-sexual meant they could be safely championed. But they also provided effective camouflage for intimate relationships that were both emotional *and* sexual.

Historians have described the way queer desire was 'suffused' into early modern culture and society. It's a vivid metaphor for the dispersal of something in such homeopathic quantities that it disappears into the atmosphere. But I don't think it's essentialist to point out that a person's sexual drive doesn't work like that: sexuality doesn't drift through the air like mist from a diffuser. It settles in varying concentrations in each individual, determining – usually for life – their experience of desire and sexual attraction.

More recently, a new generation of scholars has questioned the field's reliance on Foucault, and challenged the Eurocentric assumption that queer identities emerged for the first time in post-Enlightenment societies. Present-day theorists are giving proper attention to the history of gender nonconformity in the West and elsewhere, and treating it as a distinct (although related) aspect of queer identity. This isn't to say that queer lives have always been lived in the same way as today, but that social and cultural changes relate in complex ways to innate human desires and identities. The nineteenth century may have given Westerners a quasi-scientific language of erotic classification, but it didn't invent the fact that some people want to sleep with members of their own sex and others don't. It's possible to trace a line of descent from previous categories or discourses of queer desire to modern models of sexuality and gender identity; today's LGBTQ+ person most definitely has a place in history.

And looking back, we find Shakespeare. The determined efforts since the eighteenth century to deny Shakespeare's queerness say much more about the denigrated place of queer desire in modernity than the openness of Shakespeare's work to queer interpretation. I don't see the need to look for incontrovertible signs that Shakespeare the person was gay or bi, because I don't see anything wrong in taking it for granted that he was a queer artist, working in a culture that both enabled and frustrated his imaginative exploration of same-sex desire. For far too long, the burden of proof has been on scholars and biographers to provide 'evidence' beyond reasonable doubt that esteemed men like Shakespeare were anything other than robustly, swaggeringly heterosexual. Well, I don't accept the terms of a methodology that has homophobic distaste baked into its requirements. Why prove something that is manifestly evident to anyone with the wit to see it? As the poet Don Paterson put it, with just the right degree of irritation, in his commentary on the sonnets: 'The question "was Shakespeare gay?" is so stupid as to be barely worth answering, but for the record: of *course* he was.' I'm going to take Paterson's briskness as my guiding principle in this study of William Shakespeare, a queer artist who drew on his society's complex understanding of same-sex desire to create some of the richest relationships in literature. Shakespeare didn't just leave queer interpretations in his work for us to find. He wrote with a queer voice, informed and inspired by the culture around him: a complex and challenging mix of patriarchy and power, homoeroticism and homophobia. Discovering this world casts bright queer light on relationships in *The Two Gentlemen of Verona*, *The Merchant of Venice*, *A Midsummer Night's Dream*, *Richard II*, *As You Like It*, *Twelfth Night*, the sonnets and more. And it introduces us to a new cast of ancient and early modern writers who served as vital inspirations and mentors for Shakespeare as he learned his craft in the 1580s and 1590s.

Partly out of deference to my training and partly because I think it's the right thing to do, I've chosen to use the word 'queer' throughout this book to mean sexuality that was dissident, unusual, or athwart the erotic mainstream. It wasn't a definition that was available to Shakespeare: the word, although he never used it in print, was current in the sixteenth century in its meaning of 'odd' or 'peculiar', but hadn't yet acquired its more expansive associations to do with sexuality and gender identity. So the term is no less anachronistic than 'gay' or 'lesbian' when applied to Shakespeare's time, but unlike other modern descriptions of sexual identity, 'queer' encapsulates far more than it excludes. As an umbrella term, it embraces identities we'd recognise today as gay, lesbian, bisexual, pansexual and asexual (or ace), as well as gender identities including trans, cis and fluid. Although the focus of *Straight Acting* is on male same-sex desire, I have no way of knowing if the real people I talk about also had queer gender identities, or as what they would identify if they had our terminology. Early modern conceptions of gender difference were quite different to establishment ideas today (and rather closer to frameworks suggested by modern trans thinkers). 'Queer' is a touchstone that helps me remember that the default has never been cis and straight, and although the word has its own history of usage and abusage in the twentieth and twenty-first centuries, over the past forty years it has taken on significant political and intellectual heft. I hope it's now a term that speaks of power and continuity, rather than oppression and interruption, but not everyone will agree with me. To those readers whose own experience makes 'queer' opprobrious, I offer respectful admiration for making it through less enlightened times and ask your forbearance as the word shakes off its unhappy past.

We're about to set off on a journey back to the late sixteenth century. We're leaving behind – for the most part – the centuries of critical heritage that have accrued, barnacle-like, on Shakespeare's vast hull, to explore queer early modern England with fresh eyes. Today's queer artists and readers have interpreted Shakespeare's work in myriad ways that speak to the present and the recent past, but those creative interventions are the subject of another book. I want to describe Shakespeare's queer world as he knew it. And although my story of Shakespeare's queer lives looks a bit like a straight biography, it's not – exactly. We're going to jump over great acres of time and focus our attention on particular places and moments. This isn't an account of a queer existence from cradle to grave, with every one of the major stages in Shakespeare's life and art reduceable to a narrative that centralises his sexuality. *Straight Acting* is the portrait of an artist as a young man, which draws to a close as the Globe Theatre rises on Bankside, in the summer of 1599. Other Shakespeareans are still getting into their stride when they reach that milestone in their books; the great tragedies such as *Hamlet*, *Othello*, *Macbeth* and *King Lear* are just around the corner. But that's queer temporality for you. My book finds most to say about the obscure, poorly documented, much-fought-over period of Shakespeare's life known as the 'lost years': the era before his establishment in 1594 as a key member of the theatre company in which he'd make his name as a dramatist, the Lord Chamberlain's Men. And along the way, this queer quasi-biography gives stage time to the work of other Elizabethan writers who profoundly influenced the way Shakespeare thought about desire, sexuality and homo-eroticism: John Lyly, Christopher Marlowe and the pathbreaking queer sonneteer, Richard Barnfield.

I don't want to test your patience with a book that is too festooned with 'might haves' and 'perhaps' – although God knows it's hard to avoid when writing about Shakespeare's life. Presenting a narrative of Shakespeare's childhood in Stratford-upon-Avon, his relocation to London and his development as a writer and actor in the vibrant theatre industry of the 1580s and 1590s means primping the documentary record with inference and deduction, but never against the grain of probability. An example: I've placed him in the capital in time to witness a performance by the boy players at Paul's Playhouse of John Lyly's *Galatea* (1588), as well as a staging at one of the Shoreditch amphitheatres of Christopher Marlowe's *Edward II* in 1592. It's manifestly clear he knew both of these works intimately, and it's highly likely he saw them live on stage – but there's no paper trail that tells us so, and not every Shakespeare detective reaches the same conclusions about where he was or what he was doing at each stage of his career. More speculative still are the vignettes at the start of each chapter, where I've gone deliberately off-piste with some imagined reconstructions of particular instances in Shakespeare's artistic evolution during those murky, hard-to-decode 'lost years'. I hope that my use of storytelling is understood for what it is: a device to bring Shakespeare's world to life, and to make that world – in all its glorious unfamiliarity – vivid for readers today.

PART I

Learning

Lady Birch

Autumn 1571. Things had changed, and fast. William at seven years old understood that he was expected to become a new and different person. As he sat in the schoolroom listening to his father's steps recede down the stairs, the sequence of transformations he had undergone over the past few months took on, in his mind, a new and consequential character.

First there had been the suit of clothes: the stiff doublet with seemingly numberless pewter buttons that dug painfully into his fingers when he dressed himself in the morning, and the breeches that scratched the insides of his thighs and made him fidget. His legs felt clammy in the thick unfamiliar wool, so different to the skirts he'd known for as long as he could remember. When he'd first put on his new clothes, the household cheered, and told him to stand next to his father, both of them with their hands on their hips like a pair of player kings. William had gloried in that instant, but moments later he had cried, when little Gilbert spun like a top in the orchard with Nurse, his russet skirt flying, and Father stopped him from running to join them. He was breeched now, and shouldn't play with the women and infants.

Then, soon after, his performance at church before the bishop. No more pressing shyly into his mother's side as the family stood in the nave during divine service. In front of the town, William had appeared in his man's clothes and, with a boy's voice, he had recited his duty to God and his neighbours: to love and honour; to obey and submit; to keep his body

in temperance, soberness and chastity. This was his promise to the Lord,
his mother had said as they walked back from Holy Trinity church:
William's confirmation of the vows to God his parents had made on his
behalf at his baptism. He was old enough to reason, she'd said, and
know right from wrong.

Now another promise, and another wrench away from his home on
Henley Street. William had followed his father up the stone staircase of
the guildhall into a cavernous upper room. This time, the authority to
which he pledged was the King's New School of Stratford-upon-Avon,
his pledge to obey the master sealed with fourpence handed over by his
father and the inscription of William's name in the register. Then, all in
a rush, his father was gone. William perched on the edge of a bench with
the smallest pupils and looked warily around the room. A parliament of
boys, some known to him, some unfamiliar. Suddenly, William was
conscious of the smell of forty boys' bodies and the greasy leather of
forty satchels and a sharp top note of ink, spilling from forty inkhorns.
He was aware of the noise, too, the overlapping murmur of recited
Latin diphthongs and hard-edged consonants that meant nothing to
him, conducted by the master from a seat that seemed a species of rustic
throne. Gowned and capped and armed with the symbol of his craft –
the stinging bundle of birch sticks – the Stratford schoolmaster had the
duty of beating into William a classical education, ten hours a day, six
days a week, forty-four weeks a year, for the rest of his childhood.

We're starting the story of William Shakespeare's queer life with
the ceremonies and processes that were designed to turn him
into a 'proper' Englishman. His breeching, confirmation and
enrolment at grammar school – rites of passage that happened
within a year of one another in about 1571 – formed a three-act
coming-of-age drama in which he left infancy and entered
boyhood. But it was a coming-of-gender drama too: William
had boy-ness draped over him when he was given his first set of
breeches, the doctrinal superiority of men drummed into him

through his catechism, and masculine privilege handed to him by means of the rigorous education he received at school. William's engendering was a multistage project with shifting definitions of success; on the basis of his own experiences, eight-year-old William would have given a profoundly different answer to the question 'What is a boy?' than his six-year-old self.

William's family and neighbours, if they'd had our language and frames of reference, would have hotly denied there was anything queer about the boy's upbringing. Quite the opposite: his parents, John and Mary Shakespeare, a successful leatherworking glove-maker and his wife in the Midlands town of Stratford-upon-Avon, were doing everything they could to guarantee their son developed into a righteous, God-fearing man by making sure his gender emerged in the 'right' way. The Shakespeares understood that they had a role to play in this process, as William himself would have a lifelong duty to maintain the behaviour and mentality that identified him as a man. An awareness of the contingency of sex and gender was part of received wisdom in early modern England, and no one expected William's masculinity to bud and flower in a state of nature. It was seeded and trained by the grown-ups around him. The pernicious expression 'boys will be boys' would have had little meaning had it been current in the 1570s (it wasn't). Boys – and girls – didn't just *happen*. They were made.

Scripture taught that God had given males superior strength, intellect and imagination, and men were quick to acknowledge their right to 'compel [women] to obey by reason or force'. But anatomical theory was much less clear about the absolute distinctions between men and women. If John and Mary Shakespeare ever summoned up the courage to ask the local clergyman for an explanation of the differences between their bodies, they would probably have heard a version of physiology inherited from the second-century CE Greek physician Galen, and relayed in medical textbooks such as Thomas Elyot's much-republished *Castle of Health* (1539). Galenic medicine held that all bodies (indeed, all earthly matter) were composed of the four elements of air, fire, earth and water. Each element was associated with particular qualities of heat and moisture, and found expression in living bodies in the form of fluids, each essential to life: blood, yellow bile, black bile and phlegm. An imbalance of the fluids or 'humours' resulted in disease, or a person who was too sanguine (full of hot, wet blood), choleric (too much hot, dry yellow bile), melancholic (excessive cold, dry black bile) or phlegmatic (an overproduction of cold, wet phlegm).

Humoral balance was also said to explain the differences between male and female bodies. Men were understood to be generally hotter and drier than cooler, wetter women. Male bodily heat resulted in a finished and 'perfect' physical form that more closely resembled God's, with genitals driven outside the body by the unstoppable fire of the masculine constitution. A woman's genitalia and organs of reproduction could be imagined as a male penis and testicles turned inside out and stuck inside, languishing in the damp stasis of a less fiery feminine body (the implication of this understanding of infant gestation was that all human bodies *in utero* started out as female).

Galenic theories of sexual difference incorporated the seemingly contradictory notions that males and females were physically distinct, yet also versions of the same divinely ordained model. It's an open question how far most early modern women, with their lived experiences of menstruation, pregnancy, childbirth and menopause, adhered to the idea that their bodies were simply less finished versions of men's. But few denied that a person's humoral constitution was subject to change, and indeed did alter according to age, location, environment and health. Youngsters were proportionately hotter and wetter, and old folk cold and dry; white Europeans reached for humoral theory to explain the range of skin tones and hair texture found in people of different ethnicities or climates of origin. While sexual difference appeared to be a done deal to the parents of Stratford-upon-Avon, the very stuff of that difference – the humoral soup that made up every living being – was disarmingly fluid. Galenic medicine allowed for the possibility that people could change sex spontaneously throughout their lives; it was partly through maintaining appropriate habits of behaviour, lifestyle and health that women and men kept their bodies in the categories determined for them. John and Mary Shakespeare knew that God had made William physically male, as far as they could make out; it was their job to ensure that their son became – and remained – a boy and then a man.

Seven was a major birthday for William. If his family were like other households of middling means in the sixteenth century, they would have marked his 'breeching' – his adoption of male clothing and rejection of the skirts that all children wore during infancy – with ceremony and celebration. It was the point at which William left the world of young childhood, dominated by female caregivers like his mother and nurse, and entered a much more sex-segregated period of his life – the 'second degree of age', as one early modern parenting manual put it. No comparable ceremony existed for daughters. Girls continued in the female spheres of housekeeping and sibling-rearing, taking on greater responsibility with each passing year.

William's parents had reason to be thankful that he had passed the most perilous years of infancy. One quarter of English children died before the age of ten, most of them as newborns or babies. Mary and John had lost two baby daughters; William was their first surviving child. (The grown-up Shakespeare would learn in the most painful way possible that not every boy who made it into breeches was set fair for adulthood: his own son Hamnet died aged eleven, in August 1596.) The significant outlay on tailor-made clothes for a growing seven-year-old – breeches cost a good three shillings a pair – celebrated survival as well as the first stage in his acquisition of masculine exceptionalism. Perhaps a memory of the excitement of his new wardrobe lingered in lines Shakespeare later gave to Juliet, who interprets her hungry anticipation for her new husband Romeo as the thrill of 'an impatient child that hath new robes / And may not wear them' (3.2.30–31).

Breeching didn't just signify the confirmation of a gender assigned at birth. It indicated the point at which a boy's masculinity started to count in society at large. Seven-year-old William was marked as different to – better than – his younger brother Gilbert (still in skirts at four and a half) and little sisters Joan (just two) and newborn Anne (William's youngest brothers, Richard and Edmund, followed in later years). But the transition could entail painful loss, too: of security, comfort, motherly attention. In *The Winter's Tale*, the king Leontes – in the early stages of a manic sexual jealousy – looks on his small son Mamillius and thinks with a kind of elegiac self-pity about his own far-off days as an 'unbreeched' child (1.2.155), carefree and protected from the ravages of maturity. (In due course, the suspicious Leontes will rip Mamillius from his mother's care, a traumatic premature 'breeching' that leads to the boy's decline and death.)

Alongside William's newly visible masculinity came spiritual recognition. Boys and girls in the Church of England were confirmed, and received their First Communion, at seven – the age at which theologians believed children could understand the basics of religious doctrine. Whatever William's parents' inward confessional beliefs (it's been said that John was less keen on the new Protestant faith and cleaved to the older Catholic ways for many years), it would have been very difficult for them to keep their son separate from the key developmental phases of a Reformed upbringing. Stratford-upon-Avon's children had to show that they could recite the Ten Commandments, the Lord's Prayer and the Apostles' Creed in a public performance of faith preceded by basic training in reading and writing at the 'petty school' attached to Holy Trinity. It was a significant occasion for families with young children: the visiting Bishop of Worcester took each child – the boys awkward in newly acquired breeches – through a set of predetermined questions to establish their comprehension of Protestant belief and their awareness of the values of obedience, humility and reverence for authority. But if it was important for all children to 'order [themselves] lowly and reverently to all [their] betters', it was also necessary that boys in particular understood their destiny as 'God's priests in their own house', future patriarchs responsible for the spiritual rectitude of wife, children and servants. William's ongoing religious instruction was designed to create a generation of Protestant Englishmen sure of their superiority over inferiors, and fully aware of the scriptural precedent for male supremacy over women.

The culmination of William's entry into the 'second degree of age' – and the most significant aspect of his engendering as a middle-class male – was his admission to the town grammar school soon after his seventh birthday. This wasn't an experience shared by all boys of his age, only those of middling or wealthy backgrounds, and nor was school an institution much understood by William's parents; his father had risen in the world without the benefit of a secondary education. But it was the King's New School in Stratford-upon-Avon that, to all intents and purposes, managed William's journey through boyhood into adolescence and beyond, and it was school that planted in his imagination the 'senses, affections, passions' (*The Merchant of Venice*, 3.1.60) that would guide his life and writing. His academic inheritance came at a cost, however. The savage corporal punishment that suffused Elizabethan schoolrooms had its own traumatic effect on the bodies and psychologies of William and his schoolfellows, and established associations in these young minds between gender, power and sexuality that were to have lifelong consequences.

Registers for the Stratford grammar school don't survive from the mid-sixteenth century, but there's no question that William attended: as the son of a prosperous town alderman, he was entitled by right to an education, and his plays and poems are drenched in the language of its syllabus. Ben Jonson's assessment that his friend possessed 'small Latin and less Greek' has sometimes been taken to mean that William's schooling was truncated or patchy. But Jonson made use of any opportunity to note the depth of his own learning and the ignorance of others, and if William had even a little ancient Greek it means he'd made it to the most senior forms; almost certainly he remained at school until he was about fifteen, when his father's finances took a plunge and he was forced to withdraw from the town council. Assuming he started at seven, that's a lot of years spent in a cauldron of male privilege, which bubbled with ingredients to nourish future patriarchal power: an exclusive same-sex environment; a syllabus devoid of female authors and for the most part uninterested in women's lives; and teaching wholly devoted to the boys' acquisition of Latin, a living language of trade, law, religion and scholarship that denoted male authority and knowledge. Most crucially, it was at school that William was first introduced to the bedrock Latin texts of Renaissance humanism, such as Cicero's *De amicitia* and Ovid's *Metamorphoses*, an intoxicatingly ardent celebration of intense male friendship, and a treasure trove of queerly adventurous desire. On the one hand, William's education was designed to turn him into a conformist servant of the Tudor state, destined for a career in trade, law or the Church. But on the other, it was his gateway to a classical cultural inheritance that was rooted in a wholly unfamiliar approach to same-sex relationships, gender identity and sexuality.

Let's begin, then, with school as William experienced it in 1570s Stratford-upon-Avon.

By the last quarter of the sixteenth century, England's grammar schools had been brought under a nationwide system that prescribed staff, syllabi and timetables. Not all school leavers became clerics and lawyers, but the expansion of the school system after the Reformation was intended to educate a new class of English officials fit for the administration of the Protestant state. The Stratford schoolmaster's job was, therefore, to instil 'godly learning and wisdom' in his charges through instruction in the 'accidence and principles of grammar', by which was meant the grammar of ancient languages – most importantly Latin, with a smattering of Greek and Hebrew as well. The focus on Latin was relentless. The aim of William's teachers was nothing less than the replacement of their pupils' mother tongue (the gendering of that phrase is significant) with a new language accessible only to other boys and men of their own class. Studious schoolboys like William didn't just learn to read Latin. They spoke it, wrote it, debated in it, structured their arguments with it, thought in it.

The journey towards fluency took over William's life. First, daily prayers in the chapel next to the school at six in the morning. Then, up to the classroom, shuffling into place with satchel and schoolbooks and pens and inkhorn. Standing up to greet the master on his arrival at seven. Lessons until nine (pause for fifteen minutes to devour second breakfast brought from home). Lessons until eleven (run back to Henley Street for dinner). Lessons until three (pause again for another snack or a dash to the privy). Lessons until five o'clock in the afternoon. Then, home, with declensions or lines of verse to be learned by heart for the next day's classes. With terms structured around short breaks at Christmas, Easter and Whitsuntide, but no long summer vacation, William received about 2,000 hours of teaching per year, roughly double that of a pupil at school in most countries today. Almost all of that time was spent in learning to read, write and speak Latin.

The painstaking tedium must have been awesome. William's textbook was *A Short Introduction of Grammar* by William Lily, 200 pages long and filled with tiny, crabbed type that laid out the building blocks of Latin: the nouns, pronouns, adjectives, verbs and adverbs, with their changeable inflections and their slippery way of conjugating out of all recognition. Bit by bit, William and his schoolmates chipped their way through Lily, led by a young scholar fresh from a fellowship at St John's College, Oxford, Thomas Jenkins, who probably joined the school as a teaching assistant (or usher) in charge of the junior forms before becoming master proper in William's third year. The technique was recitation, memorisation and interrogation, a 'continual rehearsal of things learned' as Lily put it, until the total contents of the *Grammar* was lodged in the boys' brains. By the age of ten or eleven, William and his friends had worked their way through the textbook, only to begin again with a memorised portion recited anew each morning. A well-drilled form of boys could expect to parrot the entirety of Lily's *Grammar* every three months. The method worked, but even experts acknowledged it was grindingly boring. Roger Ascham, Queen Elizabeth's tutor and a leading writer on education, thought that rote-learning was 'tedious to the master, hard for the scholar, cold and uncomfortable for them both.'

Before long, William started translating classical authors into English, beginning with easy texts like *Aesop's Fables*, before moving on to more substantial writers. Soon came composition in Latin, first by retranslating texts already rendered into English, and then in making up his own material: little phrases at first, then half a dozen lines of poetry, then a whole letter or entire

speech. The set texts he still had to memorise daily were ripe
with stately words for harvesting in his commonplace book, the
personal journal kept by all literate people for jotting down 'wise
saws and modern instances', in the words of *As You Like It*'s Jaques
(2.7.156). The classroom prohibitions on spoken English – boys
above the second form had to speak Latin to each other during
lessons, on pain of a beating – gave him plenty of opportunities
to practise. As he entered adolescence, with 10,000 hours of Latin
tuition behind him, his intellect and creative vocabulary had been
transformed. Warwickshire William was now a different person
compared to the child who had commenced his education five or
so years previously: he was a Latinate scholar filled to the brim
with learned aphorisms who answered to the name of Gulielmus.

A reformation like this was an arduous process, and resistance
from bewildered pupils was met with force. William's education
pulled him from the familiar world of home and family, and the
language he had spoken from his earliest years, and fixed his attention on the dim classical past, initially glimpsed in only the most
fragmented way through the dog-eared pages of Lily's *Grammar*.
William was told that the ancients were the source of practically
all human knowledge in philosophy, law, medicine, botany,
alchemy, geography and military tactics, as well as the founding
experts in the arts of history, poetry, music and architecture, but
this golden inheritance felt a long way off to the little boy trying
to remember *amo, amas, amat*. William would have thought with
longing of the easy way he had learned his English ABC at the
petty school, sounding out the letters until he could stutter
through the first line of the Lord's Prayer (in *Othello*, Desdemona
reflects that '[t]hose that do teach young babes / Do it with gentle
means and easy tasks' (4.2.111–12)). In his early years at school,
William was severed from home life, and silenced by the abrupt
mothballing of his birth language. When Thomas Mowbray is
banished in *Richard II*, he imagines the remainder of his life spent

as a monoglot exile, his native English rendered useless by this
sudden twist of fate. His tongue, says Mowbray, is 'like a cunning
instrument cased up' (1.3.163), a vivid metaphor for frustrated
eloquence that might suggest the feelings of a chatty, wordy child
flung suddenly into a world of alien scholasticism.

But mastery of Latin came in time. And with it, the jewels of
the classical canon: the comedies of Terence; the odes, satires
and epistles of Horace; Roman political history; Virgil's *Aeneid*.
William's Latinity gave him his first taste of literary drama, as
boys in his class performed speeches from classical myth – the
only opportunity his education afforded him to imaginatively
engage with women's experiences, albeit such heightened life
events as Queen Dido's abandonment by the Trojan refugee
Aeneas. William's reading also featured modern authors from
Italy and France who wrote worthy books in Latin, and numerous works by the celebrated Dutch humanist thinker and theologian Desiderius Erasmus. A good deal of the history, philosophy
and religion that William read as a young boy was work of irre-
proachable rectitude, a headily stern brew of antique Stoicism
and Christian fundamentalism. But there were two crucial
sources of queer inspiration that occupied central spots on the
grammar school syllabus, and planted in William's mind a lifelong fascination with homoerotic same-sex relationships. Cicero's
De amicitia gave him a language to express the devotion a man
felt for his soulmate; Ovid's *Metamorphoses* inspired him with a
vision of powerfully transgressive sexuality that obsessed,
aroused and disturbed readers in Elizabethan England.

Marcus Tullius Cicero ('Tully' to early modern readers), a first-
century BCE Roman lawyer, politician and philosopher, provided
for people in the Renaissance a full-service guide to life, both
public and private. In his letters to friends and family, he set out
his theories on state service and politics; and in a series of treatises

written in his last years, he addressed the ethical questions that seemed to him most pressing as a man of affairs. Schoolboys were encouraged to see Cicero's literary style and vocabulary as gold standards, and teachers had the reassurance of knowing that the moral lessons being absorbed were precisely those a young Englishman would need (despite Cicero's unfortunate status as a pre-Christian pagan).

Few works of Cicero's – few texts of the classical era – were as familiar to pupils and general readers as his *De amicitia* ('On Friendship'), a guide to the passionate intimacies between elite men that, for ancient Romans, and male Elizabethans, represented the apogee of human relationships. Framed as a dialogue between figures from Rome's republican past, but overtly intended to represent Cicero's own feelings for the institution of friendship and for his dearest friend Titus Pomponius (known as Atticus for his love of all things Greek), *De amicitia* explained that an exclusive friendship between virtuous and elite men was a bond that should be placed 'above all other human concerns'. Such relationships weren't common, but when they blossomed, they brought into flower harmony of opinion 'about all things divine and human', not to mention surpassing affection and undying love. Apart from wisdom, wrote Cicero, 'I am inclined to believe that the immortal gods have given nothing better to humanity than friendship.' A friendship like Cicero's and Atticus's represented a far nobler bond than mere family ties, which could trudge on in sordid perpetuity even once goodwill and warmth had long gone. Friendship lived purely on love, and while it flourished, a friend was 'quite simply, another self'.

William was left in no doubt that the education he and his classmates were receiving was intended to fit them for the sort of intense affair described in *De amicitia*. Looking around the classroom, he might have pondered which of the forty boys was destined to play Atticus to his Cicero, but the treatise made it clear that such intimacy was for adults only: 'As a general rule we shouldn't commit to friendships until we've reached an age when our character and way of living are established and confirmed.' Young adulthood posed other problems, of course – 'rivalry for the same woman or for some advantage that both men can't have' waited like a snare for the unwary or the naïve.

These principles rooted themselves deeply in William's imagination, as they did in the imaginations of many boys who underwent a Renaissance education. Society offered few acceptable recipients for the powerful feelings of youth and adolescence, and those on offer tended to be abstractions rather than tangible subjects (God, England, the monarch). The people in a young man's life were lacquered with a sort of pious sealant: parents were obeyed and respected rather than adored; it wasn't expected that any man should lose his head over a wife. Ciceronian 'perfect friendship' was one of the only worldly relationships into which a man was allowed – even encouraged – to enter with abandon. During the many hours that William spent in school, he was given to understand that the most important emotional experience he would ever have would be with another man. Idealised same-sex relationships – *amicitia perfecta* inherited from classical Rome – were the model for life.

The legacy of that lesson was a rich vein of dramatic conflict. Like many writers of the time, William was to become fascinated by the apparent opposition between the ideals of the male friendship he was taught to worship, and the competing fantasies of heteroerotic courtship that culminated in marriage. Throughout his career, he explored the consequences of turbo-charged Ciceronian friendship butting up against straight seduction – two forms of romance that didn't always occupy the same air with ease and goodwill. In *The Two Gentlemen of Verona* (*c.*1588), perhaps Shakespeare's earliest play, the friends Valentine and Proteus fudge their way through their first affairs with women while toting the baggage of their longer-standing relationship with each other: 'Forgive me that I do not dream on thee,' says Valentine to Proteus, '[b]ecause thou seest me dote upon my love' (2.4.172–73). Proteus – deterministically named to suggest fickle changeability – regards his wavering loyalty towards his friend as a consequence of his burgeoning heteroerotic attraction to Silvia, the woman whom Valentine loves:

> Methinks my zeal to Valentine is cold,
> And that I love him not as I was wont;
> O, but I love his lady too too much,
> And that's the reason I love him so little. (2.4.203–6)

The awesome potency of male friendship explains the play's squalid and unsatisfactory denouement. Having fallen victim to Proteus's plan to separate her from Valentine, Silvia finds herself undefended and vulnerable in the forest. Meanwhile, Julia, Proteus's first and now discarded love, has attached herself to his service, disguised as a page called Sebastian. Proteus and Silvia meet, attended by Julia / Sebastian and watched, unseen, by Valentine. As Silvia reminds Proteus of his duties both to Julia and Valentine, the unrepentant Proteus ('In love / Who respects friend?' (5.4.53–54)) tries to rape her, before Valentine prevents the assault and denounces his friend in terms that lock the attempted rape of Silvia entirely into the related outrage of faithless friendship:

> Thou common friend, that's without faith or love,
> For such is a friend now! Treacherous man,
> Thou hast beguiled my hopes! Nought but mine eye
> Could have persuaded me; now I dare not say
> I have one friend alive; thou wouldst disprove me.
> Who should be trusted, when one's right hand
> Is perjured to the bosom? (5.4.62–68)

Valentine's invocation of abused male friendship effects a magic-
ally swift reformation in Proteus, who immediately admits
wrongdoing and apologises (to Valentine, not Silvia). The effect
on Valentine is equally miraculous: 'Then I am paid' (77), says
Valentine, generously handing over his hard-won interest in Silvia
to the would-be rapist as a token of their renewed friendship.
The revelation that the disguised Sebastian is in fact Julia prevents
the swap, as Julia and Proteus get back together and Silvia is
handed back to Valentine (Silvia says not a word after her scream
of fear at Proteus's approach). In the context of the women's
experience of exile, disguise, kidnap, attempted rape and peremp-
tory exchange, Valentine's closing line celebrating his and
Proteus's double wedding as '[o]ne feast, one house, one mutual
happiness' (173) sounds decidedly off-key.

If, as Cicero argued, a friend is 'another self', what does a man
do with those human assets – usually female – which are not
otherwise regarded as fungible? *The Two Gentlemen of Verona* was
Shakespeare's first attempt at an answer, but other writers had
addressed the topic of a woman passed as shared property
between 'faithful friends'. Shakespeare would have known the
story of Titus and Gisippus, related by the polymathic writer
Thomas Elyot as a 'right goodly example of friendship' in *The
Book Named the Governor* (1531): after Gisippus lets Titus sleep
with his wife, Sophronia, Titus returns the favour by offering to
take his place on the scaffold when Gisippus is accused of murder.
Both men vividly demonstrate the sense of shared masculine
embodiment – their 'confederated' selves, as Elyot puts it – that
the friendship grants them, in which life and wife are both held in
common (the feelings of the wife, naturally, aren't considered).

Shakespeare's later plays suggest that he wasn't satisfied with
the trafficking of silent women between male friends that he'd
read about in *The Book Named the Governor* and staged in *The Two
Gentlemen of Verona*, and nor was he finished unpicking the

threads of romance that might be shared out amongst three-
somes or foursomes of men and women, arranged in complementary and sometimes overlapping duos of friends and lovers.
In *The Merchant of Venice* (c.1596), Bassanio finds his loyalty
divided between Antonio, entangled in a messy financial bond in
which he stands to lose his life, and the fabulously wealthy
Portia, whose hand in marriage he has just won through an
implausible game of Guess the Casket. Facing a court of law
whose ruling will decide Antonio's fate, Bassanio makes it clear
that marriage and male friendship occupy adjacent spaces in his
soul – and his friendship with Antonio takes precedence in the
face of Shylock's bond:

> Antonio, I am married to a wife
> Which is as dear to me as life itself,
> But life itself, my wife, and all the world,
> Are not with me esteemed above thy life.
> I would lose all, ay, sacrifice them all
> Here to this devil, to deliver you. (4.1.282–87)

But unlike the silenced Silvia in *The Two Gentlemen of Verona*,
Portia – disguised as the lawyer Balthazar – is allowed to object:
'Your wife would give you little thanks for that / If she were by
to hear you make the offer' (288–89), she observes. The play ends
with an unexpected ménage of Bassanio, Portia and Antonio
(liberated from the bond and richly rewarded) ensconced at
Belmont, Portia's ancestral pile: the threesome is ritually enacted
as Antonio, apparent competitor for Bassanio's affections,
transfers Portia's ring (over which there has been much confected
fuss) to Bassanio, promising to stand 'surety' (5.1.254) for the
union of wife and husband. The Belmont throuple – reinforced
by Portia and Antonio's staggering wealth and Bassanio's
irresistible lovability (he brings nothing but his charm) – is a

capacious solution to the problem represented by an improvident
but wildly attractive man adored by both a rich merchant and a
landed heiress.

Not all of Shakespeare's romances end in a three-way, and he
was fascinated by the feelings of the unfulfilled third wheel – the
low-key queer best friend whose desire for the hero is discernible
at moments of particular extremity or tension. In *Romeo and Juliet*
(*c.*1595), Mercutio leverages his position as the Prince's kinsman
to remain aloof from the warfare between Montague and Capulet
(part of the youthful Montague set, he is nonetheless invited to
the Capulet feast). He also takes advantage of his role as Romeo's
intimate friend to involve himself as an active commentator on
the latter's sex life, a prurience that takes the form of repeated
invocations of Romeo's genitals and potency: Mercutio's
interpretation of the 'confederated' selfhood of Ciceronian
friendship is a proprietorial concern with his friend's penis. His
suggested cure for Romeo's frustrated desire for his initial,
unattainable lover Rosaline is a vigorous bout of masturbation:
'If love be rough with you, be rough with love; / Prick love for
pricking, and you beat love down' (1.4.272–8). At Benvolio's
objection to his raising a hue and cry for Romeo after the Capulet
ball, when they mistakenly assume Romeo is suffering the
languishing effects of excessive sex with Rosaline, Mercutio
explains that his loutish bellowing is designed to reinvigorate
Romeo and 'raise up him' (2.1.29). When he muses on Romeo's
taste for anal sex, it's a moot point whether he is imagining the
practice as a heterosexual pastime or his own queer fantasy:

> Now will he sit under a medlar tree
> And wish his mistress were that kind of fruit
> As maids call medlars when they laugh alone.
> O Romeo, that she were, O that she were
> An open-arse and thou a poperin pear! (2.1.34–38)

Mercutio's ambivalent grasp on his own sexual fascination with his friend might explain why he flies off the handle so spectacularly in Act 3. Mercutio is the first character to brandish a weapon in the confrontation between Tybalt (a Capulet) and the Montague boys that will culminate in the tragic deaths of both Tybalt and Mercutio. Tybalt's insinuating accusation that Mercutio 'consorts' with Romeo sets him off:

> Consort! What, dost thou make us minstrels? An [i.e., if] thou make minstrels of us, look to hear nothing but discords: here's my fiddlestick; here's that shall make you dance. 'Zounds, consort! (3.1.46–49)

Mercutio hears the sexual implication in Tybalt's charge (the verb 'to consort' meant, among other things, 'to have sex') and comes back with a riposte that draws on the word's simultaneous musical meaning to threaten him with both stabbing and sexual violence. In this multilayered provocation, Mercutio's 'fiddlestick' is collectively a musical device, his sword and his phallus.

Ciceronian *amicitia perfecta* had a complex relationship with queer sex. The philosophy of friendship said it was an entirely chaste affair; the reality of life – in which amity, romance, sexual desire and jealousy intermingled – argued otherwise. Shakespeare came to understand the points of provocative and dramatic overlap between *amicitia* and Eros, but it was another Roman schoolbook that stimulated him to think well outside the box when it came to sexual unions. *Metamorphoses* by Publius Ovidius Naso (or Ovid) has a strong claim to being Shakespeare's favourite work, surfacing throughout his career as a narrative source, a spring of thematic inspiration, and a treasure trove of verbal echoes – particularly in the monumental English translation by Arthur Golding, published in 1567 and one of the very few literary texts in English that found a home in the Elizabethan schoolroom. Like Cicero, Ovid lived during the turbulent first century BCE, and his *Metamorphoses* offered a swirling history of the world from its creation to the assassination of Julius Caesar – which had taken place the year before Ovid's birth. 'History' suggests something analytical and scholarly, but *Metamorphoses* was anything but. In fifteen books, Ovid provided a compendium of mythological stories that furnished western Europe with a more or less complete account of the doings of the classical gods and their human co-stars. His main purpose was to show the constantly evolving state of the world, encapsulated in acts of dramatic transformation wrought upon mortals by the gods in moments of overwhelming lust, envy or rage. Central to his vision was the notion – reassuring and disturbing by turns – that a person's soul remained unchanged through the process of metamorphosis: when the huntsman Actaeon is turned into a stag by an outraged Diana, whom he had glimpsed bathing in the woods, his man's mind persists to experience the full horror of death at the jaws of his own dogs, who '[w]ith greedy teeth and griping paws their lord in pieces drag.'

Ovid's tales were a powerful challenge to the regimes of gender conformity and sexual chastity preached by William's church and society. In *Metamorphoses*, it's usually the 'lewdness of the gods' that provides the starting point for the stories: Jupiter's abduction of Europa in the form of a bull; Daphne's transformation into a laurel tree to save her from rape by Apollo; poor Io's bitter wandering through the world as 'a cow as white as milk', a cruel sequel to her rape by Jupiter. The themes of *Metamorphoses* made it an unlikely addition to the canon of improving literature reserved for boys' education. Golding, Ovid's English champion, could hardly deny that the tales' sexual themes made them 'delectable' (or arousing) reading, but he attempted to argue that the stories were also 'fraughted inwardly with most pithy instructions and wholesome examples.' Golding's laundering was part of a long tradition of finding in Ovid a morality consistent with much chillier Christian ethics, a seemingly awkward fit made slightly easier by the apparent overlap between Ovid's description of the beginning of the world and the story of Genesis; Renaissance readers could kid themselves they were reading the Roman writer's take on the Garden of Eden or the Flood. Golding tried to make the stories appear as cautionary tales for the respectable English reader – so the tale of Icarus, who flew too close to the sun with wings fashioned by his father Daedalus, became an example of due punishment meted out to someone with rampant social ambition; and Actaeon's gruesome end could be seen as a metaphor for the wages of sinful indolence and over-fondness of hunting.

It's hard to believe that alert readers like William paid much attention to the allegedly virtuous lessons in *Metamorphoses*, but an unearned reputation for morality allowed the distinctly risqué work to remain in active classroom use, while other equally explicit classical material was banned from the shelves (and we'll get to those books later on). *Metamorphoses* was infused into the grammar school syllabus. Younger boys studied excerpts in their rhetorical textbooks, while older pupils were encouraged to read the whole thing. The pedantic schoolmaster Holofernes' puerile wordplay on 'Ovidius Naso' (4.2.123) and 'nose' in *Love's Labour's Lost* (c.1595) suggests Shakespeare might have had the Roman writer's name on the brain from an early age. It's possible he owned his own copy while at school; a Latin edition of 1502, printed in Venice, survives in the Bodleian Library in Oxford with the frustratingly vague signature 'Wm She' and the unverifiable assertion, dated 1682, that 'this little book of Ovid was given to me by W. Hall who said it was once Will Shakespeare's' (perhaps the inscription represents a bequest within the wider family of Shakespeare's future son-in-law, John Hall).

Ovid's wild imagination sparked an equally vivid response in Shakespeare. The story of Philomel and Tereus reappeared in his early tragedy *Titus Andronicus* (*c.*1589), written in collaboration with George Peele. Philomel's rape and mutilation by her brother-in-law Tereus are the source for Lavinia's terrible ordeal at the hands of Chiron and Demetrius. Like Philomel, she is raped and robbed of the means to tell of her assault by having her tongue cut out; Shakespeare and Peele go further and have the brothers hack off their victim's hands so she can't write or – as Philomel does – embroider her story. In the end, Lavinia resorts to using a copy of *Metamorphoses* itself to explain to her family her ghastly experience, inscribing the names of her rapists in the dirt with a staff. The play's final gruesome act of retributory cannibalism, in which Titus feeds the villainous queen Tamora a pie made from her rapist sons, rewrites Philomel's sister Procne's revenge on her husband: she prepares Tereus a banquet made from his own son, Itys. The ill-starred suicidal lovers Pyramus and Thisbe, an inspiration for *Romeo and Juliet* and the source for the artisans' play before the Athenian court in *A Midsummer Night's Dream* (*c.*1596), appear in Book 4 of *Metamorphoses*. The goddess of love, Venus, and her resistant love-object, the huntsman Adonis – the subjects of Shakespeare's first published poetry – have their unhappy history relayed in Book 10.

As much as it was a creative storehouse for Shakespeare's future plays and poems, *Metamorphoses* also offered a vision of sexuality that was infinitely more capacious than the options ostensibly available to him in Stratford-upon-Avon. Ovid taught him about the bisexual allure of beautiful young men like Narcissus, poised 'between the state of man and lad' and irresistible to both 'divers trim young men' and 'many a lady fresh and fair'. If Narcissus wasted away in futile adoration of his own exquisiteness, another queer icon, Orpheus, modelled a much more active pursuit of same-sex gratification. Returning from the underworld having failed to rescue his dead wife, Eurydice, Ovid's Orpheus 'did utterly eschew / The womankind', dispatching all female enquirers 'with repulse' and establishing instead a vigorously queer way of life: 'He also taught the Thracian folk a stews of males to make / And of the flowering prime of boys the pleasure for to take' (he taught Thracian men how to establish male brothels, and enjoy sex with youths).

Unsurprisingly for a world in which mortals became gods and humans wound up as animals and plants, gender was not set in stone in *Metamorphoses*. William learned of Tiresias and Scython, both of them 'sometime woman, sometime man', and of the transformative waters of Salmacis, where 'whoso bathes him [. . .] comes thence a perfect man no more', thanks to the magical fusing of Hermaphroditus and the pool's resident nymph into a 'double-shaped' intersex being. In Book 9, Iphis wrestles with the force of her love for Ianthe, 'a maiden with a maid [. . .] in love.' Her unimaginative hetero-essentialism ('A cow is never fond / Upon a cow,' Iphis complains) marks her out as a *naïf* in Ovid's fluid universe, but the gods intervene regardless, transforming her into a boy as she walks towards the marriage altar, stride lengthening, hair shortening, skin coarsening with every step. Even things that seemingly should be set in stone rarely remain so in *Metamorphoses*: Pygmalion kisses to life the statue that he lusts after, feeling the ivory beneath his fingers soften into flesh.

It's difficult to overstate the contrast that Ovid's world offered to the Protestant authoritarianism of Elizabethan England. To those with the Latin to read the crisp hexameters of the many imported editions of *Metamorphoses*, or the resources to get their hands on the English translation – and William had both – the stories opened the door to a place of desire, pursuit, transgression and magic. Ovid's work was disturbingly violent but also arrestingly pansexual, and it introduced Shakespeare to concepts, characters and ideas that would remain with him for the rest of his life.

Metamorphoses provided him with his first literary exposure to irresistibly beautiful youths, a type that was to become an abiding interest. The dewy appeal that Ovid celebrated in Narcissus, Hyacinthus and Cyparissus – queerly beloved young men – gave Shakespeare a language with which to blazon the attractions of his own male heart-throbs, from *Twelfth Night*'s Sebastian (exquisitely indistinguishable from his twin sister, Viola) to the 'fair youth' of the sonnets – all dazzling, star-like eyes, smooth cheeks and hair curled and teased like that of Apollo himself. Ovid was the source of the queered edgeland of human-immortal sexuality that Shakespeare would explore in his lyric poem *Venus and Adonis* (1593) and his comedy *A Midsummer Night's Dream*. In the latter, Shakespeare found a way to naturalise the transgressive interspecies lust of *Metamorphoses* into a folkloric woodland setting: the fairy queen Titania is compelled to fall in love with the weaver Nick Bottom, whom the sprite Puck has transformed (semi-completely) into a donkey. Ovid's flexible interpretation of gender lies behind the seemingly miraculous denouements of *As You Like It* (1599), *Twelfth Night* (1602) and *Cymbeline* (c. 1611). In all three plays, the heroine – who has spent a significant portion of the play lost to her family and living as a young man – has her original identity discovered in the final scene in a revelation received by those on stage as almost divine. The god Hymen is the agent in Ganymede's reappearance as Rosalind; Olivia breathes 'Most wonderful!' (5.1.225) at the sight of *two* beautiful Sebastians (although one of them is a Viola); 'Does the world go round?' (5.5.232) marvels the baffled king Cymbeline when he realises that his daughter Imogen has taken the form of a pageboy called Fidele. And Ovid is there too in Shakespeare's deployment of sexual violence as a plot device, from the savagery of *Titus Andronicus* to the queasy final scene of *The Two Gentlemen of Verona*.

Metamorphoses – an imaginative encapsulation of classical Rome's pagan, patriarchal and unquestionably queer attitude to sexuality and gender – was the adult Shakespeare's go-to text for creative inspiration, and the schoolbook that made the greatest impression on the young William. And he was first exposed to it in a classroom of children and adolescents, led by a teacher whose reliance on corporal punishment fostered an atmosphere that equated sexuality with power, humiliation and punishment. The high-minded idealism of *De amicitia* and the transporting fantasies of *Metamorphoses* were two aspects of William's queer education. The sexualised sadism of the teaching profession was, disturbingly, another.

William started grammar school weeks or months after his breeching ceremony, but it wasn't long before he was breeched again. This time, the word denoted the forced removal of his breeches – those iconic male garments, only recently bestowed – in order for the master to flog his bare backside. We can be absolutely sure that William was breeched repeatedly. Thrashing wasn't just a punishment for bad behaviour. It was a tried-and-tested pedagogic method to drive Latin into the brains of children, to make sure they never mistook a dative for an ablative, or confused Terence with Horace. Learning *meant* being flogged. At Louth in Lincolnshire, the grammar school's seal depicted a master in the act of beating a trouserless pupil. In the 1530s, newly qualified Masters of Grammar at Cambridge University were required to thrash a child as part of their graduation ceremony. Even in the nineteenth century – an era not known for a progressive attitude to corporal punishment – the years of William's childhood were regarded as a 'reign of terror' for schoolboys. Most teachers favoured a bundle of thin wooden rods gathered together like a stubby broom, the 'threatening twigs of birch' (1.3.24) as the Duke puts it in *Measure for Measure*. Some masters preferred a single switch, all the better for building up a stinging speed, or a paddle called a ferula, drilled with a hole to ensure the beating raised a blister on the victim's skin. It was routine for floggings to draw blood. Not infrequently, boys passed out. The 'whining schoolboy' in *As You Like It* who represents Jaques's second Age of Man had every reason to creep 'like snail / Unwillingly to school' (2.7.145–47). Parents seldom got involved.

More unsettling even than the violence in William's schoolroom was the eroticised language that attended it. Euphemisms current in Elizabethan grammar schools were preserved in phrasebooks known as 'vulgars', used by boys to develop conversational proficiency in Latin. Vulgars tell us that, among the pupils, a flogging was known as 'marry[ing] the master's daughter': an 'embrace' from 'my Lady Birch' left 'a print that sticketh upon my buttocks a good while after'. The renowned headteacher and educational theorist Richard Mulcaster was a fan of the personification of the birch as a marriage-giddy matron: in one anecdote, he was said to have once paused whimsically before commencing a thrashing of a bare-buttocked pupil to 'ask the banns of matrimony between this boy his buttocks [. . .] and Lady Birch.' To save his fellow, another schoolboy nipped in to 'forbid the banns [. . .] [b]ecause all parties are not agreed.' Both boys were let off thanks to the rescuer's quick wit.

Writers who went through the grammar school system were left with an association between buttocks (their own and other people's) and boys' education. Shakespeare's friend and writing partner Thomas Nashe castigated 'filthy' learning in his courtly entertainment *Summer's Last Will and Testament* (1592): 'nouns and pronouns', he declared, were 'traitors to boys' buttocks.' The dramatist John Marston went further. In his comedy *What*

You Will (1601), he staged a grammar lesson in which the delicate Pippo – the sort of lad who 'play[s] the lady in comedies presented by children' – is stripped and thrashed for getting in a tangle with a phrase from Lily's *Grammar*, while the master grows more and more excited about the 'juice' that flows from his victim. Early modern writers recognised that the schoolroom beatings they had endured could have a shockingly eroticised aspect, both in the sadistic arousal such punishments might produce in teachers and in the co-option of the victims into a strange erotic economy of 'marriages' between boys' backsides and birch twigs. But hardly anyone in Elizabethan England seemed to have bothered much about the notion that teachers might derive sexual satisfaction from flogging. It wasn't until the late seventeenth century that a Children's Petition to Parliament castigated the nation's schools as 'houses of [. . .] prostitution' that allowed free rein to debauched and cruel teachers. The petition drew attention to the potentially abusive intent behind the 'immodest eyes and filthy blows' of masters, who exposed pupils' 'secret parts' to humiliating punishment. When William was at school, and in the decades afterwards, there seems instead of public outcry to have been a low but persistent hum of awareness about teaching conditions in England, an understanding – but scant acknowledgement – of the lines of connection among boys' education, beating and sexuality. Nothing was done to reform the system.

Shakespeare left a glimpse of his own school years in *The Merry Wives of Windsor* (*c.*1600). In a scene which is otherwise dramaturgically redundant, neither advancing the plot nor significantly developing character, Mistress Page's young son William (the name can't have been idly chosen) is taken through his grammar lesson by the Welsh schoolteacher-parson Sir Hugh Evans. The scene is a classic set piece of lewd comic miscommunication: William gets his relative pronouns *qui, quae,* *quod* (who, which, that) mixed up; Sir Hugh makes him Latinise 'stone', Elizabethan slang for testicle; and Mistress Quickley – an atypical female presence in the classroom – mishears everything as sexualised tavern slang: she interprets *pulcher* (Latin for 'beautiful') as 'polecat' (or prostitute), 'genitive case' as 'Jinny's case' (or vagina) and *horum* – inevitably – as 'whore' (it actually means 'their' or 'of these') (4.1.27–63). Amid the bawdy word-play, little William is reserved and fearful, his mind on the birch that Sir Hugh promises will come his way: 'If you forget your *quis*, your *quaes*, and your *quods*, you must be preeches' (4.1.77–79). Sir Hugh's comedy Welshism – 'preeches' for 'breeched' – only lightly disguises his teaching habits.

One consequence of a schooling that eroticised the punishments intended to instil learning was a lifelong association in Shakespeare's mind between teaching and sex. Educational exchanges in his plays have a frequent habit of becoming (or starting out as) seductive ones. In *The Taming of the Shrew* (*c.*1591), the undercover Lucentio seduces Bianca by means of his Latin tuition, 'translating' a section of a standard school text, Ovid's *Heroides*, into a private declaration of love. During Lucentio's lesson, the somewhat misquoted line, '*Hic ibat Simois, hic est Sigeia tellus, hic steterat Priami regia celsa senis*' ('Here flowed the Simois, this is the Sigeian land, here stood the lofty palace of old Priam') becomes, 'As I told you before [. . .] I am Lucentio [. . .] son unto Vincentio of Pisa [. . .] disguised thus to get your love' (3.1.28–33). In *Henry V* (1599), Princess Katherine of France learns the beginners' English she will need for her future as the king's war-bride in a conversation with her attendant Alice that descends into French obscenity far more explicit than the double entendres of the schoolroom scene in *The Merry Wives of Windsor*. Katherine is shocked that the English for *pied* (foot) and *robe* (gown) sound unfortunately like the French for 'fuck' (*foutre*) and 'cunt' (*con*). As the princess objects, '*ce sont mots de son mauvais,* *corruptible, gros, et impudique, et non pour les dames d'honneur d'user'* ('those are evil-sounding words, easy to misconstrue, vulgar, and immodest, and not to be used by respectable ladies') (3.4.52–54). In *Titus Andronicus*, we are given a chilling reminder that the butchering rapists Chiron and Demetrius have been through a classical education: when Titus sends the brothers a scroll bearing a quotation from Horace, Chiron observes, 'I know it well; / I read it in the grammar long ago' (4.2.22–23).

In the years that Shakespeare spent at grammar school, he completed a journey from infancy to youth. He was fed an intellectual diet that centralised the ardent homoerotic feelings of Ciceronian *amicitia* and celebrated the queer sexual arrangements of Ovid's *Metamorphoses*. His education was delivered in an atmosphere of intermittently eroticised savagery meted out by men in authority to boys under their control – where a beating could be imagined as a wedding, and where boys were likelier to encounter 'Lady Birch' than they were to hear from or about actual women. His own gender identity was simultaneously assured and constantly undermined. While all the pupils in his schoolroom were boys past the age of breeching, they could take little confidence in the stability or persistence of their identity as privileged males: the garments that denoted their special status could be ripped off at a moment's notice and the wearer subjected to a degrading, obscurely sexualised punishment. Very little about the way early modern England chose to engender its men would strike us today as wholly straight. Shakespeare carried the consequences of his schooling into adult life, as did countless other boys in early modern England – some of whom became writers too, from whom Shakespeare learned or with whom he collaborated on his plays. These grammar-school boys' queer inheritances – an ambivalent legacy, to be sure – were invested in part in the Elizabethan explosion of dramatic literature, a boom in stories that excavated the possibilities of emotional and sexual relationships between men. But Shakespeare's education didn't finish at fifteen. It wasn't long before he found himself in London, a city dedicated to the pleasures and proclivities of young men, where an even richer canon of queer classical literature awaited discovery. William's training at the university of life was about to begin.

The Third University

Summer 1587. William made his way through a melee of men. He was almost there: across St Paul's to the great north door onto the churchyard and the dozens of bookshops that lined the cathedral precinct. Wherever he looked in Paul's Walk – the central aisle between the nave's soaring pillars – he saw well-dressed men posed just so in the pools of light cast down from the windows. Some were in groups, cloaks thrown over shoulders, hips tilted and shapely calves on display. Others strode in pairs, arm in arm round the nave, boot-spurs jangling and swords scraping as they made their circuit. Over the hubbub, William could hear the reedy voice of a preacher from behind the choir screen. He was inveighing against ambulatory Christians who wore out the flagstones of the cathedral with their swaggering but never deigned to get down on their knees and pray. William didn't blame them. There was far too much to hear and see and do without bothering about the cathedral's actual purpose.

He saw few women of the same class as the showily dressed gentlemen; the men's flamboyance was intended for one another – and for him. William pushed past them reluctantly. In the churchyard, he nearly walked into another cleric preparing to climb the steps of Paul's Cross, the open-air pulpit – with its decorated wooden frame it was like a pocket playhouse, he always thought. This preacher might have more luck than his colleague inside but William didn't bet on it: the crowd out here in the bookshop quarter was just as distracted, absorbed by the riches on sale.

Jerry-built stores nudged up against the wall of the cathedral. Customers lingered, browsing the pages of books piled on the outside tables and scanning the frontispieces of new releases that were pasted at eye level to advertise the stock within. There were titles here from across the continent: new editions of the classics from France, the Low Countries and Italy. His Latin gave him a passport to Europe's literature.

The world in the kind of books that he picked up was no less a playground for monied and well-born males than the middle aisle of Paul's. Dialogues and treatises of long ago, capturing the debauched conversations of gentlemen at ease on the shores of the Mediterranean, in a land unaware of the gospel of Christ, yet among a people sure of their civility and intellectual superiority. The thrill of it made William's head spin even as he marvelled that such books could be allowed. He wondered what the harried shoemaker standing at the counter, buying that year's tuppenny almanac, would make of the Moralia of Plutarch, lying for open sale with a consignment of expensive French imports. A debate – an inconclusive one – between a lover of women and a lover of boys, a philosophising sodomite who persuaded the reader of the sweetness of his scandalous desires. Without question it was licentious, bawdy, heathen and shocking (which is what made it unputdownable). The shoemaker might also call it filthy and accursed, and echo a phrase he had heard from the pulpit outside: the dialogue defended a sin not to be named among Christians. Lucky, then, that neither Plutarch nor his articulate disputants were of that faith. Lucky too that the book was in Latin, translated from Greek – two languages in which William was sure the shoemaker was ignorant. The bookshops in Paul's Churchyard offered quite different wares to William and the posing gentlemen in Paul's Walk than they did to other citizens of London.

Shakespeare didn't need any more education than he received at Stratford to access the unexpurgated heritage of classical Greece and Rome, the candid celebrations of same-sex desire by writers including Virgil, Plutarch and Lucian. His introduction to this world came as part of the homosocial whirl of London, where young writers shared ideas and commissions as well as beds, homes and lives. The metropolis itself was the country's 'third university', according to one seventeenth-century commentator – a patchwork of bookshops, taverns, freelance tutors and argumentative street-philosophers that constituted a de facto college for inquisitive youths. And as the biggest city in the land, it was also the default capital of homoerotic desire, a place where queer sex was available from willing bedfellows, cruising city gentlemen and the professional sex workers of London's male brothels. Shakespeare's literary apprenticeship took place in a city that catered for queer desires on the page, the stage and the street – and his plays show he paid attention to what was on offer.

But he didn't discover these urban novelties as a virgin bachelor. By the time he came to know London, probably from the age of twenty-three or twenty-four, Shakespeare was a married father of three, husband to a highly capable woman eight years his senior. Anne Shakespeare – born Hathaway – doesn't deserve to be made peripheral to this story, for all that her role as wife and mother might seem to place her outside a study of the queer male culture of early modern England. Her part in shaping the sexual identity of William Shakespeare is unrecoverable but also incalculable; to consider his queer life is in no way to erase the significance of his wife, or to discount the centrality of their relationship to his development as a writer. In fact, when looked at out of the corner of one's queer eye, the Anne–William marriage looks refreshingly peculiar – it wasn't particularly common (although not unknown) for a man to marry so young, to choose a woman who was considerably older, and to endow her with powers as head of a household after he upped and left for the big city. There was definitely something arsy-versy about this progression: a man was supposed to take a wife once he had established himself in the world, not when he was only a few years on from being a 'breeching scholar in the schools' (3.1.18) as *The Taming of the Shrew*'s Bianca dismissively puts it. So before we join Shakespeare in his homosocial life in London, we should consider what led him away from Stratford-upon-Avon in the first place.

When William Shakespeare wed Anne Hathaway in December 1582, he was eighteen, still a minor and unable to enter into a marriage without his parents' permission. Anne was twenty-six, an orphan with a bit of a dowry and more life experience than her husband – and she was about three months pregnant with their first child. That doesn't mean the marriage was lovelessly shotgun, nor that either party was necessarily pressurised into it to legitimise a 'natural rebellion done i'the blaze of youth' (*All's Well That Ends Well*, 5.3.6); one in four brides in Elizabethan England were already pregnant when they married. But it's difficult to believe Shakespeare had aspired to a teenage marriage. His parents expected him to do something with the education they had bestowed on their eldest son. John Shakespeare's business was in a bad way, and a learned son had the skills to help support the family in Stratford.

It's likely William was in love with Anne when he married her. One of his sonnets, tentatively dated to the early 1580s, has great fun with the teasingly masochistic energy of a young relationship: the speaker is stricken with horror to hear his lover utter 'I hate' before reassurance arrives with her addition of 'not you' (145.2, 14). There's probably a pun on Anne's surname in the phrase 'I hate, from hate away she threw' (12) (*hate away*/Hathaway), and the poem is romantically but plausibly accounted a courtship sonnet. Needless to say, we don't have any verses purporting to represent Anne's inner voice.

Romance, sex and marriage were exciting but messy. They changed things for William and Anne, as well as the Shakespeare household. William, not yet an adult in the eyes of the law, became by necessity a man. His marriage removed the possibility of attending Oxford or Cambridge, even if he had wanted to: students and fellows were required to be bachelors. Anne was now tied to an increasingly rackety family, with children underfoot and the in-laws on a slide into downward mobility thanks to John Shakespeare's unstable finances. Firstborn Susanna was followed in late January 1585 by Judith and Hamnet. Twins were double the blessing but also twice the cost. Three babies in as many years may have placed dangerous strain on Anne, ruling out more pregnancies.

We have little to flesh out the story of William and Anne's marriage: no correspondence, no recollections of offspring and neighbours, no family memoirs. Generations of mostly male biographers have painted Anne with the laziest of contemptuous strokes, picturing her as a sullen and unthoughtful burden from whom her husband escaped as soon as possible. Newer studies have treated her with more respect, revealing a woman who, as the years went on, ran an increasingly complex household in Stratford, firstly under the elder Shakespeares' roof and then as mistress of her own substantial property, New Place, which the couple bought in 1597 when William grew prosperous. Like *Twelfth Night*'s Olivia, Anne had to 'sway her house, command her followers, / Take and give back affairs and their dispatch' (4.3.17–18). The professional life of a householding married woman in a provincial town included significant responsibilities over domestic staff, financial management in the trading of grain and timber, and the large-scale manufacture of malt for brewing: Anne was an active and important member of the Stratford community. Later on, Anne helped her husband manage his extensive landholdings in Stratford and the surrounding area. Beyond Anne's evident competence, it's hard to know the true feelings of husband and wife for each other. The diverse married couples Shakespeare wrote for the stage don't follow a pattern from which we can infer an auto-biographical portrait. We're unlikely to find a model for the Shakespeares' marriage in the Macbeths, Petruchio and Katherine in *The Taming of the Shrew*, or Hermione and Leontes in *The Winter's Tale*.

We also don't know the circumstances that brought Shakespeare to London, or whether the move was accomplished in incremental steps (he almost certainly spent some of his early professional years on tour around England, traipsing a circuit like the players in *Hamlet* that took in city, court and countryside). And it was never a permanent relocation: he went back regularly to Stratford-upon-Avon, perhaps during the six weeks of Lent when public performances were banned and London social life shut down. He didn't abandon his family in a moonlight flit. But in choosing to become a playwright and actor, William was embarking on a profession that would necessarily remove him from his hometown for the majority of his working life.

There's a well-rooted theory that he was swept up as a touring player by one of the companies that passed through Stratford-upon-Avon. It's possible that he took himself off to London to scratch a living as a clerk, and ended up drifting into playwriting and acting. The first biographical snippets that circulated about Shakespeare in the century after his death suggested he got his break as a 'serviture' in the playhouse, a term that implies junior employment of many types. The lives of other middle-class writers might suggest clues. The dramatist Thomas Kyd probably began as a scrivener, or legal scribe. The poet Michael Drayton, a Warwickshire contemporary, seems to have moved to London and found work as a tutor and secretary to fund his literary ambitions. The biographer John Aubrey, in his late seventeenth-century *Brief Lives*, reported that Shakespeare served for a time as a schoolmaster. Whatever took him away from his young family, he would have been sure that his prospects beyond Stratford were brighter than those that remained at home.

To gain a footing in the capital meant recusing himself from the role of *pater familias* and adopting a sort of renewed bachelordom. Shakespeare must have been conscious of a renegotiation of his status as he joined the callow ranks of the city's young people, the 'unbaked and doughy youth of [the] nation' (*All's Well*, 4.5.3–4) jostling for advancement; for a first-born family man, some swallowing of pride may have been necessary. He was now one of the 6,000 immigrants from provincial England and elsewhere who moved every year to London, helping to refresh the numbers lost to disease and boost the city's population – which stood at 150,000 souls and growing by the time Shakespeare arrived. Newcomers had to find their tribe quickly, or face constant dangers from thieves and confidence tricksters. A seventeenth-century commentator bewailed the fate of London 'novices', likening them to inexperienced sailors turned loose onto the high seas 'ere they know either coast or compass' and winding up 'miserably wrecked' in body and soul. As Shakespeare settled into the capital city, he would have relied on the support of his friends to negotiate London's perils. He needed a place to stay where his belongings wouldn't get stolen, where the bill of fare was wholesome, and where his room-mate and bedmate was congenial.

Shakespeare's recorded biography from the ages of twenty-one to twenty-eight is almost a blank. From the baptism of his twins in 1585 to what is taken to be the first reference to him in print in 1592 – the university-educated writer Robert Greene's sideswipe at 'Shake-scene' the 'upstart crow, beautified with our feathers' (an uppity, plagiaristic actor who thinks he can pass as a poet) – he managed not to appear in the sort of documents that end up preserved in archives, although the traces of a piece of Shakespeare family financial dealing place him in

Stratford in 1587. After 1596, we can find Shakespeare in lodgings in Bishopsgate, then a house in Silver Street to the north-west of the city, and later an upscale apartment in the gatehouse of the Blackfriars district, but for the earlier years, biographers tend to fall back on the brisk vagueness of John Aubrey, who is said to have reported – although the evidence is questionable – that William 'was not a company keeper; lived in Shoreditch, wouldn't be debauched, and if invited to, writ [that] he was in pain.' With this location comes an unconvincing micro-portrait of the independent young dramatist, so dedicated to his work that even his refusals of sociability came in writing.

Aubrey's account may not have much basis in fact, but nothing is more likely than that William lived in Shoreditch in his twenties. The north-east suburbs were cheap, with plenty of room for new arrivals, and he would have had other writers and actors as neighbours and room-mates. James Burbage's splendid open-air venue, the Theatre, occupied by Lord Strange's Men and soon to be the home of the Lord Chamberlain's Men, stood on Curtain Road, close to London's other major playhouse, the Curtain (Bankside, south of the Thames, was only beginning to emerge as a theatrical neighbourhood with the opening of the Rose in 1587).

Shoreditch was less convenient for the quiet repose captured in Aubrey's observation. By the 1580s, the district was a busy strip mall of cottages and multistorey houses strung along Holywell Street, the thoroughfare that led directly north out of the city at Bishopsgate. Development was creeping into the open land of Spitalfields to the east and Finsbury Fields to the west, the rough pasture giving way to tenements aimed particularly at immigrants from France and the Low Countries. And the clamour of a rapidly urbanising district was regularly enhanced by Londoners in search of a good time at the theatres, drinking spots and gaming dens of Shoreditch, or in the nearby villages of Hoxton and

Islington, popular resorts for city-dwellers. If William had chosen Shoreditch as a removed backwater for contemplative creativity, he would have been swiftly put right. Luckily, playwriting wasn't a solitary craft. Most of Shakespeare's earliest plays are joint efforts, written with more established dramatists who had connections with London's theatre companies, the Inns of Court and the two universities of Oxford and Cambridge. *The First Part of the Contention Betwixt the Two Famous Houses of York and Lancaster* (later retitled *Henry VI Part 2*), *The True Tragedy of Richard Duke of York* (*Henry VI Part 3*), and *Henry VI Part 1* (written after the second two plays in the trilogy) were collaborations with the Cambridge graduates Thomas Nashe and Christopher Marlowe – of whom we'll hear much more; *Titus Andronicus* was written with the Oxford-educated George Peele. Shakespeare reciprocated with writing duties on other plays. Many playscripts were hashed out by pairs and teams of writers, working together in cramped shared lodgings and the smoky parlours of bustling taverns (the publican paid the bill for candles and coal, and a pint pot of ale could be made to last all night). It wasn't possible to be a hermit in a garret and write plays for the early modern stage.

Shakespeare's new bachelordom threw him into a homosocial world where professional association often meant personal familiarity, and it's extremely unlikely he lived alone in his first London years. Writerly room-sharing was a characteristic feature of a dramatist's life. Marlowe lived with fellow playwright Thomas Kyd in the early 1590s, their belongings, books and papers shuffling together in the day-to-day intimacies of cohabitation. Francis Beaumont and John Fletcher, co-writers during the 1600s, shared everything. John Aubrey noted their 'dearness of friendship': they lived together, 'lay together', and 'had one wench in the house between them, which they did so admire; the same clothes and cloak, etc, between them.' Beaumont and Fletcher seem, like Titus and Gisippus, to have achieved the fantasy of a female lover shared between 'perfect' friends. But Aubrey's remarks also tack towards a reading that sees the two men as each other's primary partner: they share a home and also share a bed ('lay together'); the female member of the household is identified ambiguously as a 'wench', a word which could imply affection or service; and their sharing of clothes marks them out as particularly close friends of the Ciceronian mould, shaping their equality and similarity in outward show.

Observers imagined that Beaumont and Fletcher's literary output, collected in a single volume in 1647, was the offspring of a queerly fertile same-sex union:

> What strange production is at last displayed,
> Got by two fathers, without female aid.
> Behold! Two masculines espoused each other,
> Wit and the world were born without a mother.

Here, sex between men stands as a rhetorical conceit for co-authorship, but the poem also asks the reader to imagine what 'two masculines espoused' might get up to beyond the conception of a literary masterpiece. If a comfortable shared bed could be the ideal place for intellectual labour – the Tudor educationalist Roger Ascham recalled bunking up with a young gentleman called John Whitney to teach him Latin, a copy of Cicero's *De amicitia* propped on the blankets in front of them – it was also the natural platform for abiding affection and emotional closeness.

Bed-sharing offered a routine context for same-sex intimacy in an age when bedsteads were expensive items of homeware and few people slept alone by choice. Even spouses couldn't always expect to have a bed to themselves; travellers looking to stay at more down-at-heel alehouses sometimes had to crawl in with the landlord and his wife (the 'second best bed' that William later bequeathed Anne indicates how well-off the couple were by the end of his life: no guest at New Place would ever need to share with Master and Mistress Shakespeare, as the family maintained their best bedstead just for visitors). Young people, students and servants of the same sex always slept in the same bed. A bedfellow might become a best friend, or more: Rosalind and Celia are long-term bedfellows (*As You Like It*), as are Beatrice and Hero (*Much Ado About Nothing*). King Henry V's bedfellow Lord Scroop turns to the bad and betrays him to the French – that the two young men had shared countless nights on the same pillow renders his treachery particularly shocking. A bedfellow brought companionable warmth to chilly sheets, and reassuring co-presence in the dark of the night. Early modern people had more opportunities than we do today to get to know their bedmates: the night's rest wasn't uninterrupted, but was typically bisected into two phases, first and second sleeps, separated by a period of late-night wakefulness when bed-sharers conversed, prayed, made plans for the next day and, not infrequently, had sex.

The boundary between sleeping chum and sexual partner was inevitably porous. The word 'bedfellow' did triple duty for someone you bunked up with, an illicit sexual partner, and the person you married (in *Henry VIII* (1613), the king has a pang of conscience at leaving '[s]o sweet a bedfellow' (2.2.142) when he plans his divorce from Queen Katherine). A bedfellow could slip between the categories of friend and lover. In John Webster's tragedy *The Duchess of Malfi* (1614), the gentlewoman Cariola is part of the knowing chatter between the duchess and her secret husband Antonio, who has come to her chamber to spend the night. 'Alas, what pleasure can two lovers find in sleep?' asks the Duchess disingenuously, and Cariola teasingly agrees: 'My lord, I lie with her often; and I know / She'll much disquiet you [. . .] For she's the sprawlingest bedfellow.' 'I shall like her the better for that,' leers Antonio (3.2.10–14).

Platonic co-sleeping could easily – and unremarkably – become something more. In the Restoration, the diarist Samuel Pepys recorded an interrupted night in the same bed as a servant of the Earl of Sandwich: the two men 'fell to play with one another' and got very little rest. In the occasional legal cases that have come to light detailing unwanted queer sexual attention, the setting is often a shared bed, and the persons involved are fellow servants, apprentices or temporary residents of an inn obliged to huddle together under the covers. Shakespeare understood that there was something powerful and complex about the various sorts of 'lying with' that men and women experienced at different times and in different contexts. In *Othello* (1603), the villainous ensign Iago makes Othello believe his wife has been unfaithful with the handsome lieutenant Cassio, in part through relating a (fictional) experience of nocturnal seduction by the man he happened to be sharing a bed with:

> I lay with Cassio lately;
> And, being troubled with a raging tooth,
> I could not sleep. [. . .]
> In sleep I heard him say 'Sweet Desdemona,
> Let us be wary, let us hide our loves.'
> And then, sir, would he gripe and wring my hand,
> Cry 'O sweet creature!' and then kiss me hard,
> As if he plucked up kisses by the roots
> That grew upon my lips: then laid his leg
> Over my thigh, and sighed, and kissed; and then
> Cried 'Cursed fate that gave thee to the Moor!' (3.3.413–26)

Iago's fantasy of comradely co-sleeping becomes passionate queer sex under the cover of dreamt adultery. The invented incident is plausible precisely because it is so possible: in a shared bed, to 'sleep with' someone becomes a thoroughly indeterminate business. The simultaneous meanings might account for Othello's subsequent dismayed confusion about what he has been told: 'Lie with her! Lie on her! We say lie on her, when they belie her. Lie with her! That's fulsome' (4.1.35–37). The young Shakespeare of those early 'lost years', making his way in a London of shared lodgings and overlapping lives, knew very well that 'lying with' could sometimes mean 'lying on', and that beds shared for convenience could soon become beds shared out of mutual desire.

Early modern London also provided more direct means to get a man into one's bed, and part of Shakespeare's urban education was the discovery of these metropolitan facilities. Services that catered to male sexual desire formed one of the biggest businesses in the city. Boys and young men could be acquired in several of the thousand or more alehouses in the city. There was a male brothel in the village of Hoxton, run by a powerful underworld family that managed a chain of bawdy houses. Queer sex workers were a recognisable type. John Marston pictured the male prostitute – shaved, scented and ready for action – soliciting for passing trade:

> A goat doth stand before a brothel door,
> His clothes perfumed, his fusty mouth is aired,
> His chin new-swept, his very cheeks are glazed.

The capital had a profusion of male-dominated spaces that facilitated, in a more ad hoc way, the needs of gentlemen who wanted and renters who offered, from the backrooms of taverns to the busy colonnades of the Royal Exchange on Cornhill. Paul's Walk, the nave that led east to west through the cathedral, was a combination of gentlemen's club, fashion runway and cruising ground, where men struck business deals, flaunted their imported silks and lace, and picked up boys and women. Young men who could be 'hired to sin against nature', as the translator John Florio put it in his definition of *catamito* or 'ganymede', plied their wares under the lofty vaulted roof of London's mother church. Who knows if Shakespeare ever availed himself – but when the railing Thersites characterised Patroclus as Achilles' 'male varlet' and 'masculine whore' (5.1.15, 17) in *Troilus and Cressida* (c.1602), playgoers recognised in his accusation the terminology of the modern city.

There was, then, no shortage of queer sex in Shakespeare's London, and not all of it fell under the hair-raising prohibitions of the Tudor church and state. Sodomy was forbidden by the Bible (Genesis 19 and Leviticus 18) and outlawed by statute: the Buggery Act of 1533 laid down the death penalty for the 'detestable and abominable vice of buggery committed with mankind or beast', which marked only the start of a practitioner's punishment. Darkness, hellfire everlasting, and an eternity of pain awaited such sinners in the next life, as *The Book of Common Prayer* (1559) and the official homily 'Against Whoredom and Adultery' (1547) made very clear. But if the wages of sin were difficult to ignore, the job description itself was harder to find. Most people knew the general principle of buggery – it was 'preposterous amor', said the early Tudor polemicist John Bale, love placed in the wrong order, what we'd call anal sex – but English law had very little to say about the queer sexual menu more generally. Many foreign jurisdictions prosecuted intercrural (between the thighs) and oral sex, as well as mutual masturbation and same-sex kissing and fondling. None of these activities appeared in English legislation, and queer sex between women was totally ignored. The dragnet capaciousness of later laws against 'gross indecency' were centuries away.

When anti-queer preachers thundered from the pulpit at St Paul's that sodomy was 'detestable and abominable', 'among

Christians not to be named', a 'horrible vice', and 'the use that nature abhorreth', the promenading gallants in Paul's Walk and their queer pickups could be forgiven for tuning out the fury as sound signifying very little. Hardly anyone in Shakespeare's England was ever successfully prosecuted for consensual sodomy. The law was framed – presumably unintentionally – to make it almost impossible for a court to reach a conviction. The legal theorist Edward Coke explained that for buggery to have taken place, there had to be penetration – *res in re*, or 'thing in thing' – as well as emission of semen. And it had to be witnessed. As the majority of queer sexual encounters weren't spectator sports (some were, no doubt), it was seldom possible to persuade someone to convict themselves with their own testimony. Vanishingly few people ever found themselves labelled a 'bugger' or 'sodomite' as defined by law. In the long reigns of Queen Elizabeth and King James combined (1558–1625), only one person was convicted for sodomy in all of the home counties surrounding London.

This wasn't deliberate toleration, and there was nothing even approaching civic acceptance of queer sex. Religious law was wielded through the 'bawdy courts', an ecclesiastical magistracy that fined and shamed parishioners who gave way to 'uncleanness' or 'wickedness of life'. Anything queer that fell shy of full-on sodomy was liable to raise the alarm among the snoops of the church courts, although for the most part the clerks had their hands full with the more visible consequences of straight sexual misconduct: unmarried pregnant women and girls bringing feckless seducers to the bench, and abandoned illegitimate babies who would have to be brought up by wet nurses and foster families paid by the parish. If Shakespeare's England gave no quarter to queer sexuality in theory, there was in practice a vacuum of surveillance, regulation and punishment. The word 'sodomy' conjured up terrible associations with Biblical cataclysm, but that wasn't necessarily the word men applied to their sexual practices with each other, whether their activities fell under that definition or not. When bedfellows slept together, or masters extracted sexual favours from apprentices, or best friends took things to another level, they might have regarded themselves as guilty of sinful carnality – behaviour that was against God's injunction that we go forth and multiply – but few would have recognised their behaviour as the kind of thing that led to the scaffold. England's fundamentalist state religion kept overt discussion of queer sex well out of the public sphere, but the consequence wasn't erasure of queer desire: it was merely the suppression of a language with which early modern people could articulate the everyday intimacies of same-sex eroticism.

Men like Shakespeare did have a queer language at their disposal, however: Latin. Educated Englishmen knew *why* the street slang for a male sex worker, or any youth who took the receptive role in anal sex, was 'ganymede'. They knew the ancient story of the irresistible Phrygian boy seized by Jupiter – in the form of an eagle – to be his servant on Mount Olympus. In the version relayed by Ovid, Jupiter 'did burn [. . .] in love' for Ganymede, whose installation as the god's new sexual plaything enraged Juno, Jupiter's wife. In fact, some awareness of the Ganymede myth was widespread. Taverns and alehouses called the Eagle and Child depicted Ganymede's abduction on their signs. When Shakespeare transformed Thomas Lodge's prose romance *Rosalind* (1590) into his comedy *As You Like It* (1599) and retained the disguised heroine's pseudonym of 'Ganymede', he was confident that a good proportion of the audience understood the name's significance in myth and in contemporary London. Rosalind-in-drag certainly brings a ganymedic, power-bottom energy to her role as a forthright, rosily pretty youth in love with the strapping Orlando, a man strong enough to floor a champion wrestler and carry his servant Adam through the Forest of Arden.

Most of the queer classical canon didn't make the transition to popular culture. The sexual histories of Greece and Rome were privileged knowledge in early modern England, intended only for Latinate men like Shakespeare who – it was hoped – understood that the habits of long-gone pagan societies had no place in a modern Protestant nation. But it's not at all clear that those with the learning to read about the queer sexual cultures of the ancient world – the allure of beautiful boys, the easy acceptance of relationships between older men and younger male lovers, the widespread sexualisation of enslaved people of all genders – were so ready to abhor them. Among the English-language sermons, news pamphlets, novellas, dramas, lyric poetry and works of history, theology and philosophy that were laid out for sale in the bookshops of Paul's Churchyard was a parallel literature of classical queer desire, freely available to buy or browse but forbiddingly printed in foreign languages. The publishing boom of the European Renaissance brought this heritage from printing houses across the continent to London, where it found a market among educated readers keen to discover the ins and outs of relationships that the church said were 'not to be named among Christians'. If Shakespeare went shopping for sexual knowledge in his early years in the big city, his instructors would have been some of the most respected heroes of ancient literature. In fact, it would have been difficult to avoid learning the queer facts of life.

Even venerated classical poets like Virgil took enthusiastic detours into intensely homoerotic territory. Renaissance intellectuals loved Virgil not just for the *Aeneid*, but because he was thought to have foretold the advent of Christ: the fourth in Virgil's collection of ten *Eclogues* (pastoral poems) told of the 'glorious birth' of an 'infant king' ushering in a new golden age. But only a few short pages before this apparent prophecy of the nativity lay less virtuous material: the second *Eclogue*, in which

Corydon the shepherd is possessed with 'fierce desire' for 'heavenly fair' Alexis, the beloved boy of his own master. Most of the short poem is delivered in Corydon's increasingly desperate voice, as he begs Alexis – his 'lovely care' – to stay with him in his humble cottage, where they will live off the land and enthral each other with their singing and piping. Corydon's realisation that Alexis looks down on his gifts tilts him close to breakdown – 'What frenzy, shepherd, has thy soul possessed?' – and he ends the poem yearning for a less haughty lover who can give him what he wants.

When the second *Eclogue* was given to younger readers, they were told that the story was merely a 'symbolic picture' of an 'ill-formed friendship' between two contrasting men, Corydon a middle-aged rustic and Alexis a smooth young urbanite. More worldly adults could see that it was an overt account of sexual obsession. The translator Abraham Fleming, who produced the first English edition of the *Eclogues* in 1575, regarded the Alexis–Corydon relationship as autobiographical: Corydon was to be interpreted as a stand-in for Virgil, and Alexis, explained Fleming, was a slave in another man's ownership whom Virgil craved.

Other Roman poems explored the sexual exchange of enslaved youths between men without bucolic euphemisms. The poet Catullus, whose extremely graphic work was available in numerous Latin editions printed on the continent, wrote a poem warning his friend Aurelius to keep his hands off his favourite boy, or he would subject Aurelius to the traditional punishment for adulterers: sodomisation with a root vegetable. Few experienced readers of Roman literature could delude themselves that the queer relationship narrated in Virgil's second *Eclogue* was anything other than sexual (or at least, that Corydon's unfulfilled desire was wholly carnal). The name 'Alexis', like 'Ganymede', became shorthand in cerebral circles for a younger male lover. Among the outrageous claims said to have been made by Christopher Marlowe when he was informed upon for heresy was the declaration that St John was 'our saviour Christ's Alexis', who 'used him as the sinners of Sodoma'.

Shakespeare knew the *Eclogues*; *As You Like It*'s lovelorn shepherds are lifted from its manicured pastures. He also knew his Plutarch. Thomas North's monumental translation of Plutarch's first-century CE *Lives of the Noble Grecians and Romans* (1579), on which Shakespeare would later rely for his Roman plays, painted a vivid picture of the ancient world, queer sex and all. While flicking through Plutarch's potted biographies in search of inspiration for stories that would eventually become *Julius Caesar* (1599), *Coriolanus* (c.1606), *Timon of Athens* (c.1607) and *Antony and Cleopatra* (1607), Shakespeare would have learned of the heart-stopping beauty of Alcibiades and the devotion of his admirer Socrates, as well as Alcibiades' less-than-devoted loyalty. 'Alcibiades was held of Socrates by the ears,' reported Plutarch (the younger man was keen to hear what the philosopher had to say), but 'he gave his other lovers hold which Socrates never sought for'.

Another work by Plutarch, his *Moralia*, was so popular that it circulated in Latin and French as well as the original Greek and inspired a whole new genre of reflective, self-revelatory nonfiction, of which Montaigne's *Essays* (1580) was the prime example. But early modern writers didn't emulate Plutarch's chapter titled 'The Dialogue on Love', in which a group of men discuss the relative merits of love for boys or love for women (a frequent topic in Greek and Greco-Roman literature). Pederasty tends to go hand in hand with misogyny: one of the disputants, Protogenes, declares it's impossible to feel true love for women, 'any more than flies feel love for milk or bees for honey'. There is, he says, 'only one genuine love: the love of boys'. He talks loftily of friendship and virtue, but his friend Daphnaeus points out that Protogenes hangs around the wrestling gym and whisks attractive youths away for sex.

When Plutarch's *Moralia* was translated into English for the first time by Philemon Holland in 1603, he struggled with this exchange. Holland warned his readers that although Protogenes spoke a language that seemed to contain elements of the *amicitia perfecta* familiar to Elizabethan society, the disputants were actually defending what the translator called 'cursed and detestable filthiness', or sodomy. It made the dialogue 'more dangerous to be read by young men than any other treatise of Plutarch.' Translating *Moralia* – making it accessible to a wider readership including women and non-Latinate lower-class men – obliged Holland to include a content warning. Educated readers of Latin and Greek literature already knew that queer sex positivity (supposedly an outrage in Shakespeare's Protestant society) could be carried within texts that promoted intimate male friendship (a celebrated institution in the sixteenth century). One aspect of Shakespeare's Latinate male privilege was his ability to see that queer sex and queer love overlapped in the ancient world – despite the fact that his own culture tried to keep them quarantined from each other as execrated 'sodomy' and valorised 'friendship'. Shakespeare understood that there was an unspoken rule in operation in early modern England: writers who engaged with the queer literary heritage of Greece and Rome, either through translation or creative re-imagining, were expected to retain the convenient fiction that the love between males celebrated in antiquity was sexless comradeship.

Scrubbing a text free of sex could have the unintended consequence of drawing readers' attention to even racier material. In 1579, the poet Edmund Spenser established the fashion for English pastoral when he published an adaptation of Virgil's *Eclogues* called *The Shepherd's Calendar*. The ardour between Spenser's passionate shepherds Colin Clout and Hobbinol was deliberately meant to invoke Corydon and Alexis, but Spenser didn't want to be seen as openly advocating sexual immorality. In annotations to *The Shepherd's Calendar* provided by the unknown editor 'E. K.' – who may be a literary invention by Spenser himself – the reader is firmly informed that the friendship between Colin and Hobbinol is entirely free of 'disorderly love, which the learned call pederastic'. Indeed, wrote E. K., the shepherds should be understood as something like Alcibiades and Socrates, as relayed in Plutarch's *Lives*: lovers of each other's souls, not bodies. In case the English reader were to raise their eyebrows like Daphnaeus in *Moralia*, E. K. insisted that no one should 'think that herein I stand with Lucian or his devilish disciple [. . .] Aretino, in defence of execrable and horrible sins of forbidden and unlawful fleshliness.' In denying sodomy, E. K. had given the sexually curious reader their next point of reference.

Shakespeare certainly read the hugely popular *The Shepherd's Calendar*, but Lucian and Aretino were slightly more niche. If he'd followed E. K.'s inadvertent clue, he'd have been richly, if eye-openingly, rewarded with the most candid erotica available in the sixteenth century. The work of Lucian, a Greek writer of the second century CE, was known in England in Latin translation, and E. K. was thinking of the dialogue known as 'The Loves', which is – like Plutarch's in his *Moralia* – a discussion about the merits of boy-love and love for women. Now regarded as 'pseudo-Lucian' – that is, by a different writer of the fourth century CE who was copying his style – 'The Loves' captured late-antiquity queerness at its most self-confident and indolent. Two friends, Lycinus and Theomnestus, amuse each other with stories of seduction. As Theomnestus is equally drawn to the lads of 'the oily wrestling schools' and 'women at their fairest', he asks the less highly sexed Lycinus to rule on which kind of love is best. Lycinus obliges by relating a debate he had previously adjudicated between two old friends: Charicles, who loves women, and

Callicratidas, who prefers young men. Callicratidas's preference is for butch youths of about twenty, educated and muscular, and he defends his choice as 'the only activity combining both pleasure and virtue.' It is precisely because sex with men isn't required for the perpetuation of the species, he argues, that it exceeds love of women in metaphysical worth. As a bodily activity based on aesthetic appreciation, it's a sign of the civility of society, an indication that Greek men have moved beyond the mere hard-scrabble desperation of seeding the next generation. Callicratidas wins the argument – Lycinus rules that all men should marry, but 'only the wise be permitted to love boys' – and, back in the framing dialogue, Theomnestus gives a rousing encomium on the 'waves of enjoyment' that course through him when he fondles and kisses his boyfriend. Lucian's 'The Loves' really left very little to the imagination, and E. K. might have regretted drawing readers' attention to it.

Lucian's 'devilish disciple' Pietro Aretino was a Tuscan poet and dramatist whose notoriety lay in a volume familiar mostly by repute: his *Sonetti Lussuriosi*, or sixteen 'Lustful Sonnets'. Written in 1525, they accompanied an album of highly graphic engravings known as *I Modi*, or 'The Positions', produced by Marcantonio Raimondi after drawings by Giulio Romano (Romano is the only Renaissance artist Shakespeare ever mentioned by name – he is said to be responsible for the lifelike finish on the 'statue' of Hermione in *The Winter's Tale* (1611), and erudite theatregoers would certainly have clocked that the astonishingly convincing model is supposedly the handiwork of someone known for pornography). Swiftly banned in Italy, surreptitious copies of the poems and the pictures spread throughout the continent and into England, where 'Aretine's Postures' soon became shorthand for notably athletic depictions of adventurous sex between men and women (Ben Jonson later had his aspirant English sophisticate Lady Politic Would-Be of *Volpone* (c.1606) observe that 'for a desperate wit, there's Aretine; / Only his pictures are a little obscene' (3.4.96–97)). Ten of Aretino's sixteen sonnets champion anal sex between men and women, making him the era's most vigorous proponent of the practice as a pleasure rather than an unspeakable shame: in Sonnet 2, the female speaker notes 'there isn't a man who isn't a bugger', as her male partner promises: 'This time I will do it in your cunt, and in your rear another; both in your cunt and your arse my cock will make me joyful, and you happy and blissful.' Nothing about the poems or engravings was coy. Any lingering questions that twenty-something Shakespeare might have had about the 'forbidden and unlawful fleshliness' decried by E. K. would have been swiftly resolved by the illustrated sonnets of Aretino – or the murmured descriptions of them that passed as current among the polyglot readers in his literary circles.

The third university – London itself – was Shakespeare's prompt to remake himself as a worldly man-about-town, part of the homosocial swell of the big city among a bookish, ambitious crowd of playwrights and actors. Men involved in the commercial theatre industry had more reason than others to think of themselves as active participants in the process of classical rediscovery: James Burbage had reached for the ancient languages (Greek, *theatron*; Latin, *theatrum*) when naming his new purpose-built playhouse the Theatre in 1576. The wonky wood and plaster polygons that rose in the northern and southern suburbs, echoing the stately stone amphitheatres of the Roman Empire, were the Renaissance in real estate, an homage gratifyingly recognised by foreign observers: 'Its form resembles that of a Roman work,' said a Dutch commentator of the Swan playhouse, built in 1595 at Paris Garden on the Bankside. Let's allow ourselves the possibility that during his 'lost years' of youthful self-discovery, Shakespeare also came to know something of the queer classical

Renaissance, the storehouse of Latin and Greco-Roman literature
that gave cultural expression to the feelings of same-sex desire
ineffectually outlawed by Elizabethan society.

Shakespeare certainly understood the dynamics of a queer
male relationship that went well beyond the tenets of *amicitia
perfecta*, although it wasn't until *Twelfth Night* (1602) that he wrote
a queer couple in the classical mould, embedding in an already
decidedly fluid story the most overt depiction of a same-sex
romantic couple he would ever put in a play. The shipwrecked
Viola transforms herself into the young man Cesario in order to
serve Duke Orsino – who promptly falls in love with his new
servant. Cesario is sent to woo Countess Olivia on Orsino's
behalf, and the lady is smitten with the young man too, unaware
that she has fallen for a woman. Threaded through the comedy
of queered misapprehension – Orsino desires Viola but believes
she is a man; Olivia thinks she has feelings for a man who is
actually Viola – is the story of Viola's identical twin brother
Sebastian, the plot device who will resolve the hetero-romantic
confusion by supplying Olivia with a husband, freeing Viola to
marry Orsino. But Sebastian is very much more than a *deus ex
machina* fiancé for Olivia. He is also the adored younger lover of
the sailor Antonio, a privateering enemy of Orsino. Teasing
Sebastian and Antonio's relationship from the convoluted plot of
Twelfth Night allows us to see the classical building blocks
Shakespeare used to construct his most fully formed queer
couple: a strong dose of Corydon's yearning desperation in
Antonio, plenty of Alcibiades' irresistible beauty in Sebastian,
and a resounding echo of the ancient world's understanding of
sexual relationships between older and younger men in the
candour and intensity with which Antonio articulates his feelings
for Sebastian. As the play unfolds in the Mediterranean setting of
Plutarch's *Moralia* and Lucian's 'The Loves' – Illyria (the Croatian
coast), 'Candy' (Crete), and 'Messaline' (Marseilles), Viola and

Sebastian's hometown – we come to understand that the Antonio–Sebastian plot is a crucial third strand in the story, alongside the Viola–Orsino–Olivia triangle and the gulling of Olivia's steward, Malvolio. We can reconstruct the chronology of the men's affair from the recollections dotted throughout the play, resuscitating the narrative of their meeting, falling in love, parting, reunion – and the final unresolved conflict between their queer love and the marriage Sebastian contracts with Olivia.

Sebastian and Antonio's meet-cute is dramatic, the former clinging to a piece of flotsam, the latter happening to sail past in his ship. Antonio plucks the younger man from 'the rude sea's enraged and foamy mouth' (5.1.78), a rescue he frames as a stunning encounter with almost sacred beauty:

> [I] [r]elieved him with such sanctity of love;
> And to his image, which methought did promise
> Most venerable worth, did I devotion. (3.4.361–63)

Antonio's instant adoration puts him in the same category as Olivia and Orsino: he is a victim of the preternatural erotic power wielded by the Messaline twins. Viola and Sebastian have the capacity to strike onlookers with immediate and lasting love. Olivia is likewise smitten after only a few minutes' interaction with Viola: 'How now? / Even so quickly may one catch the plague?' (2.1.294–95) she marvels. For Antonio, Sebastian's bewitching looks shine out as the boy battles to stay afloat in the choppy waters of the Adriatic Sea.

It's quickly made apparent that whatever religiose sentiments Antonio might utter when speaking of Sebastian, the feelings he is describing are just as carnal as those produced by Viola in Olivia and Orsino. Following his deliverance from the shipwreck, Sebastian lives with Antonio for nearly three months, hiding his elite status and his name. He goes by 'Roderigo' and spends all his

time – 'No interim, not a minute's vacancy, / Both day and night'
(5.1.95–96) – with his rescuer, who soon harbours for him a
rampaging love 'without retention or restraint' (5.1.81). And no
mystery: informed by descriptions of Viola, Sebastian's precise
clone, we know that the young man possesses a spectacularly
epicene appeal, all smoothly 'rubious' lips and youthful effeminacy
that is thrillingly 'semblative a woman's part' (1.4.32, 34). Sebastian's
beauty sinks deeply into Antonio, nourishing his conviction that
the youth possesses a soul as rare as his appearance.

Antonio's absolute devotion explains the actions that bring
him to Illyria. Sebastian's foreboding soul prompts him to shed
his identity as 'Roderigo', leave Antonio and head for Orsino's
court. Antonio is shattered, not just by the loss but by the
revelation of Sebastian's aristocratic heritage, which places the
equality of their relationship in jeopardy: given such disparity,
Antonio bleakly reinterprets their months together as the 'bad
entertainment' (2.1.33) offered by a social inferior to a superior.
Both men are unmoored by the recalibration of their relationship:

ANTONIO. If you will not murder me for my love, let me be
your servant.
SEBASTIAN. If you will not undo what you have done – that is,
kill him whom you have recovered – desire it not. (2.1.35–39)

For Antonio, losing Sebastian is fatal, and the blow to his status
that comes with service is a price worth paying for continued
proximity to his lover. Sebastian in turn claims that the abjection
Antonio would feel in waiting on him will lead to his own death,
a fear that forces his departure, almost in tears as he takes his
leave.

Sebastian's independence doesn't last long. Antonio considers
the danger he faces in Orsino's territory, after a career preying on
Illyrian shipping, and resolves to follow Sebastian regardless: 'I do

adore thee so / That danger shall seem sport, and I will go!'
(2.1.47–48). Sebastian offers the most token resistance when they
meet up again, but Antonio's invocation of the 'desire, / More
sharp than filed steel' (3.3.4–5) that spurred him on erases the
awkwardness of reunion. And any irregularities in their relationship are solved in the relocation to Illyria: Antonio now takes the
role of cossetting older lover, protecting the naïve and 'skill-less'
(3.3.9) Sebastian from the hazards of travel: he recommends an
inn, promises to arrange their meals, advises on sightseeing and
presses on Sebastian some money in case his 'eye shall light upon
some toy' (44–45) he wishes to buy. Such servant-like activity as
facilitating bed and board is drained of shameful servility for
Antonio by the fact that it is he who provides both physical and
financial protection for Sebastian. Amid all this lovers' domesticity, the sexual puns in the scene pass almost unnoticed: 'There
shall you have me,' (42) Antonio promises Sebastian when they
arrange to meet at a nearby tavern; 'I'll be your purse-bearer,'
(47) says Sebastian as he takes Antonio's money – 'purse' being
slang for scrotum.

It's from this position of contented intimacy that things unravel
for Antonio. The consequences of two identical, seemingly male,
Messaline twins abroad in Illyria begin to blossom out of control.
Antonio is arrested while protecting the disguised Viola – whom
he takes for Sebastian – from assault by Andrew Aguecheek.
Antonio is astonished when 'Sebastian' does not immediately
return his money for prison expenses, and suffers an agonising
sense of betrayal that his lover has spurned him. The real
Sebastian also finds himself threatened with violence by
Aguecheek and Sir Toby Belch, but he is saved by Olivia who –
thinking him Cesario, Viola's male alter ego – bundles him into
her house as fast as she can. Sebastian, misty with confusion but
willing to be 'ruled' (4.1.64) by the assertive Olivia, complies, as
he does shortly afterwards when Olivia proposes marriage.

Somewhat adrift without Antonio – 'His counsel now might do me golden service' (4.3.8) – Sebastian nonetheless goes with the flow of 'this accident and flood of fortune' (4.3.11). His new wife is, after all, a rich and powerful countess.

Antonio must go through one more painful confrontation with Viola, the un-Sebastian who has unwittingly broken his heart. Brought into the throng of Act 5 and presented to Orsino and Viola as the 'notable pirate' (5.1.69) responsible for attacks on richly loaded vessels, Antonio justifies his foolhardy visit to Illyria as a result of 'witchcraft', the irresistible love he felt towards the 'ingrateful boy' (76–77) by Orsino's side. The only inter-pretation Antonio can place on this 'Sebastian's' bafflingly cruel rejection of him is that the boy sought to evade his own impris-onment through 'false cunning' (86), by denying all knowledge of the man to whom he owed his life.

Antonio's sanity seems in danger of slipping entirely off its axis when Orsino reveals that for '[t]hree months this youth hath tended upon me' (99), calling into question the reality of everything that has passed between Sebastian and him. His salvation comes with the real Sebastian's entry, bringing on stage both Messaline twins for the first time in the play and striking Orsino, Olivia and Antonio – the twins' three lovers – with amazement. Although Antonio learns of Sebastian's marriage with Olivia, his loss is partly remedied by the fact that he receives in Sebastian's greeting some of the most passionate language of all the various unions and reunions that make up Act 5:

> Antonio! O my dear Antonio!
> How have the hours racked and tortured me
> Since I have lost thee! (5.1.218–20)

We leave Antonio in much the same position of open-ended intimacy that characterises the other Antonio's situation at the end of *The Merchant of Venice*: a spouse-without-portfolio, or floating lover, within a conventional heteroerotic marriage between a wealthy heiress and a somewhat useless charmer. Antonio's ambiguous resolution is captured in his final words, delivered fresh from the shock of the twins' identicality: 'Which is Sebastian?' (224). He means, of course, 'How can one tell the two siblings apart?' But is there also a lingering question of which way his Sebastian will swing – lover, friend or husband, or all three? Amid the deferred conclusions at the end of *Twelfth Night* – Viola and Orsino's marriage must wait until she has retained her women's clothes, the wronged and vengeful Malvolio must be placated – the question of what to do with Antonio's powerfully affectionate and erotic feelings for Sebastian is left hanging.

London gave Shakespeare the opportunity to learn things about queer sexuality that were seldom expressed or discussed in Stratford-upon-Avon. His teachers were the laurel-garlanded poets of classical antiquity, as well as the sex workers who trudged a beat in Paul's Walk or in taverns that had a certain reputation. But his education in same-sex desire also came via the everyday intimacies of homosocial domesticity and creative labour: the shared beds, and shared sheets of manuscript paper, that characterised the interwoven lives of collaborative dramatists in the late sixteenth century. Co-living with other young men allowed Shakespeare to put into practice some of the ideologies of male friendship he'd been taught at school, and his discovery of the adults-only classical erotica available in Paul's Churchyard showed him the limits of what his society was prepared to accept: Elizabethan England could cope with a chaste male soulmate in the Roman mould, but educated Englishmen were on their honour to keep quiet about the queer sexual adventurism within the pages of Plutarch, Virgil and Lucian. A man's Latinity was his pathway to queer sexual knowledge, should he choose to take it, and ancient literature was the source of the code-words of queer male desire familiar to those with a classical education: the figures of Ganymede and Alexis, the *Morals* of Plutarch and the dialogues of Lucian. To have the characteristics of an 'antique Roman' (5.2.341), as a despairing Horatio asserts in the final moments of *Hamlet*, was to demonstrate values of self-sacrifice, courage and loyalty; it was also – for some in Shakespeare's circle – to share that era's understanding of sexual desire between men. Shakespeare's own sexual experimentation is beyond recovery, but evidence of his fascination with queer male relationships stands out from the pages of *Twelfth Night*, commanding attention just as Sebastian's beauty demands devotion from Antonio.

But if the world of classical queer desire was a sophisticated coterie taste available to only a few, Shakespeare's next queer discovery was a crucial part of London's popular culture. It was the theatre that had drawn Shakespeare to London in the first place, and it is to the playhouses – indoor and outdoor, featuring adult professionals and companies of children – that we now turn. Shakespeare's education, at school and the university of life, was over. It was time to go to work.

PART II

Living

3

Galatea's Children

The first weeks of 1588. He'd been waiting in the narrow lane, watching groups of finely dressed people, more men than women, enter the choirmaster's house in the southern yard of the cathedral. The doorkeeper had refused to take his sixpence until the bell pealed four, to allow the gallants and gallant wenches (his words) time to take their place in a space no bigger than a gentleman's hall. Now the path was empty. William dropped a coin in the pot and followed the beeswax glow up the stairs and into Paul's Playhouse.

The gentry claimed the best seats, of course, but even from the back, the room dazzled. Beyond the spectators, resplendent in their feathered hats, the stage occupied the far end of the hall, flanked by candelabra that drew William's eyes to the brightly painted façade. The play, a new comedy called Galatea, *fresh from performance at court, had already started: William was in time to see two boys march offstage to a blast from the cornet players in the gallery. The next arrivals sent a rustle around the room. Here was a ten-year-old Cupid, tripping barefoot across the boards, bare in fact of almost everything apart from his bow, quiver, golden wings and – William now saw – a slip of cloth around his waist. Cupid was in pursuit of another vision, a costly wall painting come to life: a teenage nymph, a periwig of silken threads piled on his head and a gauzy robe circling his shoulders.*

The room was heavy with perfume and tobacco, the haze growing denser and the heat from the candles more noticeable as the performance continued. Sweat shone on the bodies of the players. Their fluency and gracefulness with the witty script were remarkable. The story brought extraordinary things onto the stage: youths decked as goddesses and gods; unspoken love and magical transformation; a world that was drawn from the treasure troves of Metamorphoses *and the* Eclogues *but charged with something rich and courtly. It seemed astonishing to William to hear boys talk about seduction and magic with such knowing confidence. Any schoolboy could parrot some Ovid. These performers commanded the room and bewitched the crowd.*

All too soon, it was over. Music from above marked the end of the play, and the audience rose from the benches, ladies shaking out flattened skirts and men pressing their damp foreheads with embroidered handkerchiefs. William was carried by the movement of the crowd towards the stairs, but he could see two gentlemen lingering behind as some of the boys emerged again from the tiring house at the back of the stage, their faces still half painted, to have coins pressed into their hands by the admiring spectators. The congratulations continued as the choirmaster's servant went from light to light, snuffing out the expensive candles until only a patch of gold remained on the chattering party of men and boys at the end of the hall. William didn't stay to see more, but followed the departing spectators into the cool of the winter evening. The alley that led away from the choirmaster's house crossed Carter Lane, only a few yards from the Bell Inn, the departure point for the Warwickshire carrier and the sorting house where he received letters from home. In all the months that William had been in London, he had never felt further from the predictable respectability of Stratford-upon-Avon than he did then, as night closed in on the cathedral precinct and the door to Paul's Playhouse shut behind him.

If Shakespeare was on the lookout for glamorous experiences that only London could provide, there was one key destination in the last years of the 1580s: the tiny playhouse, slotted into the hall of a building at the foot of St Paul's Cathedral, that was home to Paul's Boys, England's most well-connected and modish theatre company. The big commercial houses in the suburbs weren't yet leading the theatrical vanguard. The fashion was still, in the closing years of the decade, being set by a group of courtier-impresarios and their company of boy actors, trained by the best orators and musicians England could provide.

The theatre industry that Shakespeare joined when he arrived in London was undergoing a period of transition. The travelling companies that criss-crossed the country, dipping into the capital to do a season in a tavern before taking to the road again, were being edged out by larger companies, new mega-troupes like the Queen's Men or Lord Strange's Men, which enjoyed noble or even royal patronage. These big companies toured too, taking hits such as *The Famous Victories of Henry V*, *The Troublesome Reign of King John* and *The Tragical History of King Leir* to towns across the country. Shakespeare was probably a member of the Queen's Men for a while; he later rewrote their crowd favourites as *Henry IV Parts 1* and *2* (1597–98) and *Henry V* (1599), *King John* (c.1596) and *King Lear* (1606). But London was increasingly the focus. The new purpose-built playhouses in Shoreditch and on Bankside – the Theatre, the Curtain and the Rose – offered year-round playing and much greater certainty of regular income. At the urban playhouses, spectators had to pay a penny (or more) just to walk through the door; on tour, managers were reliant on the largesse of the audience to toss a coin in a hat after the show. Staying in the city required a wider repertoire of work (no one could expect the same audience to return for repeated perform-ances of just a few plays). Shakespeare was to benefit from the boom in demand for new writing: the ever-shifting and recon-stituting commercial troupes gave themselves longer London seasons, and began offering decent wages for performable scripts. Shakespeare could earn one pound per act, or up to six pounds for a completed play, at a time when an actor might earn five shillings per week.

As theatre-making became a more permanent feature of the capital city, the Corporation of London – the local authority – took an increasingly dim view of the whole enterprise. Officials distrusted commercial drama as a matter of course. Plays attracted crowds, and crowds meant the risk of disorder. Regular afternoon performances encouraged citizens to spend their working days in idleness at the theatre. Stories featuring lechery and rebellion put ideas in spectators' heads and made the urban poor dissatisfied with their lot in life. The city passed ordinances restricting the times and places of performances, and compelled the taverns that had welcomed touring companies to bar their doors to drama. The new amphitheatres were built in the suburban sprawl of Middlesex and Surrey, not within the city walls. Only the fact that the queen summoned London's troupes to perform at court – which required them to 'rehearse' their plays in public – prevented the Corporation from banning plays outright. They might have wanted to rid the city of the crowds and time-wasting inseparable from drama, but theatre companies had support from aristocracy and royalty.

And the more glittering the connections, the safer a company was from civil interference. Since medieval times, juvenile cathedral choristers had performed plays on special occasions for the monarch, and from the 1570s, two of these choirs developed theatrical offshoots, semi-autonomous companies that staged plays in public (garnished with music and song) on the days when the boys weren't needed for divine services. Boy companies operated with the blessing of both the church and the royal court, and this twin protection gave them a commercial advantage over the more embattled adult players in the 1580s.

At intervals throughout his career, Shakespeare and his fellow adult actors had to compete with a parallel but distinct style of performance: casts composed entirely of child stars, boys who ranged in age from seven or eight to strapping late adolescents, blessed with dazzling singing voices and endowed with the services of the country's best writers. From the 1570s until 1590, then again from 1599 until about 1613, companies of boy actors exerted an outsize influence on theatrical fashion, establishing themselves in bijou indoor playhouses in the heart of London despite civic disapproval. When the Players in *Hamlet* (1601) abandon the city and come to Elsinore because of the threat posed by a new 'eyrie of children' (a competitor company ensconced, like Paul's Boys, in an upper room), the conclusion is that the 'boys carry it away' (2.2.339, 360): Shakespeare was to become ruefully aware that his greatest artistic challengers were a posse of teens and tweens. Boy companies managed to be both enmeshed in elite society, but also edgily countercultural. Ambitious writers like Ben Jonson, John Marston and John Fletcher used them to push innovative new forms of drama, satire and tragicomedy. Dramatists could take greater risks with plays performed by children: the unpaid schoolboy actors didn't backchat about their lines, and political subtext seemed more excusable to the authorities when delivered by youngsters (although the companies' periodic closures tended to be because they'd overstepped the mark and offended the very people from whom they drew their protection).

In his first months in London, Shakespeare absorbed the history of the boy players. He learned that Sebastian Westcott of St Paul's was the first choirmaster to make his theatrical 'rehearsals' public in 1576. His example was followed by a singing teacher in the Chapel Royal, who launched the Children of the Chapel in a room in what had been the Blackfriars monastery. By the mid-1580s, the two had merged (the Children of the Chapel would return as a separate entity in 1600), leaving Paul's Boys – now under a new impresario, Thomas Giles – the leader of the field. Until its closure in 1590, Paul's Playhouse enjoyed a reputation built over fourteen years as the place for fashionable, witty plays, expertly performed by several generations of young actors (the company experienced ongoing turnover of personnel as the boys grew up). Forming a profitable dual leadership with Giles was one of the most famous writers in the country, John Lyly. Already widely adored for his revolutionary prose works, which gave literary English the sort of dazzling *sprezzatura* of continental classics, Lyly was Paul's Boys' house dramatist. He was a suitable figure to lead such a high-class establishment: he had an MA from Oxford, a rich wife with lands in Yorkshire, a future as a Member of Parliament, and a long-treasured but unfulfilled hope to become Master of the Revels, the courtier with responsibility for licensing plays. (He was also grandson of William Lily, whose grammar book had been the bane of Shakespeare's childhood.) Like society dramatists since, he enjoyed putting portraits of real people in his plays. The scholar Gabriel Harvey advised, 'all you that tender the preservation of your good names' to stay on the right side of Lyly, or he would deploy his 'apes' at Paul's to 'make a play of you, and then is your credit quite undone for ever and ever.'

Harvey's characterisation of the Paul's actors as 'apes' figured them as obediently imitative chorus boys, but those in the know were more likely to think of them as precocious artistes who operated at a higher level of sophistication than common-or-garden adult players. In Marston's *Antonio's Revenge*, written for Paul's in 1602, a character scornfully dismisses as 'player-like' the kind of performance to be found in less stylish theatres: bosom-striking, foot-stamping, copious weeping. In contrast to the 'over-doing' grown-up actors on the suburban stages, Paul's Boys offered finely carved studies in human action, more artful than the performers in the inn-yards and amphitheatres. Part of this reputation for excellence was musical. As singers, they formed the best choir in the land, selected from the 'fairest voices of all the cathedral churches in England', according to the French-born linguist Claudius Holyband. Their value was also driven by scarcity. What with singing at religious services, and attending the choir school, the boys could only perform as actors once or twice per week during the social season that stretched from November to March. On winter afternoons, Paul's Playhouse was the place to be for courtiers, city gallants, foreign visitors and young dramatists keen to soak up one of the cultural highlights of the city.

Audiences were offered an extensive repertory, from earnest morality plays to translations of newly fashionable Greek tragedies. But it was Lyly's comedies that drew the crowds. *Campaspe* (1583) was set in the same languid world as the classical literature that Shakespeare could buy in Paul's Churchyard: Alexander the Great and the celebrity portraitist Apelles fall in love with the beautiful Theban prisoner Campaspe, amid some light philosophising from guest stars Aristotle, Plato and Diogenes. His *Sapho and Phao* (1584) took the rom-com intrigue further: a ferryman is rendered irresistibly sexy by Venus, which causes no end of trouble in the court of Queen Sapho (a figure with no relation to the queer poet of Lesbos). Lyly recognised that the choristers of Paul's were not just articulate schoolboys. He saw that their talents made them quadruple-threat performers: his plays gave a platform to the boys' virtuosic ability to act, sing, dance and tumble. In the late 1580s, Paul's Boys were famed for their physical deftness, linguistic quickness and aristocratic following.

It didn't hurt that Paul's Boys had long been Queen Elizabeth's favourite actors, invited to court more often than any other company. In their heyday, they appeared before the queen every winter, sometimes numerous times; this unprecedented royal favour prompted Westcott to build the theatre for public performances into the hall of his grace-and-favour home in the cathedral precinct. Paul's Playhouse was tiny, seating about a hundred spectators, but it kept its audience warm and dry (unlike the roofless amphitheatres) and had the necessary kit: a stage wider than it was deep, with two entrances and a central curtained opening known as the 'discovery space'; a gallery above for musicians, and an interior window through which the young actors could poke their heads; a good stock of costumes and stage props; and great branches of candles that lent flickering glamour to the late-afternoon performances, so different to the flat winter daylight of the outdoor theatres. Everything about the playhouse denoted sophistication, including the entry price: a seat cost up to sixpence, six times as expensive as a standing ticket at the Theatre or the Curtain.

The little theatre at Paul's was unique to Shakespeare's eyes. He was used to boy actors on the public stage. The companies he worked for trained teenaged apprentices to play the female roles, thereby ensuring a steady supply of new talent and keeping the stage free of women (a desire driven as much by misogyny as by any ostensible wish to save women from the loss of reputation that would come from public performance). But Paul's offered transgressive display of a wholly different order: the boys crossed boundaries of age, gender and status with virtually every role, upending conventional assumptions about what schoolboys should do and say. Shakespeare had never been witness to such staging and commodification of boys. They were primped and costumed and adorned for the entertainment of the adult audience: the very production values at Paul's spoke to an awareness of the boys' allure.

Boy companies were remarkably upfront about their appeal, given the opposition from a vocal anti-theatrical religious minority who had no doubt that players made a spectacle of themselves purely to provoke sexual desire. One commentator deplored the 'pretty upstart youths' of the Chapel Royal, who 'profane the Lord's Day by the lascivious writhing of their tender limbs, and gorgeous decking of their apparel, in feigning bawdy fables gathered from the idolatrous heathen poets.' Almost every subclause ticked off another category of sin: the boys breached the Sabbath by playing on Sundays; they moved in outrageously alluring ways; they wastefully adorned their bodies with silks and satins; they lied in impersonating others; and their plots were far too sexualised and – moreover – drawn from the pre-Christian myths of the Greeks and Romans. The polemicist Stephen Gosson warned of 'consorts of melody, to tickle the ear; costly apparel, to flatter the sight; effeminate gesture, to ravish the sense; and wanton speech, to whet desire to inordinate lust,' a sensory smorgasbord that suggests he was thinking of the boys' playhouses, where small orchestras – 'consorts' of professional musicians – played in the gallery (at this point, most music in the amphitheatres was provided by the actors on the main stage).

Shakespeare must have rolled his eyes at opinions like these. He knew religious extremists regarded his workplace as ground zero for sexual malpractice. The pamphleteer Philip Stubbes had recently conjured a vision of pornographic extravagance when he described a stage play as a cavalcade of 'kissing and bussing' that drove credulous spectators to imitation: aroused and inspired, wrote Stubbes, the crowd couple up and 'in their secret conclaves (covertly) they play the sodomites, or worse.' But notwithstanding the lurid accusations of the anti-theatrical campaigners, Shakespeare recognised that there was something provocative about the work of Paul's Boys, and the plays of Lyly in particular. Lyly had developed a form of drama that drew attention to the body of the actor, that platformed the queer allure – and the pederastic nature – of the boy-player convention in ways designed to be appealing to male and female theatregoers. Central to Shakespeare's realisation was the example of Lyly's romantic comedy *Galatea*, which he wrote for a royal premiere before the queen at Greenwich Palace on 1 January 1588. The play was the talk of the town in the first weeks of the new year.

Thomas Giles and John Lyly had shepherded the boys onto a couple of wherries at Paul's Wharf and directed the boatmen downriver to the sprawling red-brick palace on the south side of the Thames. The queen watched plays in her Great Chamber, the final state room in the sequence that led to her private apartments. The royal Office of the Wardrobe had spent the day draping every available surface with fine tapestries, while workmen threaded the ceiling with the spider's web of copper wire needed to suspend a constellation of wax candles. By the time the boys arrived at Greenwich, the queen's throne was in place on its dais, and the Office of Works' carpenters had fastened the wooden banks of seating firmly to the walls (no one wanted to be responsible for a collapsing bleacher filled with nobles). The crowded Great Chamber didn't have a tiring house (backstage area), or anything that could be used as one, so the playing space was flanked by painted canvas tents that functioned as wings: it was here the boys sat in the gloom waiting for their cues, or fumbled through a quick costume change before re-entering as a new character.

The show began late – the court kept hours that ordinary people seldom saw. It wasn't until ten o'clock at night that the queen made her torchlit entrance into the Great Chamber, and the boys – who had been waiting silently in their tents as the room filled up with chattering courtiers – could begin (naturally, with a flattering prologue addressed to Her Majesty).

Galatea was calculated to enthral its audience of politicians and royal hangers-on. Reworking the rural setting of Virgil's *Eclogues* and taking inspiration for his cast of meddling gods and bewildered mortals from Ovid's *Metamorphoses*, Lyly could not have been more attuned to the literary tastes of the crowd. And he gave his classical models a thrilling domestic familiarity by planting them in the unlikely setting of north-east England.

The play takes place in long-ago Humberside. When Viking raiders destroy a temple dedicated to Neptune, the angry god whips the North Sea into a deluge. Water covers the land: '[t]hen might you see ships sail where sheep fed, anchors cast where ploughs go' (1.1.33–34) – a set of images lifted wholesale from Ovid's description of the great flood in Book 1 of *Metamorphoses*. The sea god's conditions for release from the miserable flood are chilling. Every five years, the people of Lincolnshire must bring forth 'the fairest and chastest virgin in all the county' (1.1.48), tie her to a tree and leave her as a peace offering for Neptune. No one is quite sure what happens after that, but it involves the arrival of a terrifying monster called the Agar, who either drowns the girl, devours her, or conveys her to Neptune.

The shepherd Tityrus, unlucky father to a beautiful and virtuous daughter, Galatea, takes matters into his own hands. As the date of the sacrifice approaches, he dresses her as a boy and orders her into the woods to wait out the lethal visit from Agar. Galatea is affronted ('an honourable death is to be preferred before an infamous life' (1.1.83–84), she protests) but Tityrus won't be budged, and Galatea is dispatched into the wilderness.

Woodland Lincolnshire is busier than one might assume. Along with a trio of wisecracking brothers who have been shipwrecked on the Humber shore and depart severally into the woods to seek their fortunes, the forest is also a playground for the gods. Diana, virgin goddess of the hunt, pursues big game with her nymphs. Their iron-clad virginity outrages the little love god Cupid, who plots to shoot his love arrows at the nymphs so that they will all fall queerly in love with one another: Cupid can't wait to see them 'so confound their loves in their own sex' that they'll go crazy with lust and 'practice only impossibilities' (2.2.7–8, 9–10).

Of more interest to Galatea is the young man she discovers alone, like her, in the forest. Melibeus is an exquisite youth and the two are instantly captivated by each other; what Galatea doesn't know is that 'Melibeus' is really the female Phillida, also evacuated to the woods in male disguise by her protective father. Phillida and Galatea wrestle privately with their growing feelings, each conscious that to fall for a boy would reveal her protective disguise, even as they take the freedom afforded by male drag to flirt boldly with each other. 'Seeing we are both boys, and both lovers,' suggests Phillida, 'that our affection may have some show and seem as it were love, let me call thee mistress' (4.4.16–18). Under cover of this conceit, Phillida and Galatea fall in love.

Meanwhile, Cupid's pranks cause havoc among Diana's maidens. The same-sex love dart has worked in an unexpected way, with the entire nymph corps falling in love with the disguised Galatea and Phillida, whom the nymphs naturally take to be boys. Diana despairs (it's not a good look for the goddess of chastity to have her followers mad with desire) and sends her pining nymphs to arrest Cupid, thereby enraging Venus, the goddess of love, Cupid's mother and the chaste Diana's most implacable enemy.

The play moves to its conclusion. The arrival of Agar is tremblingly anticipated, but the monster proves a no-show when the virgin presented for sacrifice – poor plain Hebe – fails to whet his appetite by being insufficiently beautiful. Neptune threatens a renewed cataclysm in retaliation for all this mortal promise-breaking (beautiful girls put in breeches and hidden in the woods; plain ones offered up to a monster who has a strict fairest-only rule), but it's the discord between Diana and Venus that creates the space for resolution: Diana agrees to restore Cupid to his mother on the condition that Neptune abandon his quinquennial virgin sacrifice.

With Lincolnshire safe from Agar's ravages, Galatea and Phillida emerge from the forest to a welcoming committee comprising their fathers and a whole panoply of gods and nymphs. Their disguise is lifted and if the girls are briefly dismayed – 'Unfortunate Galatea, if this be Phillida!' (5.3.120) – it doesn't take long for the purity of their love to win out. 'I will never love any but Phillida,' swears Galatea. 'Her love is engraven in my heart with her eyes' (135–6). Neptune is nonplussed and Diana prudishly outraged at this apparently unnatural coupling. Venus, however, regards the girls' devotion as a win for the power of love. 'I like well and allow it,' she declares. 'They shall both be possessed of their wishes, for never shall it be said that nature or fortune shall overthrow love and faith' (143–45). Assured that the girls' love is to be lifelong, Venus takes it upon herself to transform one of the girls into a young man in order to allow them to marry. With the consent of the gods and the girls' fathers, the wedding party departs for the nearest chapel (the land of pagan temples has now become one of parish churches) – where, at the porch, one of the girls (we never learn who) will undergo a transition and become male in order to permit the solemnisation of their goddess-granted nuptials.

Galatea, restaged at Paul's in the weeks after its premiere and published in 1592, acted like imaginative fertiliser on Shakespeare's brain. Lyly was doing something that he had never seen before in re-situating Ovidian myth in the distant English past. Underlying *Galatea* was the story of Iphis and Ianthe from Book 9 of *Metamorphoses*, and the act of transformation that sees Iphis become a man through the intercession of the goddess Isis. But even more startling was the way that Lyly used the resources and capacities of the theatre to significantly ramp up the impact of his play. *Galatea* wasn't just a tale about two beautiful virgins falling in love with each other. It was a living drama in which the bodies of the performers playing Galatea and Phillida – boy actors portraying girls disguised as boys, one of whom *becomes* a boy – served a vital function in the story's exploration of desire and transformation.

Lyly understood that his boys-playing-girls-playing-boys brought on to the stage a sort of titillating irony. Paul's Boys traded in knowing artifice whatever the play – any story required them to embody some category of person other than their own – but *Galatea* marked a step up in the sophistication of this sort of layered impersonation. The 'disguises' adopted by Galatea and Phillida are – in fact – simply the usual attire of the young actors performing the roles. In hiding the characters' femaleness, Lyly asked his audience to 'see' the actors' male bodies, and to incorporate their identity as boys into the love plot of the play.

Not everyone would have been willing or able to do so. Some spectators reconciled themselves to the boy actor tradition – either in all-boy companies or on the adult commercial stage – by regarding it as a bloodless convention. The writer Mary Wroth thought boys could perform the gestures of femininity well enough, but to watch a 'delicate play-boy act a loving woman's part' was to observe action without passion. Others invested completely in the idea that the performer on stage was female. After attending a production of *Othello* on tour in Oxford in 1610, student Henry Jackson recorded the deep impression that the dying Desdemona had made on the audience: 'stretched out on her bed she begged the spectators' pity with her very facial expression' (Jackson wrote in Latin, a language that inscribed the femaleness of the boy actor playing Desdemona into the grammar of the sentence). Wroth's and Jackson's responses depended on the ability of the spectator to either see through or ignore the boy in front of them. Lyly was demanding that his boys be noticed, whatever unexpected thoughts and feelings that provoked in his spectators.

Galatea established the London theatre as a place of queer and trans possibility – at least for those inclined to detect it. Lyly gave vent not only to the same-sex desires of Galatea and Phillida, but to the capacity for trans self-determination that existed in myth as well as early modern notions of physiology. Venus's ruling – 'I like well and allow it' – retrospectively endorses the characters' queer relationship, and grants one of the lovers the body they require in order to live the truth of their 'love and faith' within the security of marriage. This was a female-to-male transition that was understood to be eminently feasible: in Montaigne's *Essays*, the philosopher related the story of a young female-presenting person whose hitherto-hidden male sexual organs were thrust out when they 'strained [themselves]' in an act of physical exertion. According to Galenic theories of the human body – in which female genitalia were understood to be an interior, inverted form of a male penis and testes – any woman whose body was 'hot' enough to shake loose their sexual organs was potentially a trans man (male-to-female transition wasn't understood to be spontaneously possible in the same way). Boy actors playing female characters who disguise themselves as young men might have become a convention on Shakespeare's stage, but the conceit tapped into powerful and unstable contemporary notions about gender and sex.

Where Lyly went, other dramatists followed. In the years after *Galatea*, up to the closing of the theatres by Parliament in 1642, seventy-five surviving plays featured a heroine, played by a boy, in male disguise. Given the quantity of lost plays that were staged but never printed, we'll never know quite how often the English stage deployed the boy-playing-a-girl-playing-a-boy trope, but it was evidently regarded as powerfully appealing. As *Twelfth Night*'s Malvolio finds of Viola/Cesario, the 'well-favoured' (1.5.160) youth has a threshold allure that the steward can't quite put his finger on: he's 'as a squash is before 'tis a peascod, or a codling when 'tis almost an apple: 'tis with him in standing water, between boy and man' (1.5.157–59). The young lady disguised as a youth, performed by a boy – and the same description applies to Sebastian, a youth performed by a youth – appears to hover between sexual and temporal states; between the bulgingly phallic squash, and the slender, vulvic pea-pod; between the prematurity of adolescence and the readiness of adulthood.

It didn't take long for Shakespeare to tap into the erotic promise and genderqueer potential that some early modern theatregoers understood to exist in the juvenile boy actor. He brought the conceit into his early comedies *The Two Gentlemen of Verona*, with Julia disguised as Sebastian, and *The Merchant of Venice*, with no fewer than three cross-dressed young women. Portia, Nerissa and Jessica all adopt 'the lovely garnish of a boy', as Jessica's lover Lorenzo approvingly puts it (2.6.45). When Portia and Nerissa take on new identities as a lawyer and his clerk in order to win Antonio's release from Shylock's bond, the two women linger on the confusingly sexy consequences of their disguises. Portia sees herself and Nerissa 'accoutred like young men' (3.4.63) in the boisterous company of other men, bragging about their imagined sexual conquests (which is certainly not the nature of the sombre character of a lawyer she actually adopts). It's a sufficiently stimulating fantasy that both women find themselves thinking about the male sexual organs their disguises will imply: it will be thought 'we are accomplished / With that we lack' (61–62), says Portia.

Two of Shakespeare's plays show most clearly the evolution of his Lylian inheritance, as he worked through the inspirational effects of *Galatea* on his imagination. *A Midsummer Night's Dream* is, at the level of plot, effectively *Galatea* redux: confused humans – Demetrius and Lysander and Helena and Hermia, and the bumbling amateur actors led by Nick Bottom and Peter Quince – find themselves caught in the crossfire of battling immortals when they head into the woods. Shakespeare advertised his debt to Lyly in Act 2 Scene 1, when he restaged *Galatea*'s

confrontation between Cupid and a Nymph of Diana as the opening salvo in the Titania–Oberon dispute: Puck, Oberon's right-
hand sprite, squares off against a Fairy follower of Titania.
Shakespeare gives Puck much of Cupid's amorous disruptiveness:
the 'love-in-idleness' (2.1.168) magical flower, source of the potion
that spreads disorder amongst the young lovers and bewitches
Titania into adoring the ass-headed Bottom, is Cupid's arrow in
another form. And the desires triggered by Puck's interference are
as queerly atypical as the 'new conceits' and 'strange contraries'
(*Galatea*, 3.1.1–2) that affect Lyly's nymphs: the disdained Helena
becomes a boy-magnet as both Demetrius and Lysander fall over
themselves to sleep with her, and Titania is pushed towards cross-
species consummation when she takes the metamorphosed
Bottom to her 'flowery bed' (3.1.129).

But it wasn't until *As You Like It* that Shakespeare really
engaged with the iconic image of *Galatea*: two boys, in love,
seducing each other in the Virgilian utopia of the greenwood.
Although Shakespeare took his story from Thomas Lodge's
Rosalind, Galatea and Phillida's courtship was the guiding model
for the central relationship in the play between Orlando and
Ganymede, the revealingly named alter ego that Rosalind adopts
when she escapes into the Forest of Arden. *As You Like It* was the
first time that Shakespeare had built a play around the queer
allure of the boy actor. He encouraged – urged – his audience to
pay attention to the overlapping bodies that the actor playing
Rosalind materialised on stage: the young noblewoman and the
forthright woodsman Ganymede of the narrative, and the real-
life body of the multitalented performer playing the part.

As in the woods of *A Midsummer Night's Dream* and *Galatea*,
numerous strands of plot converge on the Forest of Arden in *As
You Like It*. It's a place of exile for the virtuous Duke, whose rule
has been usurped by his wicked brother; it's where the good
Duke's daughter Rosalind flees in company with her cousin

Celia, the bad Duke's daughter; and it also provides a hiding place for put-upon young gentleman Orlando, whose own brother plots his death (families truly are hell in this play). Meanwhile, disparate communities of shepherds and foresters make their livings in the space left by these urban refugees, who have brought their courtly habits of poetry-writing and hunting into the countryside.

Orlando and Rosalind first meet, and begin to fall in love, when the latter witnesses the former triumph in a wrestling match. But banishment intervenes before the relationship can proceed. To ensure her safety on the road, Rosalind – 'more than common tall' – opts to disguise herself as a 'swashing and a martial' youth (1.3.115, 120). The ever-overlooked Celia merely smears her face with dirt and wears very unattractive clothes: her chosen pseudonym 'Aliena' underscores the racist early modern association between darkened skin and foreigners. The girls' adventure, for all it begins in heartache and fear, is rapidly becoming a bit of a lark: Rosalind imagines arming herself with a cutlass and striding about with a boar spear. From the beginning, she's alive to the queer associations of her male guise, resonantly named 'Ganymede'. And in case anyone should miss the implication, Rosalind spells it out: she's calling herself after 'Jove's own page' (1.3.124). Her new name and identity give her the licence to take the lead in wooing Orlando, whom she rediscovers – much to her delight – in the forest.

There's nothing in the story to stop Rosalind – now safely in the Forest of Arden and near her father's campsite – shedding her Ganymede disguise and presenting herself demurely to Orlando to continue their courtship in a conventional manner. Instead, Rosalind cleaves to the masculinity that gives her such freedom, a decision that casts the Rosalind–Orlando affair as an exercise in queer love-play. She proposes what is ostensibly a 'cure' (3.2.406) for the besotted Orlando: he is to come and woo Ganymede as if the boy were Rosalind, and Ganymede will perform such a convincing impression of infuriating changeability that Orlando will soon give over the very idea of love.

It's entirely part of Rosalind's plan that she doesn't put off Orlando in the slightest: soon, Ganymede and Orlando are a couple. Rosalind/Ganymede ropes in Celia to play the priest and 'marry' them (4.1.125). The queer wedding that takes place offstage in *Galatea* – two girls who look like boys, one of whom transitions to male in the instant of marriage – is dramatised in *As You Like It* with the male-presenting Rosalind/Ganymede and Orlando. It's not a fully legal marriage, to be sure (although early modern law understood that spoken vows *per verba de praesenti*, or given in the presence of witnesses, constituted a binding union) but the powerful words 'I take thee, Rosalind, for wife' (137) and 'I do take thee, Orlando, for my husband' (139) are uttered by two young men, attired as such, on a public stage.

Shakespeare leaves it to Celia – watching in astonishment as Rosalind plays fast and loose with her society's ideas of gender, sexuality and decorum – to raise the question of what's really going on under Ganymede's performance:

> You have simply misused our sex in your love-prate. We must have your doublet and hose plucked over your head, and show the world what the bird hath done to her own nest. (4.1.201–4)

It's an understandable eruption of anger – Celia, herself devoted in decidedly queer ways to her cousin, stands to lose the intimacy she enjoyed with Rosalind if the latter marries Orlando – but her imaginary punishment of Rosalind draws sudden and vivid attention to the body on stage. This fantasy of exposure – Rosalind/Ganymede stripped of her clothing – invites two conclusions and more than a few interpretations. The first conclusion is that Rosalind has 'fouled her own nest' through her behaviour with Orlando, a vivid metaphor that can only imply a literal or figurative transformation of her female genitalia. Perhaps Celia suggests that the naked Rosalind would bear the signs of insatiable lovemaking; or possibly that her male-presenting behaviour as Ganymede will have effected a physical alteration to her very body, like Montaigne's spontaneously transitioning Frenchman.

We can draw another conclusion from Celia's threat: that this is a moment at which Shakespeare wants us to recognise the boy actor himself, to reflect on the body beneath the costume, and understand that Rosalind/Ganymede (and Celia, for that matter) bring their boyness to bear on the appeal that they wield on stage. It's a tactic Shakespeare deployed rarely but forcefully: some years later in *Antony and Cleopatra,* the boy actor playing the Egyptian queen would reflect, at a moment of intense emotional duress, that she can't bear the thought of being taken in chains to Rome where public mockery will accompany her progress through the streets, and '[s]ome squeaking Cleopatra' (an adolescent actor) will 'boy my greatness / I'the posture of a whore' (5.2.220–21). It's a confident – even hubristic – line that invites the audience to note that the actor they are watching on stage is leagues ahead of the imagined Roman performer. But to register the dramatic irony of the line, the spectators in the theatre must first really *see* that Shakespeare's Cleopatra – the paragon of female erotic allure 'whom everything becomes' (1.1.49) (who is made irresistible by every characteristic and fashion) – is a teenage boy.

In an adult playing company, it was the squeaking Cleopatras who bore the chief responsibility for generating on-stage sex appeal designed to titillate men and women in the audience, and Shakespeare seized on the idea that Rosalind/Ganymede captured the queer, fluid effect of the disguised heroine embodied by a boy. In an almost unprecedented move, he wrote an epilogue to *As You Like It* to be spoken by Rosalind – *almost* unprecedented, because there are very few other early modern dramas in which the epilogue is voiced by a female character, and *Galatea* got there first (although whether we are to imagine that Galatea has at this point, beyond the end of the story, already been transformed into a man by Venus, we are left to ponder).

Rosalind's epilogue is in some ways a conventional appeal for applause. But she also positions herself as an active participant in the romantic lives of the playhouse audience:

It is not the fashion to see the lady the epilogue, but it is no more unhandsome than to see the lord the prologue [. . .]. I am not furnished like a beggar; therefore to beg will not become me. My way is to conjure you, and I'll begin with the women. I charge you, O women, for the love you bear to men, to like as much of this play as please you; and I charge you, O men, for the love you bear to women – as I perceive by your simpering none of you hates them – that between you and the women the play may please. If I were a woman, I would kiss as many of you as had beards that pleased me, complexions that liked me, and breaths that I defied not. And I am sure as many as have good beards, or good faces, or sweet breaths, will – for my kind offer – when I make curtsy, bid me farewell. (Epi., 1–23)

Thanks to her deft wooing and matchmaking in *As You Like It*, Rosalind has turned into a sort of sex expert in the ways men and women negotiate their pleasures and preferences. The epilogue brings the playhouse audience suddenly into view, characterising them as an erotically charged crowd of potential lovers – women who love men and men who 'simper' towards the women they like. But the dynamic that Rosalind invokes is not nearly as hetero-conventional as that seems. When Rosalind requests that 'between [the men] and the women [in the audience] the play may please', she means that she hopes approbation from both sexes will ensure the play's success. But she also hints that the play itself, and perhaps the characters in it, belong in the space between a man and a woman: she drops an erotic double meaning that positions *As You Like It* as a sex aid for courting couples. And there's more: Rosalind both declares that she's a lady and denies she's a woman ('[i]t is not the fashion to see the lady the epilogue'; '[i]f I were a woman . . .'), and then raises the notion of kissing her way through the playhouse audience to secure their approval – implicitly the male spectators, but the sentence allows for the possibility that Rosalind includes well-complexioned and sweet-breathed women. Rosalind of the epilogue – who brings with her the recent memory of her identity as Ganymede – is an omni-lover, flexibly male or female, and potentially available for the enjoyment of anyone in the audience.

Were these queer moments intended for everyone? Rosalind's pose in the epilogue fashions the character as cheerfully, if not voraciously, fluid and bisexual. Earlier in the play, Rosalind/Ganymede had offered the worldly observation that 'boys and women' are 'cattle' of the same colour in their wilful responsiveness to being wooed by men (3.2.414–15), conjuring not just the queer conventions of pastoral romance, but capturing something of the sexual politics of early modern England as well. However much godly Englishmen should be expected to resist it, attractive youths were understood to be just as much of a sexual temptation as beautiful women. But it's difficult to believe that all members of the audience, at the Globe during *As You Like It* or Paul's during *Galatea*, responded in the same way to such queer dynamics. It's more likely the theatre acted as a beacon – and a haven – for people whose gender identity and sexuality found fewer safe harbours elsewhere. The vision of trans masculinity invoked by the many disguised heroines of early modern drama might have offered consolation or encouragement to gender-nonconforming people in the audience. London's playhouses had a reputation as spaces where men and women could be seen exceeding the bounds of acceptably gendered behaviour. In a satirical poem about the Jacobean indoor theatre, *Notes from Blackfriars* (1617), the writer Henry Fitzgeffrey affected horror to see an unaccompanied 'woman of the masculine gender' settle down among the fashionable male gallants. The gender-nonconforming Mary Frith, or Moll Cutpurse, a working-class cavalier who was punished by London's ecclesiastical court for wearing men's attire, had their fame confirmed when a sympathetic play about them – *The Roaring Girl* (1611) by Thomas Middleton and Thomas Dekker – was staged at the Fortune theatre (the character of Frith was played by a boy, but the real-life Frith appeared on stage as an after-piece to play the lute and sing a song). In a society that was overwhelmingly hostile to overtly expressed gender or sexuality variance, theatres stood out for the more expansive vision found on their stages and in their auditoria.

But as Shakespeare's epilogue to *As You Like It* suggests, the liberality of the stage had a potentially darker aspect. Rosalind's final speech was the first and only time that Shakespeare drew such forthright attention to the boy actor as a sexually available figure, and it calls into question the conditions under which boys and young men worked in the adult and children's companies. It's not easy to uncover the forms of sexual exploitation that existed in early modern playhouses. Among cases of child sexual assault that survive in court or church archives, there are no explicit records of abuse within theatre companies – which isn't to say that such crimes didn't take place (and theatre troupes certainly didn't escape accusations of mistreatment). It's difficult to believe that boy actors escaped abuse or unwanted sexual attention, and Shakespeare was well aware that the erotic charge borne by a boy player on stage carried over into the real world.

Willingly or not, his own junior colleagues were required to entertain punters: Ben Jonson described how Richard Robinson, the leading lady of the King's Men in the 1610s, dressed as a woman to be taken out for dinner by a male admirer. Edward Dering, a wealthy theatre fan in the early seventeenth century whose account book records the first known purchase of the First Folio, paid out gratuities to boys at the Blackfriars and Cockpit (another indoor playhouse). The anti-theatrical campaigner William Prynne condemned men 'who have been desperately enamoured with players' boys thus clad in women's apparel, so far as to solicit them by words, by letters, even actually to abuse them.' That the boy companies were held to be titillating for men was so widespread a view as to be the subject of jokes. Thomas Middleton satirised the Children of the Chapel at Blackfriars as a 'nest of boys able to ravish a man'. Thomas Dekker, in his mock-conduct manual *The Gull's Horn-book* (1609), considered a few pennies handed out at the playhouse as money well spent for any dissolute gallant who wished to 'purchase the dear acquaintance of the boys'.

Boys were certainly recognised as sexual temptation for women, too, but the lustful audience member was most commonly imagined as male, turned on both by the femininity of boys-playing-women and by the masculinity of the youths themselves. Comments later in the seventeenth century, after the introduction of female performers, looked back to a time when male theatregoers ran wild for attractive boy actors:

When boys played women's parts, you'd think the stage
Was innocent in that untempting age.
No: for your amorous fathers then, like you,
Amongst those boys had playhouses Misses too.
They set those bearded beauties on their laps,
Men gave 'em kisses and the ladies, claps.

If the Restoration gallant's foible was his habit of seducing actresses, his predecessor earlier in the century did exactly the same thing with the boy players, who in their wigs and gowns made a dazzling spectacle. Boys who played female roles had every assistance from costume and cosmetics to look the part: garments like hooped underskirts, bum-rolls and bodices built a convincingly feminine silhouette, while costly hairpieces made out of silk were teased into the latest court styles. A fucus (or paste) of white lead covered up any skin breakouts, and a final dusting of crushed oyster shells gave the boys the lustre of true stars. The Oxford theologian John Rainolds urged his readers to beware 'beautiful boys' in female costume; just as a man might get sinfully aroused by looking at a painting of an attractive woman, or a particularly curvy statue, so the artifice of a convincing female impersonator could work dangerous magic on the average hot-blooded male.

But as the reference to 'bearded beauties' in the Restoration verse suggests, the boys' masculinity was part of the lure, too. Playwrights wrote parts for witty, knowing youths that were then embodied by lively, articulate young actors – and plenty of dramatists dialled up the innuendo when writing for the boy companies. When the half-Italian John Marston, in *Antonio and Mellida* (1599), called his two smart-aleck pages Cazzo (Italian slang for penis) and Dildo (the meaning of which hasn't changed), he wanted his audience to notice the phallic terms attached to these young servants. Marston had a particular obsession with the worldly-before-his-time pageboy. In *What You Will* (1601), a company of angry young servants stages a mock court case against the 'profane use we are put to'. High on the indictment list is the master, who is as 'libidinous as Priapus' and for whom his page does service both as a sexual bait – 'he keeps me as his adamant to draw metal after to his lodging' – and a sort of preparatory fluffer: 'I am his frotterer or rubber in a hot-house.'

It was widely understood that adolescents and young men in the theatre were vulnerable to sexual exploitation. Ben Jonson alludes to the issue in *Poetaster* (1601), his Roman satire for the Children of the Chapel. The braggart Tucca tries to hire out his pageboys by the week to the actor Histrio. Part of his bargain-driving includes the accusation that the 'mangonizing' (slave-dealing) Histrio will 'sell 'em for ingles', or pimp the pages out as prostitutes (3.4.210–11). Shakespeare wasn't as blunt as Jonson, but the pimpability of boys connected to the theatre lies behind the Induction of *The Taming of the Shrew* (*c*.1590). A nobleman and his friends make the drunken Sly believe he is an amnesiac lord and set him to watch a group of travelling players. For additional hilarity, the nobleman orders his pageboy, Bartholomew, dressed 'in all suits like a lady' (Ind., 1.106), into Sly's chamber to keep him company and pretend to be his wife. A tumescent Sly tells Bartholomew to undress and come to bed; seduction is only avoided when Bartholomew explains that Sly is under doctor's orders to abstain from sex for two nights.

A scandal that engulfed the Children of the Chapel gives us a glimpse of some of the anxieties about the boy companies that circulated in Shakespeare's London. In December 1600, thirteen-year-old Thomas Clifton, son of a Norfolk landowner, was snatched off the street as he walked from his father's lodgings in Smithfield to Christ's Hospital grammar school in Newgate. Thomas was dragged south to the Blackfriars playhouse, where he was brought into a 'company of lewd and dissolute' players (in the words of his father's subsequent lawsuit) who revealed their intention to press the boy into service as an actor. As later became evident, the kidnappers knew very little about the boy, and they didn't seize him because of any abilities on his part in acting or singing. Thomas was probably taken simply because his looks were right for the company.

When Thomas's father objected, he received a shock. Nathaniel Giles and Henry Evans, the adult managers of the company, informed him – curtly – that they had the authority to take anyone's son in the land, be he gentry or nobleman, and Clifton had no right of appeal. The newly re-established Children of the Chapel needed an influx of talent, and Giles possessed a Royal Commission that empowered him to take as 'many children as he [. . .] shall think meet, in all cathedral, collegiate, parish churches, chapels, or any other place or places [. . .] within this our realm of England' in order to furnish the queen's Chapel Royal with 'well-singing children'. The businessmen running the Children of the Chapel had taken advantage of the commission of impressment intended for the royal choirs to acquire – kidnap – boys for the theatre company they ran for their own personal profit. It was a deeply shabby situation.

Clifton was the first person affected by theatrical impressment with the social clout to kick up a fuss. Appalled at his son's 'base restraint and misusage', he pulled strings to secure Thomas's release. Then he hit the Children of the Chapel with a lawsuit that dwelt on the 'corrupt and undue purposes' by which his son had been 'abusively employed' in the 'vile and base manner of a mercenary player'. Clifton's complaint wasn't with the notion of choral impressment (although, as he pointed out, Thomas couldn't sing): it was that his boy had been forced into the murky, morally questionable world of the theatre, where he'd be prey to cynical exploitation – or worse – by men like Giles and Evans. Behind the glamour and sophistication of the Children of the Chapel and Paul's Boys lay a disturbing institutional framework that allowed the trafficking, exploitation and objectification of boys and young men for the entertainment of Londoners.

Shakespeare came to understand something of the workings of the boy companies in the years after the premiere of Lyly's

Galatea in 1588, although unlike many of his contemporaries he never wrote a play for them (and for most of the 1590s the theatres at St Paul's and Blackfriars were mothballed due to political missteps on the part of their adult managers). Phillida and Galatea remained on his mind, as did the exploitative nature of the labour that boy players were put to – in his own and competitor theatre companies. He knew how to draw attention to the erotic appeal of the young actors on stage, in female attire and out of it, and he understood that their subjection and vulnerability were in themselves a powerful lure for some spectators. Even late in his career he hadn't finished objectifying his boy actors. In *Cymbeline* (1610), when the imperilled princess Imogen disguises herself as the boy Fidele to seek service with the Roman general Lucius, she provokes bewildered erotic fascination in virtually every man she meets – and not just because they detect the girl beneath. As her servant Pisanio lays out the course she must take, he seems to imagine the creepy harassment that a solitary youth is prey to: Imogen/Fidele will have to '[f]orget that rarest treasure of your cheek, / Exposing it [. . .] to the greedy touch / Of common-kissing Titan' (3.4.160–63). In picturing the coarsening effects of sunshine on Imogen's hitherto-untanned skin, Pisanio reaches for a simile that figures the sun-god as an over-affectionate groper, slobbering kisses on every young man he can reach. Pisanio's concern is well founded. Before too long, Imogen/Fidele has dazzled a boy who turns out to be her long-lost brother ('Were you a woman, youth, / I should woo hard' (3.6.68–69)) and succeeded in winning an intense affection from Lucius that is even more remarkable for the speed with which it is kindled. Indeed, when Imogen swiftly cuts herself free from Lucius's service, the Roman general – still thinking her to be Fidele – reflects bitterly on the ambivalent pleasures due to a man who seeks satisfaction from the pursuit of youth: 'Briefly die their joys / That place them on the truth of girls and boys,' he says (5.5.106–7). Like Viola and Sebastian, the obedient Messaline twins in *Twelfth Night*, Imogen/Fidele has an overwhelmingly potent queer allure that is made even more powerful by her position as a vulnerable youth in service – a vulnerability shared by the boys in indentured employment in the adult troupes and the children's companies.

The male- and female-presenting boy actors of Shakespeare's London were a complex aspect of early modern England's queer culture. Their gender nonconformity helped establish the city's theatres as places of queer self-expression that were (marginally) safer than elsewhere, but their lives as objectified and eroticised boys in service exposed them to risk and exploitation. There's no evidence, for good or bad, of Shakespeare's own relationships with his boy-actor colleagues, but his presentation of girls-disguised-as-boys in *The Two Gentlemen of Verona*, *The Merchant of Venice*, *As You Like It*, *Twelfth Night* and *Cymbeline* shows that he was well aware of the dramatic and erotic potential contained within the boys' bodies beneath the female costumes. He had John Lyly to thank for showing him how to harness that particular aspect of early modern English theatre culture, but Shakespeare's most significant queer theatrical mentor was a figure much closer to him in age, status, background and profession, who had made his name in the adult commercial companies which toured the provinces and were making an increasing splash in the big London amphitheatres. Enter Christopher Marlowe, Shakespeare's tough – albeit doomed – queer twin.

4

Kings and Minions

Early 1592. It gave William an odd feeling to know he would be sharing the bed with four of his own severed heads. The wax models of Suffolk, Say, Cromer and Cade were wrapped in a blanket, tucked up in the bedstead for safekeeping while they awaited their next outing in The Contention, his chronicle about Henry VI. He worried he'd become fixated with heads in that play, although it couldn't be denied the audience loved seeing the piked remains of Lord Say and Sir James Cromer kiss, to the jeers of the soon-to-be-beheaded rebel Jack Cade, and he admitted it was a nice touch to have Queen Margaret lug round Suffolk's head like a babe in arms. But he needed a new tone for his English histories, something with less of the feel of the executioner's scaffold. He hoped the play in his hands would help.

He pushed the heads carefully to one side and climbed into the bed, then settled against the bolster, his boots hanging over the side. He wouldn't normally have made himself at home in a prop, but he was here to read and it happened to be the only place in the tiring house that got plenty of light. Besides, it meant he'd be out of the way while Pembroke's Men readied themselves for the afternoon's performance of Edward II. The tirewomen had already set out the costumes, masses of them, a trousseau of cloaks and jerkins and gowns on every actor's peg.

He didn't have long. They'd sound the trumpets in an hour, and the bookkeeper would need the manuscript to prompt the show. Kit had sweet-talked the old man into letting him read it in the first place.

William's Henry VI plays might have been part of Pembroke's repertory, but that didn't mean he was still a company man. He was with Lord Strange's Men now, and therefore an interloper at the Theatre, for all that he knew the old playhouse like his own home. Players weren't keen on foreign hands getting hold of their assets.

He'd already seen Kit's chronicle play twice, crammed with hundreds of others in the yard. But to read it like this was a privilege. William had known after his first viewing that he'd have to borrow the prompt copy if he was ever going to understand what Kit had done with the material. It wasn't like he could buy the script; Kit had waited three years before putting his Tamburlaine the Great through the press. William couldn't hang around that long for Edward II. Now, he read and absorbed: he saw new detail in the play's structure; the complementary excesses of the king and his favourite Piers Gaveston, and the queen and her lover Mortimer. Unobtrusively, he made notes.

He was dimly aware, as he sped through the handwritten pages, of activity in the tiring house. The actors were marking their entrances and exits in preparation for the approaching performance, checking the cursory stage directions in their own parts against the instructions in the scene plot nailed to the tiring house wall. Some of them muttered through their lines at double speed. William finished reading (he noticed that Kit included a severed head in his final scene, too) and looked up. 'Edward' and 'Gaveston' were dressed: Master Nicholls with a golden coronet, Master Cooke in the company's most expensive slashed doublet. Parts in hand, they were walking through their first scene. Cooke dropped to his knees at his lord's feet. Gently, Nicholls pulled him up, took him in his arms and kissed him on the lips. As they embraced, Nicholls's crown – tarnished gold leaf on wood – slipped, coming to rest on Cooke's velvet hat. 'Gaveston' took it off and smiled.

That's not how the play ends, he said.

The career of Christopher Marlowe is almost as hard to trace in the tangle of late Elizabethan theatreland as Shakespeare's.

Companies merged, thrived, dwindled, went bankrupt and were born again under a new patron; personnel slipped between payrolls and impresarios like the pioneers of a start-up industry that they were. But the early 1590s saw plays by both men briefly converge in the repertory of the short-lived Pembroke's Men, a troupe under the protection of Henry Herbert, second Earl of Pembroke. (Herbert's wife, Mary Sidney, was herself an important poet; their two sons, William and Philip, would be the dedicatees of the First Folio in 1623.) Pembroke's Men contained within its ranks several young members who would go on to star in the Lord Chamberlain's Men, although its shareholders – two of whom, Lionel Cooke and Robert Nicholls, appear speculatively in the vignette above – were less distinguished actors who had no great futures. Among the plays owned by Pembroke's Men, which they took on the road and performed in London, were Shakespeare's *The First Part of the Contention Betwixt the Two Famous Houses of York and Lancaster (Henry VI Part 2)* and *The True Tragedy of Richard Duke of York (Henry VI Part 3)*, and Marlowe's *Edward II*. All three later appeared in print under the company's name. *Edward II (c.*1592) – Marlowe's story of the medieval king destroyed by ambitious barons who cannot bear the monarch's relationship with Gaveston, his beloved male favourite – was to have a transformative effect on the way Shakespeare wrote history plays, and provided the model for *Richard II* (1595), his most lyrical and moving historical tragedy.

If anyone deserves to be the subject of a book on queer early modern lives, it's Marlowe. His reputation is intoxicatingly glamorous. A university intellectual who failed to complete his MA because he was busy spying for the queen, he wrote (or co-wrote) seven smash-hit plays and a good deal of fashionable verse while embroiling himself in the struggles of late-Elizabethan statecraft. He held dangerously advanced religious beliefs that teetered on the edge of heresy, and harboured a temper that flashed out in violence and street brawls. In spite of his enemies, he owned up to his desires: those 'that love not tobacco and boys were fools', he was said to have bragged. And to top it all, he was dashingly good-looking: a portrait dated 1585 shows a well-dressed twenty-one-year-old with a leonine sweep of chestnut hair and a piercing gaze. That he died in mysterious circumstances before his thirtieth birthday, stabbed in the eye, has cast over his wild life and untimely death an air of queer martyrdom. In contrast to Marlowe the sexy iconoclast, Shakespeare's life can't help but seem a little pedestrian.

The two men invite, even demand, comparison. Born the same year, two months apart (Marlowe the elder), they were both first surviving sons to middling craftsmen in the provinces – Marlowe's father was a shoemaker in Canterbury, Kent. Both came to tower over their contemporaries: Marlowe's *Tamburlaine the Great* (*c.*1587) was among the most emulated plays of the 1580s and 1590s, and dramatists were lifting phrases from *The Jew of Malta* (*c.*1590) and *Doctor Faustus* (*c.*1592) until the middle of the seventeenth century. Marlowe and Shakespeare trod the same ground in the early 1590s: they were neighbours (Shakespeare in Shoreditch, Marlowe a few steps south in Norton Folgate), as well as colleagues and perhaps co-writers with Pembroke's Men at the Theatre and Strange's Men at the Rose. After Marlowe's death, Shakespeare would plant two acknowledgements of the loss in *As You Like It*. The countrywoman Phoebe, besotted with Rosalind/Ganymede, honours the wisdom of a line from Marlowe's erotic poem *Hero and Leander*:

Dead shepherd, now I find thy saw of might,
'Who ever loved, that loved not at first sight?' (3.5.81–82)

Elsewhere, the philosophical clown Touchstone reflects that for a man to have his poetry misunderstood strikes him 'more dead than a great reckoning in a little room' (3.3.14–15) – not merely an echo of *The Jew of Malta*'s 'infinite riches in a little room' (1.1.37), but seemingly an allusion to the alleged cause of Marlowe's violent death: an argument over the 'reckoning', or bill, in a Deptford eating house.

Marlowe was the contemporary whose death cleared the way for Shakespeare to dominate the drama of the late 1590s and 1600s, but he was also the predecessor whose astonishing achievements gave Shakespeare an example for imitation, and a height to surpass. Scholars have traced allusions to Marlowe's work in twenty plays by Shakespeare. Early in his career, Shakespeare found himself inspired by the ambitious, amoral anti-hero of Marlowe's *Tamburlaine* when he created Aaron in *Titus Andronicus*, who launches a bid to control Rome through his mistress, the new Empress Tamora. The continuing popularity of *The Jew of Malta* probably lay behind Shakespeare's own decision to write a play that peddled in – but also called into question – his society's virulent anti-Semitism, *The Merchant of Venice*. Marlowe's influence on Shakespeare continued long after the older poet's death: there's more than a touch of Faustus's satanic overreaching in Macbeth's witch-inspired ambition to seize the crown of Scotland. *Edward II* was different. Written at a time when both Marlowe and Shakespeare were experimenting with the history play genre, it represented a breathtaking leap forward in the form that was to have significant consequences for Shakespeare, who had just completed his own sprawling history cycle carved out of the English chronicles. *Edward II* showed Shakespeare how to create a new form of tightly focused historical tragedy in which the monarch's desires came into direct conflict with his duty to govern. Marlowe's pioneering history play wasn't just an innovation in form. The kingly desires he dramatised were partly inspired by queer political scandals in the recent histories of England's neighbours, where besotted rulers had upended convention and outraged their ruling classes. The troubles of early modern Europe's queer kings would furnish Marlowe with material for a radical queer drama – one that would serve as a vital lesson for Shakespeare.

It's fortunate for Marlowe's unassailably queer modern reputation that his work demonstrates an abiding interest in same-sex desire, because biographers have doused cold water on elements of his steamily transgressive life. They've pointed out that there's little evidence his espionage work was much more than low-level couriering between England and the continent. His two street fights, which brought him before the law, aren't signs of a particularly fiery nature in an age when violence was frequent and writers were forever lashing out (Shakespeare got mixed up in a brawl in 1596; the cerebral Ben Jonson killed a man in a duel). And his fetching portrait, discovered in Corpus Christi College, Cambridge, is no more likely to be Marlowe than any other young man of the same age – of which there was a store in a university town.

The less sexed-up version of Marlowe's troubled life depicts a dazzlingly talented writer whose final two years brought a series of disappointments and humiliations – chief among them arrest for currency counterfeiting in the English-controlled Dutch town of Vlissingen – that fed his anger and resentment. He had made enemies in his work in government intelligence circles, and when phrases from his plays appeared in blood-thirsty anti-immigrant libels that were displayed on London's streets, those enemies sought to press their advantage. Marlowe was questioned as part of the investigation into the anonymous libels, and soon afterwards the Privy Council received a note from one Richard Baines – someone Marlowe had known well in Vlissingen – setting out, in malicious detail, the outrageous and heretical views allegedly held by the poet. Baines didn't hold back. Among other things, Marlowe apparently thought that Moses had led his followers into the wilderness to kill off those who knew the secret of his entirely non-divine magic tricks; that he himself could write a much better holy book than the New Testament; that St John the Evangelist had sex with Christ; and the killer line about tobacco and boys that has attached itself to Marlowe for centuries. Baines could not have put together a more egregious mix of heresy, treason and sodomy – a classic trifecta of sin – if he'd tried. His note wasn't a character profile, but a character assassination that drew on the most potent of his society's fears.

Marlowe held views that skirted close to religious scepticism – more than one of his contemporaries mentioned his atheistical tendencies – and his queerness was something that blazed brightly in his plays and poems. But the poison-pen letter that dropped into the Privy Council in-tray spoke chiefly of Baines's eagerness to paint him in the murkiest colours imaginable. Neither Marlowe's religion nor his queer identity is likely to be truly found in bad faith testimony. We need to look to his work to discover the queer feeling he captured in his art – a theme he explored from the beginning of his career.

By the mid-1580s, Marlowe was down from Cambridge and beginning to make waves in London. He was a poet already: his translation of Ovid's poems of seduction, the *Amores*, although not published until 1599, is probably a university work. In the city, he became a playwright. Like Shakespeare, he was creatively stimulated by the performances of Paul's Boys and the Children of the Chapel. With the help of Thomas Nashe, he wrote a John Lyly-ish boy-company play about the most famous lovers in history (one that Shakespeare would recall when writing *Antony and Cleopatra*). *Dido Queen of Carthage* (c.1587) took the story of Dido and Aeneas's affair from Virgil's *Aeneid* and restructured it as a five-act erotic thriller. Cupid ensures that

Dido falls hard for Aeneas when he washes ashore in Carthage, while Dido's sister Anna pines for Iarbus, Dido's discarded suitor. Meanwhile, the gods Venus, Juno and Jupiter wrangle over the destiny of Aeneas and his band of refugees from Troy: Juno wants to wreck the Trojans on the high seas; Venus – Aeneas's mother – naturally wishes to see him settle in Italy and establish the city of Rome.

Some scholars think *Dido* was Marlowe's first work of drama, and if so, it's noticeable that he chose to lift the curtain of his theatrical career – quite literally – on a scene that staged his society's most iconic representation of queer seduction. The play opens in the heavenly realm with a 'discovery' – a *coup de théâtre* in which the drapes to a recessed area are suddenly swished aside to reveal a striking tableau – that was designed to grab the audience's attention and transport them instantly to the epic world of Virgilian myth:

Here the curtains draw; there is discovered Jupiter dandling
Ganymede upon his knee, and Mercury lying asleep. (1.1.*SD*)

Marlowe loses no time in letting his spectators know what they're watching. 'Come, gentle Ganymede,' says Jupiter straight away, 'and play with me; / I love thee well, say Juno what she will' (1–2).

Those familiar with the classics would hear in these opening words an echo of the first lines of Book 1 of the *Aeneid*, which blamed Aeneas's sufferings on 'haughty Juno's unrelenting hate' of Troy, in part because Ganymede – a Trojan mortal – had supplanted her in Jupiter's bed. It was clever of Marlowe to frame the beginning of his *Aeneid*-inspired play with the same threat of Juno's displeasure that sparked off Virgil's epic poem.

But most of the audience at the expensive indoor theatres knew that the *Aeneid* doesn't start with a sex scene. In staging the Jupiter–Ganymede tryst, Marlowe not only brought the character of Ganymede onto the English stage for the first time, but he also produced the first dramatic representation of explicit queer sexual foreplay, and did so in a way his audience would understand.

Marlowe's Ganymede knows what he wants from the unusual domestic *ménage* in which he's found himself. Juno has it in for him: he can't top up a wine cup without her beating him around the head. Jupiter promises to sort it out. He'll tie up his wife and confine her to the cosmic void, he thunders. Satisfying though that sounds to Ganymede, he's after something a little more tangible, a bit less Olympian. If Jupiter wants his fun, Ganymede needs a treat: he'd like – as well as Juno's wedding jewellery – an earring and a new brooch to pin on his hat. And then, he says while perching on Jupiter's lap, 'I'll hug with you an hundred times' (48). Deal done, the couple are prevented from going any further by the arrival of Venus, unimpressed that Jupiter 'can sit toying there, / And playing with that female wanton boy' (50–51) while her son Aeneas is in peril on the sea.

Marlowe brings us from the giddy heights of Mount Olympus to the contested sexual battleground of the early modern English household. The sensational opening scene of *Dido Queen of Carthage* dramatised the Ganymede story as a version of one of the most familiar and visible forms of queer relationship in Shakespeare's England, that of the young servant who is rewarded for sex with his master, while others in the house respond with (understandable) jealousy. Ganymede's trinkets are payment for services rendered, and compensation for the physical injury he receives from his master's wife.

Marlowe didn't bring queer desire into his play to exoticise the story, or make the mythical world seem even more fantastical. Quite the opposite: the short opening scene made conflict between the gods familiar, and gave an accessible, understandable shape to the erotic discord that was to come. The canoodling Jupiter and

Ganymede – preoccupied with each other and all the limb-entangling activity they've got in mind – also presented a dramatically effective contrast to the heroic Aeneas, who nobly forsakes all hope of epic sex with the beautiful Dido in order to found Rome.

The Ganymede scene tells us something about the way Marlowe depicted same-sex feeling in his writing. He was interested in it for its own sake, but he also thought deeply about the way that queerness interacted with other sorts of erotic and emotional bonds. Like Shakespeare, he was fascinated by the conflicts that could arise between the social demands of straight marriage and the bodily demands of queer desire. But Marlowe also looked beyond the confines of the marital home. Just as *Dido Queen of Carthage* explored the way a straight romance affected the political history of a great empire, Marlowe's *Edward II*, which was to have such an influence on Shakespeare's writing, depicted the politically motivated destruction of a passionate relationship between a king and his male lover. And while he found the origin of the story in England's chronicles, it was the recent histories of Scotland's King James VI (later James I of England) and France's King Henri III that showed Marlowe how relevant it was for his own time. Behind the tragedy of Edward and Gaveston lay a pair of political cautionary tales from the experiences of England's nearest neighbours.

The activities of King James VI were well known in England. As the child of Mary Queen of Scots and her English husband Henry Stuart, Lord Darnley, both of whom were great-grandchildren of Henry VII, the first Tudor king, he had a high ranking in the English succession from the moment of his birth. Observers south of the border kept an eye on the doings of the Scottish crown prince.

He wasn't a prince for long. Soon Darnley was murdered, and Mary had been forced off the throne and locked away until she was able to make her escape to England, where she would eventually be executed for plotting against Elizabeth. The one-year-old James, confined to Stirling Castle, was king, although he was monarch in name only. His unstable nation went through regents with alarming speed: three of them before the little boy's fifth birthday, the first two shot by clan enemies. The cycle of violence and retribution was so bad that James assumed full kingly powers before he'd reached adolescence: by 1578, aged twelve, he was in charge, and it was time to leave the fortress at Stirling and meet his people. As he did so, those members of his family with a view to influence and power made haste to Scotland to pledge allegiance to the boy king.

Chief among the new courtiers was a French aristocrat called Esmé Stuart, Seigneur d'Aubigny, cousin to James's father. Aubigny had glittering connections in France, where he was a Gentleman of the Bedchamber to Henri III, and he was rich, worldly and ambitious. Leaving behind his wife and four children, Aubigny made for Edinburgh in the summer of 1579 with a sizeable retinue of exquisitely dressed French aristocrats and plenty of cash. Presented to the king, he laid himself on the floor and called on 'the King of Heaven to bless his Majesty with perpetual felicity'.

James's upbringing had been one of utter removal from the world, in the hands of loveless tutors and upright noblewomen who had raised him from infancy. As he entered his teenage years, he was surrounded by the hard faces of his councillors, mistrustful men who jockeyed for power amid religious dispute and political crisis. James's short experience of kingship was hardly more splendid than his secluded childhood. His was a life of stone castles and the iron skies above Edinburgh's Holyroodhouse.

Handsome, fashionable Aubigny was a vision from another world and James, now thirteen, fell for him at once. In the presence chamber at that first meeting, James raised Aubigny from his prostrate position, 'embraced him in a most amorous manner' and proceeded to endow him with gifts and favours that made him the most powerful man in Scotland after the king. As James grew into adolescence, Aubigny was his constant companion, and fount of the only male affection the teenager had ever known. The thirty-seven-year-old was evidently a parental figure to the fatherless James, but with his flattering manners and alluring appearance, he was also something more – the first in what would become a long line of beloved men who made James feel adored. And James rewarded Aubigny's love with reckless generosity.

The titles and privileges kept on coming: Earl – and then Duke – of Lennox, Great Chamberlain of Scotland and First Gentleman of the Chamber, and the lordships of five substantial estates. James's Privy Council deplored the 'inward affection' between the two. It was said that the king 'can hardly suffer [Aubigny] out of his presence, and is in such love with him, as in the open sight of the people, oftentimes he will clasp him about the neck with his arms and kiss him.' The Scottish Church, the Kirk, saw him as a Catholic conspirator, despite his perfunctory conversion to Protestantism. Foreign observers were under no illusions as to who was in charge: the Spanish ambassador reported that James's French friend was governing both king and country.

The nobility and the Kirk moved against Aubigny in August 1582. They denounced him as a leech on the nation, and to ensure that he couldn't claim protection from the king, a posse known as the Lords Enterprisers seized James and kept him far away from his favourite. Months passed until the king accepted the nobles' demand that Aubigny must leave. He finally sailed for France in December, determined to return. It wasn't to be. Aubigny died in May 1583. Not long afterwards, the king received his embalmed heart, which had been spirited out of France without his widow's knowledge.

The king, overwhelmed with grief and impotent rage at the Lords Enterprisers, turned to poetry. He commemorated his love for Aubigny in a 'Metaphorical Invention of a Tragedy Called Phoenix': envious 'ravening fowl' attack an exquisite foreign bird, who is driven away and burned to ashes. (The poem closes with a glimmer of hope: it is implied that the phoenix's offspring, born out of her ashes, will return to marry the grief-stricken poetic speaker.) If the poem's real-life resonance wasn't clear enough, James made sure that his readers would understand the identity of the tormented bird. He included the poem in a collection with the self-effacing title *The Essays of a Prentice in the Divine Art of Poesy*, which he published in 1584. In the preface to 'Phoenix', James planted an acrostic in which the first and last letters of each line spelled out a name, running column-wise down left and right of the page: 'ESME STEWART DWIKE' [Duke]. The king wanted it proclaimed to everyone how rare and envied their love had been.

The book advertised the eighteen-year-old king's learning and sensitivity to his own people, but just as importantly to readers in England, the realm he was likely to inherit. Beautifully bound and decorated copies were sent to the queen's ministers. English readers bought it in droves, keen to understand the man set to become their monarch. In discovering his politics and piety, readers of 'Phoenix' were also presented with the king's passionate feelings for Esmé Stuart, Duke of Lennox and Seigneur d'Aubigny, and the constitutional upheaval the affair caused.

A man like Marlowe – involved in back-channel diplomatic work as England's statesmen prepared for a new reign – would have been immediately drawn to the political and emotional dynamics of the James–Aubigny affair. Perhaps he was already contemplating a play inspired by the story, although he would need to find a way to obscure his debt to Scottish current affairs: playwrights weren't permitted to stage stories about living rulers (when James became King of England, the Master of the Revels had to shut down a London production of 'The Tragedie of Gowrie', a real-life thriller about another attempt to abduct the Scottish king). It was the fallout from a comparable scandal in France that gave Marlowe the crucial imaginative connection he needed to the reign of Edward II, and set the scene for his revolutionary new take on the history play.

From 1574 until his assassination in 1589, Henri III of France had startled everyone by the excessive favour he showed to a small troupe of young male aristocrats who became known as the king's *mignons*, or minions. Royal favouritism wasn't unusual in the courts of Europe, but Henri's minions came from otherwise-obscure noble families who had seemingly done little to deserve the king's notice. And because Henri – a slender young man with a weakness for high fashion – liked to use his favourites as an extension of his kingly body on which he could drape the trappings of royal magnificence, it wasn't long before rumours started circulating about the epicene youths and their flamboyant style. The minions' middling rank and sudden advancement stoked fears about the stability of the different estates, and raised questions about what precisely these boys had done in exchange for such lavish attention from the king.

The Parisian diarist Pierre de l'Estoile reported as early as 1576 that the minions were causing comment on the streets. It wasn't just that they were self-important and haughty, but also that their 'paint [cosmetics], and effeminate and unchaste apparel' outraged more sober citizens. They flaunted dish-sized ruffs, doublets snatched to vanishingly narrow waists, and tiny trunk hose that showed off an expanse of thigh. The minions pinned their long hair into the styles favoured by court ladies, topping their up-dos with miniscule velvet hats that they wore 'like whores in the brothel'. Satires in print and manuscript characterised the minions as 'deceitful Ganymedes', and soon the libellous verses had breached all decorum in their savage attacks on Henri and his favourites. One poem, ascribed to the poet Pierre de Ronsard, gives a vivid sense of the gossip:

> The king, it is said, embraces, kisses, and licks
> The fresh faces of his dainty minions day and night:
> They, to obtain money, offer him in turn
> Their fulsome buttocks and suffer the breach.

Ronsard attacks Henri III for lavishing the nation's cash on his lovers; the poem goes on to wish that the king's father had also confined himself to unreproductive anal sex rather than produce 'another Nero from his noble seed'.

The explosive rumours about Henri and his minions were the product of highly unstable politics. Henri was the third son of Henri II and Catherine de' Medici to sit on the French throne, and none of them had shown any inclination or ability to produce an heir. With the family line nearly extinct, the crown was set to pass to another royal house, the Bourbons, whose head was Henri of Navarre, leader of the Protestant faction in France. An extremist party known as the Catholic League was formed with the express purpose of keeping the Protestants away from power. Hatreds that had come to a head with the massacre of French Protestants on St Bartholomew's Day in August 1572, which took place less than a week after Navarre's controversial marriage to Henri III's sister Marguerite, seemed to be rising again. Catholics and Protestants were at one another's throats. In the context of financial, religious and political chaos, Henri's expensive tastes and lissom minions were an easy target.

Satires and libels poured off the presses, and in 1588 an anonymous Catholic League writer made a chilling association between French politics and English history in a pamphlet titled *Histoire Tragique et Memorable de Pierre de Gaverston* – 'The Tragic and Memorable History of Piers Gaveston'. Purporting to be the story of 'the minion of Edward II, King of England', the author had another target in mind: Henri's 'arch-*mignon*', the much-rewarded Duc d'Épernon. *Histoire Tragique et Memorable* drew scandalous equivalence between Henri's obsession with Épernon and Edward II's love for Gaveston. The pamphlet sensationally threatened Henri and Épernon with the same violent ends as their medieval forebears: an excruciating death at the hands of powerful enemies.

Sir Edward Stafford, the English ambassador in Paris, quickly sent the pamphlet to Sir Francis Walsingham, the queen's Secretary of State, noting it was 'the vilest book that ever I saw'. King James, still thinking of Aubigny, tried to get his hands on a copy. The statesmen of England and Scotland wanted to keep abreast of the ways in which intense and queerly inflected royal favouritism was understood, and how it was put to propagandist use by the intemperate politicians of France. That the scandal-mongers of Paris were reaching into England's medieval past in search of analogies for their current disasters was deeply concerning, to say the least.

But this was invaluable material for an eagle-eyed dramatist who understood English and French affairs, and had access to texts printed in both countries thanks to his Channel-hopping intelligence work. Marlowe was fascinated by it all. The politics of England's closest neighbours were dominated by the romantic psychodramas of kings who found their chief emotional support in attractive male favourites, the ambitions of whom were widely mistrusted by the aristocratic establishment. Moreover, a French commentator had found a dramatic parallel for their ruler's queer desire in the records of English history. Marlowe saw the clear potential in Edward II's story, newly back in intellectual circulation, and in 1591 or 1592, he set to work on a play the chief theme of which was the impact on the state of the monarch's overwhelming desire for his male favourite. Marlowe would make a revolutionary queer tragedy out of queer history, which spoke to the queer politics of the nations next door. His *Edward II* would change Shakespeare's approach to historical storytelling forever.

It was a good time for a chronicle history play of this sort. Shakespeare's own four-part Wars of the Roses saga, the three *Henry VI* plays and *Richard III*, had helped set the fashion for the genre. Battle-filled dramas about the ghastly consequences of bad government and civil strife were hugely popular and carried a propagandist message pleasing to the authorities: they demonstrated to London spectators their good fortune in living under a stable monarchy. Shakespeare and Marlowe had grateful recourse to the bumper two-volume *Chronicles of England, Scotland and Ireland* (the second edition of which was released in 1587), a jingoistic history of the British Isles edited by Raphael Holinshed and revised by Abraham Fleming. Holinshed's *Chronicles* and other narrative histories provided a rich stock of source material for historical dramatists. Playwrights picked their way through the densely printed pages of the history books, teasing out plot lines and character arcs, and choosing which events to highlight, which years to compress, and which historical personages to make their stage heroes and villains.

Marlowe's dramaturgical surgery on the twenty-year span of Edward II's rule (1307–27) was transformative – necessarily so, given that Holinshed was comprehensive in his historical storytelling (the Edward section was 30,000 words long). Playing fast and loose with history, Marlowe reshaped the narrative to centre the story on Edward and Gaveston – who died only five years into the reign – and make it the abiding concern of the embattled king for the rest of his life.

Newly crowned Edward welcomes his adored favourite Piers Gaveston back to the court, and grants him princely wealth along with a fistful of aristocratic titles. He wants to 'share the kingdom with [his] dearest friend' (1.1.2). By the end of the first scene, the barons are up in arms that a mere favourite has such influence in the state. They threaten to fling 'the glozing head of thy base minion' at the king's blood-spattered throne (1.1.133). Soon Edward's wife, Isabella, complains to her supporters that she has been supplanted as conjugal spouse:

> For now my lord the king regards me not,
> But dotes upon the love of Gaveston.
> He claps his cheeks and hangs about his neck,
> Smiles in his face and whispers in his ears,
> And when I come, he frowns, as who should say,
> 'Go whither thou wilt, seeing I have Gaveston.' (1.2.49–54)

Edward tries to place Gaveston next to him on the throne, the position claimed by Isabella, and the barons drag Gaveston away to banishment; Edward, with despairing irony, suggests partitioning the kingdom among the power-hungry nobles and leaving him 'some nook or corner' where he might 'frolic with my dearest Gaveston' (1.4.72–73).

A temporary reconciliation lasts long enough for Gaveston to be recalled (and married off to Edward's niece), before Edward's open desire for his lover and his financial extravagance blow apart the truce. Gaveston is captured and summarily killed; Edward vows to put the rebelling nobles to the sword in revenge for the murder of 'my lovely Piers' (3.1.8). As each side digs in, Isabella turns to Mortimer, leader of the rebel barons and aspirant warlord, who plans to rule the country through the queen and her young son.

Edward takes to the field in the name of 'Good Piers Gaveston, my sweet favourite' (3.1.228), supported by Hugh de Spencer, an eager courtier keen to step into Gaveston's shoes. The fight goes first Edward's way, and then the rebels', and the king is seized and compelled to resign his crown to his son. Mortimer, now Lord Protector, glories in his triumph to Isabella: 'Be ruled by me, and we will rule the realm!' (5.2.5). Isabella bleakly consents to her husband's murder. When the king's captors cannot induce his death by vicious mistreatment ('O Gaveston, it is for thee that I am wronged,' cries Edward as he is roughed up (5.3.41)), Mortimer procures an assassin called Lightborn to kill him in such a way that 'none shall know which way he died' (5.4.24). In the aftermath of the king's death, the young Edward III regains control, punishes his mother and executes the traitorous Mortimer.

When Marlowe reached the final paragraphs of the account of Edward II's reign in Holinshed's *Chronicles*, he could see the makings of a viciously vivid piece of theatre in the description of the king's murder at Berkeley Castle:

[T]hey came suddenly one night into the chamber where he lay in bed fast asleep, and with heavy featherbeds or a table (as some write) being cast upon him, they kept him down and withal put into his fundament an horn, and through the same they thrust up into his body an hot spit [. . .] the which passing up into his entrails and being rolled to and fro, burnt the same, but so as no appearance of any wound or hurt outwardly might be once perceived.

The *Chronicles* doesn't come right out and say that Edward and Gaveston were sodomites (although it drops clanging hints with comments about the king's 'disordered manners' and the lovers' 'voluptuous pleasure' together), but Marlowe would hardly have missed the brutal implication behind the savagely allegorical anal spitting: Edward II, who allowed his passions to get the better of him, is dealt with in condign fashion, fucked to death at the hands of a usurper's agent.

Marlowe was a playwright who gloried in the ability of theatre to bring forth eye-popping extremities and acts of violence, and the power of a well-turned stage direction to set a theatre company's inventive brains whirring and come up with a spectacular special effect. In *Tamburlaine the Great*, a two-part epic about a fourteenth-century Central Asian conqueror, the imprisoned emperor Bajazeth 'brains himself against the cage' (*Part 1*, 5.1.304 *SD*), immediately followed in the same action by his wife Zabina; and a pair of defeated kings are harnessed to Tamburlaine's chariot 'with bits in their mouths' while the conqueror holds the 'reins in his left hand, in his right hand a whip, with which he scourgeth them' (*Part 2*, 4.3.0 *SD*). These sensational moments got audiences talking, and Marlowe took care to script them with a degree of precision.

All the more surprising, then, that his dramatisation of Edward's murder shows exceptional restraint, even ambiguity, in precisely how the king is made away with. The sinister Lightborn – the character is Marlowe's invention – is an expert in outlandish murder techniques (suffocation with silk, mercury poured down the throat), but although he demands a fire and a spit made 'red hot' (5.5.30), Edward appears in Marlowe's telling to be crushed to death by Lightborn's henchmen Gurney and Matrevis:

> LIGHTBORN. Run for the table.
> EDWARD. O spare me, or dispatch me in a trice.
> LIGHTBORN. So, lay the table down and stamp on it,
> But not too hard, lest that you bruise his body.
> MATREVIS. I fear me that his cry will wake the town,
> And therefore let us take horse and away. (5.5.110–15)

Nothing about the text prevents an interpretation in line with the *Chronicles'* ghoulish narrative (the red-hot spit is a Renaissance version of Chekhov's rifle, waiting in the wings to be put to use) but in a play that is in other respects fairly free with stage directions that call for explicit action – in the previous scene featuring the abused Edward, his captors 'wash him with puddle water, and shave his beard away' (5.3.36 *SD*) – their absence at this crucial moment leaves open the possibility that Marlowe intended Edward to meet his death in a less abject way.

Perhaps Marlowe was unwilling to pander to the bigoted sadism in Holinshed. If so, it was a fitting culmination to a play that goes out of its way to fashion Edward as the emotional focus of the story, and present his love for Gaveston as powerful, consequential and – crucially – comprehensible within the framework of a popular drama that required audiences to empathise with the feelings of the central characters. Marlowe was doing something new in creating a queer tragic lead in *Edward II*, and he did so in expectation that audiences would be on his hero's side.

It was received wisdom in early modern England that Edward and Gaveston had had a sexual relationship, a fact most writers regarded as a reflection on Edward's poor rule and susceptibility to bad influence. The poet Michael Drayton – something of an Edward obsessive, with at least three versions of the story to his name, told variously from the points of view of Gaveston, Isabella and Mortimer – figured the king's lover as a 'girl-boy', an 'incestuous shameless Ganymede' who supplanted Isabella in the royal bed. In the 1620s, the aristocratic writer Elizabeth Cary judged Gaveston 'a fit instrument for a brothel', whose 'bewitching' charms beguiled Edward away from his French queen.

Marlowe makes Gaveston an overt replacement for Isabella, too. 'Villain,' she cries, ''tis thou that rob'st me of my lord'

(1.4.160). 'Madam,' snaps back Gaveston, "'tis you that rob me of my lord' (1.4.161). Isabella bitterly resents her humiliating exclusion, and draws on the chief classical model for a woman abandoned in favour of a youthful male sexual partner that Marlowe had staged in the opening tableau of *Dido Queen of Carthage*:

> Like frantic Juno will I fill the earth
> With ghastly murmur of my sighs and cries;
> For never doted Jove on Ganymede
> So much as he on cursed Gaveston. (1.4.178–81)

Gaveston's vision of the royal entertainments he plans for the king – pages dressed liked 'sylvan nymphs' (1.1.58), topless menservants as satyrs, a nude boy playing Diana – gives a clear sense of the queer delight both men take in the male body.

But where Marlowe departs from his sources – and many other versions of the Edward–Gaveston story – is the romantic heft he grants his two central lovers. His play doesn't portray their relationship as a symbol of a decaying monarchy. Neither are saints, and both have moments of foolishness and brutality, but Marlowe makes their scenes of leave-taking and reunion as moving as any similar instances in early modern drama. As Gaveston prepares for banishment, the two men are almost wordless with grief. They exchange lockets containing each other's portraits, and Gaveston manages the wry observation, amid tears, that it is 'something to be pitied of a king' (1.4.130). It's the ambitious and intolerant nobles who express contempt for the couple: '*Diablo*! What passions call you these?' scoffs the Earl of Lancaster (1.4.319). Gaveston's execution is presented as flagrantly illegal ('flatly against the law of arms' (3.1.121)), and in his final moments, Edward achieves a sort of saintly resignation in the face of torment.

Marlowe's radical intervention in the discourse around Edward and Gaveston was to recognise that the issue wasn't 'diabolical' desire, whatever phobic fulminations the playwright put in the mouths of the king's enemies. Instead, he saw the contradiction in terms that hobbled Edward's desire to forge a life with his sexual soulmate on the basis of classical *amicitia perfecta*, the model to which elite men had been educated to aspire. Edward – the creation of an early modern mind, for all that he is a medieval character – regards Gaveston as his other self, the second half of his heart whose return to court completes his own identity:

> What, Gaveston, welcome! Kiss not my hand,
> Embrace me, Gaveston, as I do thee.
> Why shouldst thou kneel? Know'st thou not who I am?
> Thy friend, thy self, another Gaveston. (1.1.140–43)

Worthy though this sentiment is for a man, it's an impossibility for a king, whose position as a monarch anointed by God to rule removes his right to give away his soul to another, and particularly another man with a taste for royal trappings and executive power. The tragedy that Marlowe crafts for Edward draws its power from the king's thwarted desire to create a relationship with his lover on equal terms. A king, of course, can have no equal.

Like the other destabilising power couple in the play – Queen Isabella and her lover, the usurping Mortimer, who 'do kiss while they conspire' (4.6.13) – Gaveston and the king find that affairs of the heart become matters of state when monarchs are involved. As with James VI and Aubigny, or Henri III and Épernon, Edward and Gaveston face opprobrium from a nobility that can't conceive of a sexual passion that also speaks a language of Ciceronian desire, of shared hearts and twin souls. Favouritism itself isn't necessarily the problem as far as England's powerful aristocrats are concerned: as Mortimer's uncle points out, citing classical example and echoing the language of sixteenth-century France, '[t]he mightiest kings have had their minions' (1.4.391). Gaveston's overt ambition – his desire to rise to the level of the king's adoring expectations – is what finally dooms him in the eyes of the hostile nobility. Marlowe's achievement in *Edward II* was to dramatise the clash among three competing human urges: sexual passion, the need for love, and the desire for power. But his revolutionary move was to refract those urges into a study of queer kingship, and make his play a tragic contest among sodomy, *amicitia perfecta* and monarchy.

Edward II raised the stakes significantly for Shakespeare. He had already begun thinking through the dramatic implications of the conflict between *amicitia perfecta* and marriage. In *The Two Gentlemen of Verona*, written perhaps four years before *Edward II* appeared on stage, Proteus and Valentine must negotiate their desire for each other as well as their potential brides, Julia and Silvia. And Shakespeare had his own experience of carving out a historical story from Holinshed's *Chronicles* in the *Henry VI* plays and *Richard III*. Now Marlowe was showing him how to take things even further, by pitting queer passion against kingship; Edward loves Gaveston as much as he loves his crown, but he can't have both. Other plays of the 1580s and 1590s had explored comic fantasies of straight royal romance (kings in love with poor country girls whom they cannot marry), but Marlowe's queer innovation elevated the chronicle play to the level of tragedy. Edward's queer desire is part of his tragic fall, although Marlowe is careful to show that it's not the cause. The king is a complicated blend of qualities, praiseworthy and problematic, and his queerness is an aspect of this portfolio of human characteristics that, the play suggests, comes into conflict with the rigid demands of rule. It was a newly nuanced way to depict the national story. Inspired by Marlowe's dramatisation of queer history, Shakespeare's next history plays were to be themed around the destructive clash between royal duty and individual desire.

Shakespeare embarked on his second burst of history play-writing – the second tetralogy (four-part story) of *Richard II*, *Henry IV Parts 1* and *2* and *Henry V* – with Marlowe's *Edward II* at the forefront of his mind. In each episode of the second tetralogy, the royal central characters must wrestle with desires that are incompatible with kingship, and undergo an emotional shock – or worse – as the price of giving them up. In *Henry IV Parts 1* and *2*, the king's seemingly prodigal son Prince Hal shows his mettle by rejecting the royal bad influence, Sir John Falstaff, who keeps Hal carousing in an Eastcheap tavern among thieves and sex workers. If the fat knight seems a world away from a smooth court favourite like Gaveston, his impact is regarded as similarly baleful: Henry IV despairs at his 'degenerate' son whose folly and self-absorption remind him so strongly of the deposed and murdered Richard II (*Part 1*, 3.2.128). *Edward II*'s barons recoil at the notion of an all-powerful royal favourite seizing the nation's purse strings for his own enrichment; Shakespeare's Henry IV puts an end to Hal's 'barren pleasures [and] rude society' (3.2.14) with grifting hangers-on. There's no space in the official edifice of princehood and kingship for a male friend in the Falstaffian mode: greedy, self-serving and ambitious for personal gain, but also loving, indulgent and devoted to pleasure. Buried deep down in Falstaff's ebullient frame is a conception of male intimacy as ardent and exclusive as Gaveston's – and it is brutally extinguished by Hal at the moment of his coronation. 'My king! My Jove! I speak to thee, my heart!' cries Falstaff in the closing moments of *Henry IV Part 2*. 'I know thee not, old man,' replies the new Henry V (5.5.46–47).

Shakespeare showed most clearly his career-long debt to Marlowe in *Richard II*, written soon after the publication of *Edward II* in 1594. Marlowe inspired Shakespeare to become even more ambitious in his dramaturgical pruning, and showed him how to sacrifice comprehensiveness for impact. Shakespeare's earlier dramatisation of Henry VI's long rule had required three full-length plays and a cast that must have tested the capacities of even the biggest theatre companies. But he was able to compress Richard's two-decade reign into a tight narrative composed of incidents plucked from the king's final two years, presenting a monarch whose grip on power tumbles precipitately from his grasp rather than one (as Holinshed relates) who had spent a life-time battling his aggrieved aristocrats. Shakespeare's jumping-off point for his story was the year in which Richard 'began to rule by will more than reason', according to Holinshed's *Chronicles*, and to give way to his 'inordinate desires' and wilful urges.

Wearied by a chivalric spat between powerful nobles Henry Bolingbroke and Thomas Mowbray, Richard summarily banishes them both. And when Bolingbroke's father, John of Gaunt, dies, Richard immediately absorbs the old man's vast wealth to fund an unnecessary war in Ireland. In exile, the dispossessed Bolingbroke seethes, and decides to return to claim his patrimony. As more noblemen fall behind Bolingbroke, his campaign morphs from a mission to rectify Richard's illegal seizure to a fully fledged royal coup. Richard is captured and pressured to give the crown to Bolingbroke, who claims right to rule by descent from Edward III – the king who had brought the turmoil to an end at the close of Marlowe's play. Confined to a grim castle, Richard is finally dispatched by murderers hired by Bolingbroke's followers, as Bolingbroke – now King Henry IV – makes a half-hearted offer to atone for his usurpation.

Marlowe's model of a vacillating, financially irresponsible king who is overpowered by aggrieved barons, forced to give up his crown and imprisoned in a castle where he meets a violent end, was the basis on which Shakespeare constructed *Richard II*. Although the bones of the story were to be found in Holinshed, it wasn't inevitable that Shakespeare would shape them in the way he did. He had Richard's eventful twenty-two-year reign from which to carve a play: promising raw material filled with revolts and French wars that lent itself to a treatment in the mould of the *Henry VI* plays. *Edward II* gave him a framework and a dramatic language for the powerful conflict between anointed kingship and wilful self-absorption.

Shakespeare drew heavily on Marlowe's Edward for his portrait of Richard, a vain and self-centred monarch whose flaws lead him to make poor choices, but who shows loyalty and sensitivity to those around him. Egged on by his favourites, Bushy, Bagot and Green, Shakespeare's king is a spendthrift, bankrupting the nation with pointless extravagance. John of Gaunt deplores the 'rash fierce blaze of riot' (2.1.33) that characterises the court, and execrates the flatterers – 'caterpillars of the commonwealth' (2.3.166) in his son's words – who pull the king whichever way they please. Shakespeare doesn't depict Richard as overtly queer, and his sympathetic queen doesn't suffer the same rejection as Edward II's wife. But he wanted his audiences to think that Richard's opponents suspected him of queer immorality. Diverging from the sources, Shakespeare made his play's unnamed queen an adult woman (the historical Queen Isabella, Richard's second wife, was nine years old when the king was deposed in 1399) and allowed Bolingbroke a queer-phobic sneer: he accuses Bushy and Green of 'sinful' interference in Richard's sex life, by usurping the 'royal bed' and making the queen miserable with unspecified 'foul wrongs' (3.1.11, 13, 15). Bolingbroke's distaste persists into *Henry IV Part 1*: the new king remembers Richard as a 'skipping' monarch who relished spending time with 'beardless' boys (3.2.60, 67).

Like Marlowe's Edward, the flawed but human Richard rises above the hostility of his enemies to emerge as a deeply sympathetic tragic anti-hero. His serious error of judgement – illegally seizing the wealth rightfully due to Gaunt's heir – is twisted by Bolingbroke from a valid example of kingly overreach into a morally questionable *casus belli* that allows him to take the throne by force of arms. In the face of unjust punishment, Richard assumes a dignified majesty that is strikingly at odds with the unstable new rule bodged together by the usurping Henry IV. Confined to Pomfret Castle, he emerges as a kingly Boethius, channelling his 'still-breeding thoughts' (5.5.8) into a prison philosophy that grants him insight into the reasons for his fall. And another Marlovian figure who suffers calamity was on Shakespeare's mind as he wrote his historical tragedy. Attempting to come to terms with deposition, Richard calls for a mirror and addresses his reflection with lines that echo Doctor Faustus's astonishment at the sight of Helen of Troy: 'Was this the face that launched a thousand ships, / And burned the topless towers of Iliam?' (5.1.99–100):

> Was this the face
> That every day under his household roof
> Did keep ten thousand men? Was this the face
> That, like the sun, did make beholders wink? (4.1.281–84)

Behind Shakespeare's powerful new historical storytelling – his ability to fashion a tragic hero who comes to understand his own flaws – lay Marlowe's innovations in *Edward II*, the queer historical tragedy inspired by queer current events.

When Shakespeare's *Richard II* was printed in 1597, two years after its stage premiere, it was advertised on the title page as a 'tragedy' – the same word that was applied to his *Richard III*, also published that year (although written c.1592). The two Ricardian tragedies demonstrate Shakespeare's approach to historical storytelling before and after the appearance of Marlowe's *Edward II*. Shakespeare's violent drama about the monstrous last of the Plantagenets drew on Tudor propaganda and popular traditions of stage ultra-villainy to create the compellingly awful Richard Duke of Gloucester, later Richard III, who connives and kills his way through the play. In the final act, Richard shakes off a brief stab of conscience kindled by a ghostly visitation from his victims – his brother, his wife, his two nephews, his closest ally and more – to lead his forces to unrepentant defeat at Bosworth Field. The self-reflective, anguished Richard II is a very different stage anti-hero, journeying from the political missteps and foolish discourtesies of the early acts to a bleak realisation that the demands of kingship are incompatible with the emotional needs of a man:

> I live with bread like you, feel want,
> Taste grief, need friends. Subjected thus,
> How can you say to me I am a king? (3.2.175–77)

Shakespeare's dramatic art was a beneficiary of Marlowe's new and subtle dramaturgy in *Edward II*. Marlowe had looked outwards, to the real political landscape of the late sixteenth century, where England's neighbouring countries were led by kings unable to accommodate their queer selves to the hostile environment of early modern monarchy. Marlowe's gift to Shakespeare was a queer dramaturgy that took seriously the range of ways in which a person might love, and the intemperate things which a powerful person might be driven to do by that desire.

By the start of 1592, Shakespeare was beginning to catch up with Marlowe. At the Rose playhouse on Bankside, theatregoers had the chance to directly compare the successes of these twin dramatists: *The Jew of Malta* and *Henry VI Part 1* (with its vivid portrayal of the gender-nonconforming French warrior Joan of Arc) played on alternate days on four occasions that spring. Each man was developing his audience-pleasing repertory, from Shakespeare's comedies and English histories (*Titus Andronicus* was his only tragedy at this point) to Marlowe's more attention-grabbing achievements in *Tamburlaine* and *Faustus*. Marlowe's immersion in the politics of Scotland and France in his preparation for *Edward II* seems to have tilted him in the direction of current events (or as current as the Master of the Revels permitted him to be). His final play, *The Massacre at Paris* (1593), based on the long aftermath of the 1572 St Bartholomew's Day massacre, returned him to the setting of the recent French civil wars and allowed him to revisit the relationship between King Henri III and his beloved Duc d'Épernon. Marlowe's early death at the end of May 1593 left his queer historical dramaturgy to be developed by others. But by then, the citizens of London had other things on their mind. Plague descended on the city in the summer of 1592, and devastated the way of life of everyone connected to the theatre. The epidemic was to force Shakespeare to take a sudden professional swerve, and develop his queer art in an entirely new way.

Toys for the Inns of Court Boys

October 1592. Eventually, London became intolerable.

They said plague deaths exceeded a thousand per week, a number so terrifying that William could only look at the shuttered doors of the Curtain and the Theatre with relief. With the pestilence in full roar, a tightly packed audience would be food for worms within days.

Londoners found other things to occupy their time, in any case. In the unseasonal mildness of early autumn – in another year, ideal playgoing weather – William saw city-dwellers working frantically to protect their families from the cloud of poisoned air that was billowing through town, parish by parish. Housewives sluiced their doorsteps, and placed bundles of rue at the windows. Few people left their lodgings without a nosegay of sweet herbs. Those who were able escaped to houses out of the city, where the clean air seemed to promise health and safety.

The afflicted suffered a sequence of horrors. Raging fever, convulsions, the eruption of buboes in groin and armpit, a sickening necrosis of the skin and, before too long, an incessant bloody flux that left victims delirious as they lay in soiled sheets. Most died in a few days. Stricken houses were boarded up with everyone inside, a livid red circle painted on the bolted door along with a scrawled prayer: Lord have mercy upon us. William knew this was uncharitably severe but, like everyone else, he turned his face away from the marked houses and hurried past, lest any fumes seeped out of cracks and knotholes. It wasn't safe to be outside: the already plague-tainted air was deteriorating further with the effusions that emanated from the slowly decaying bodies of the dead. The only wise course of action for Londoners with nowhere else to go was to stay at home, seal the windows, and pray to God.

Prayer only helped those who could quieten their fearful minds, and the pestilence occupied everybody's thoughts. His friend Tom Nashe didn't stop writing about it, filling page after page with visions of a hot-spurred plague, and the sound of wheels grinding through the street as carters called out for new corpses. But William couldn't bear to bring this apocalypse into his work. With the news of every squalid and unhallowed death, the need within him grew to hear of something succulent and delightful, to be charmed – and to charm others – with tales of desire. He wanted to think of bodies that were vital, entire, vigorous and hot, not infected and mortified and cold. William's imagination insisted that death – if it had to be thought of at all – brought with it divine transformation, not the interment of a shroud-wrapped corpse in a mass grave. His mind turned to his favourite storehouse of delight and fantasy. Even as God rained down punishment for man's sin today, William was thinking about man's pleasure tomorrow.

Plague was a frequent and unwelcome visitor to the teeming capital, and when citywide deaths from the disease topped thirty per week the authorities swung into action, closing theatres, animal baiting rings and bowling alleys in an attempt to stop the spread of corrupted breath. The purpose was understandable, even if the science was flawed. Bubonic plague wasn't airborne. It was spread by fleas that lay dormant in the seams of linen shirts and sheets, tiny agents of chaos awaiting revitalisation by the warmth of a human body. Throughout Shakespeare's life, his theatrical work was brought to a periodic hard stop as the playhouses shut down because of plague (bubonic, pneumonic and septicaemic), and theatre companies either toured to such towns as would admit them or looked to their patrons for financial support. When plague struck for the first time in the career of the twenty-eight-year-old dramatist and actor in summer 1592, it's likely the upheaval caused him to consider his profession: there's no doubt that the rackety life of a theatre man looked more precarious than ever at that time. Within a year, Shakespeare transformed himself from a little-known playwright into a widely adored writer of published verse, some of it strikingly homoerotic. His long lyric poems *Venus and Adonis* (1593) and *Lucrece* (1594) made his national reputation, with the former bringing him immediate fame as a writer of queerly arousing poetry aimed squarely at a young male readership centred on the universities and London's Inns of Court. And as he innovated in the face of disaster, Shakespeare also turned to a new literary patron whose life and artistic interests demonstrated his own queer desires: Henry Wriothesley, third Earl of Southampton.

Shakespeare knew about plague. There had been an outbreak in Stratford-upon-Avon in the year of his birth, and his parents praised their luck in making it through the pestilence unscathed. But the epidemic that ravaged London and closed the playhouses from June 1592 until the start of 1594 – aside from two quickly terminated winter seasons – was shockingly lethal. More than 15,000 people – ten per cent of the capital's population – died in twenty months. The city's economy was devastated as trade collapsed and high-spending gallants fled to the country. Passers-by gave the ever-growing numbers of beggars a wide berth, afraid of infection. Even if the Privy Council hadn't banned public entertainments, few would have had the resources or inclination to visit the theatre. For the first time in Shakespeare's professional life, there was simply no audience in London for drama.

People began paying more attention to the preachers who had always campaigned against godless vanities like plays. The minister William Perkins rushed out a treatise in 1593 that laid the blame for the plague on the depravity of the populace. Almost everyone accepted that rampant disease was divine punishment for sin. As the clergyman Thomas White had put it during an earlier outbreak, 'The causes of plague is sin, if you look to it well, and the cause of sin is plays; therefore the cause of plagues are plays.' The pestilence was the perfect opportunity for religious extremists to say, 'I told you so.'

Shakespeare's movements during the nearly two years of plague closure aren't clear. He surely didn't stay in London; the theatrical suburbs of Shoreditch and Southwark were disproportionately hit by infection, and the non-stop tolling of the parish death knell would have been a clear message to depart. He probably toured with the Lord Strange's Men, who trailed around southern England, or Pembroke's Men, who made for the Herbert seat at Ludlow near the Welsh border. Other writers secured an invitation to their patrons' estates (in the last months of his life, Marlowe spent time with the courtier Sir Thomas Walsingham in Kent). It's likely Shakespeare was back in London for the short intervals of tentative playing that resumed at the Theatre and the Rose at the starts of 1593 and 1594, before surging infection rates closed the playhouses again. And he must have returned to Anne and the children, still at Henley Street in Stratford, to offer thanks that they and he were in health and free of the sickness ripping through the city where he made his living. The good health of the children was a sadly fleeting reassurance: Anne and William's son Hamnet was to die, possibly of the plague, within three years.

Wherever he was based, it was an emotionally exhausting time for someone whose life was tied to the enjoyments of theatre and literature, and perhaps the turmoil and anxiety left him unwilling to address the topic directly in his work. Unlike some of his contemporaries, Shakespeare made few references to the impact of the plague on everybody's lives. The social dislocations that came with stern public health regulations are only occasionally glimpsed: in *Romeo and Juliet*, suspicion of an 'infectious pestilence' (5.2.10) confines Friar John to a quarantined house, meaning he can't bring Romeo word that Juliet's apparent death is merely a drugged sleep. Mostly, 'plague' is an epithet in Shakespeare, tossed casually into speech or hurled bitingly as an insult, its pungency dependent on an audience's implicit knowledge that the word contained a world of fear and loss. Other writers were less circumspect about invoking its terrors. Thomas Nashe made a speciality of lurid accounts of plagues current and historical: victims stricken and dead within the afternoon, entire families wiped out, a single tomb that yawned to receive a hundred coffins.

Shakespeare had no reason to question his society's assumption that plagues were sent by God – in *Timon of Athens* (*c.*1606), he would write of Jupiter casting 'sick air' over a 'high-viced', or outrageously wicked, city (4.3.110–11) – but he must have struggled with the idea that it was all the fault of players and poets. He didn't believe that the pleasures of literature led to plague, but he could see that other people did. There was nothing like cataclysmic death to make earthly delight seem transient. 'Fond are life's lustful joys, / Death proves them all but toys,' wrote Nashe in 1592. Self-renunciation – like the pestilence – was in the air during those years.

Shakespeare realised it was time to make a creative swerve that would take him away from the commercial stage and into the more rarefied world of print literature. Far fewer people could read than had the capacity to attend plays – perhaps one third of England's men and one in ten women were confident readers, although rates were higher in London – but print was the route to literary immortality, and the number of new poetry books, novellas and romances was growing year on year. None of Shakespeare's plays had yet been published, and although the market for printed commercial drama was expanding, it was doing so from a small base, and with very uncertain conventions around authorship and ownership (when *Titus Andronicus* and *The First Part of the Contention*, or *Henry VI Part 2*, were published in 1594, his first plays to make it through the press, they appeared without Shakespeare's name on the title pages). In 1592, with the theatres closed, it wouldn't have seemed to Shakespeare that his fortune or his fame lay in playbooks. Nor was he ever likely to join the chorus of disapproving commentators adding their ha'penny worth to discussions about plague-struck London's moral failings, for all that religious books were by far the most widely produced and bestselling texts in the country. Instead, he leaned enthusiastically into what Nashe had called 'lustful joys', writing a long poem in that first plague year that was the most erotic thing he had ever composed. *Venus and Adonis*, about the goddess of love and her ultimately tragic pursuit of an irresistible huntsman, was a full-throated rebuttal to the idea that bawdy thoughts had brought down God's vengeance on London, and a daringly queer fantasy that gave its mostly male readers a first-person view of the seduction of a beautiful youth.

Shakespeare made a canny decision when he chose to write a classical erotic mini-epic. Booklet-length lyric poems that recounted tales of transgressive desire – a form that later literary critics called the 'epyllion' – were becoming all the rage, a popularity sustained in large part by young men. The greatest concentration of such readers was to be found in London's Inns of Court, where print and manuscript erotica – the sorts of things that moralist Philip Stubbes castigated as 'prophane schedules, sacrilegious libels, and heathenical pamphlets' – circulated freely. Authors of epyllia used less sulphurous language to advertise their tales, but the titillating purpose of these 'pleasant fables' and 'delectable discourses' was clear: they were sexual fantasies that transported the reader to a magical space of desire and transformation. And a significant selling point was the importance that epyllia placed on the youthful male body, a subject calculated to appeal at a time when lightly veiled queer romance satisfied the accepted reality that men could feel desire for boys as well as women. Along with other privileged Londoners, many of the Innsmen had fled the plague, but they'd be back with the cooler weather. And when they were, Shakespeare would have a delectable treat ready and waiting for them.

The Inns of Court – The Honourable Societies of Gray's Inn, Middle Temple, Inner Temple and Lincoln's Inn, and their subsidiary Inns of Chancery – were London's ancient seats of legal learning and practice, dense communities of lawyers and students who occupied a patch of the expanding urban sprawl between the cities of London and Westminster, at that time a separate municipality at the other end of the Strand. The Inns might have been part of the notional 'third university' spread across the capital, but these inner-city campuses had few lofty dreaming spires. Unlike the colleges of Oxford and Cambridge, the societies didn't have endowments for the construction of impressive stone quadrangles. The mostly brick and timber buildings went up in an ad hoc fashion, and usually in rackety ways – at Gray's Inn, they'd hitched an extra floor of residential chambers onto the chapel roof. But in the crowded bustle of pre-plague London, the Inns' gardens and walks – designed with perambulating Socratic conversations in mind – offered peace and fresh air to lawyers and students.

Not that they were a particularly scholarly bunch. The Inns might have been institutions of higher education, but they weren't universities. Lectures and mock trials were sporadic affairs. Students were unsupervised and didn't follow a syllabus. A junior member was expected to buy a law textbook and fend for himself. Unsurprisingly, well-to-do young men at the Inns – most of whom took up residence at seventeen or eighteen – found other things to occupy their minds and bodies. Being fashionable was a popular distraction. Attending plays, visiting the tailor, taking a turn in Paul's Walk, drinking, gambling and whoring all took up time. Onlookers were aghast. The theologian Joseph Hall regarded the hands-off approach at the Inns as catastrophic: 'Where there are many pots boiling, there cannot but be much scum,' he warned. He said youths sent by their parents to become lawyers learned to 'roar instead of pleading' – to become urban louts instead of refined barristers.

The Inns turned a blind eye to their members' misbehaviour. As far as the heads of the societies were concerned, theirs were communities of men, not academies for children. It wasn't their job to cosset. Students who progressed to an Inn of Court from the sheltered world of the university regarded it as a brutal introduction to masculine independence. The seventeenth-century antiquary Simonds D'Ewes recalled with a shudder his removal from the 'full breasts' of St John's College, Cambridge – his 'dear mother, from which I had sucked so much variety of learning' – to the macho bustle of Middle Temple.

Residents squeezed into shared chambers and shared beds, so making friends with the right sort was important: 'The unknown man is known by his companion,' one Polonius-like guardian wrote to his charge at Inner Temple. Cultivating relationships with other men was regarded as an art, and the rhetoric of passionate *amicitia perfecta* fuelled emotional intimacies between members. Certainly, the language of institutional togetherness could become fervent. A masque during the post-plague Christmas entertainments of 1594 featured a 'device of friendship' that staged the personified figures of 'Graius' (Gray's Inn) and 'Templarius' (Inner Temple) alongside classical exemplars of faithful friends – and queer lovers – including Theseus and Pirithous, and Achilles and Patroclus.

If the authorities hoped that virtuous friendships would keep the Innsmen from indulging in youthful excesses, then they hadn't reckoned with the insatiable popularity of erotica. Leaflets of poetry – printed, copied or composed in manuscript – were the units of currency in a vigorous market of literary exchange. Sultry poems were passed from hand to hand, and chamber to chamber. Innsmen who learned to live it up in the big city were just as keen to read about the sorts of sexual adventures that were available on their doorstep.

This was the milieu of John Donne's elegies, the metaphysical poems too hot for print. Unknown numbers of Donne's friends at Lincoln's Inn read hand-copied sheets bearing his visions of full-bodied passion three decades before their publication. But it was also the context for some fantastically unliterary smut, much-shared erotica that titillated its male readers with visions of sexual extravagance, exoticism and religious transgression. Sometimes an author tried to achieve all three: 'A Proper New Ballad of the Countess [who] would be a Notorious Woman Out of Italy and of a Panderess or Promotor of Love among the Augustine Nuns,' read one comprehensive title. Just as exciting were the gigglingly priapic penis jokes which abounded in manuscript collections, such as this acrostic found in an early seventeenth-century poetic miscellany:

> A maiden fair of the green-sickness late,
> P ity to see perplexed was full sore;
> R esolving how to mend her bad estate,
> I n this distress Apollo doth implore
> C ure for her ill. The Oracle assigns:
> K eep the first letters of these several lines.

Innsmen loved talking, reading and writing about penises. There was a barrack-room humour to it, of course, but their fascination was also a constituent part of the homoerotic togetherness that was so important at the Inns. Cocks and balls pranced across puns, poems and jests, and no doubt decorated privy walls and the backs of library benches as well, a baldly bodily counterpart to the high-flown language of classical *amicitia perfecta* that the Inns propounded about themselves. While they were unquestionably schools of poetic hetero-seduction, the Inns of Court were also places that understood the satisfaction young men found in thinking about their own and their friends' bodies.

Into this ready market arrived the epyllion. The new publishing format packaged erotic fantasies into inexpensive books that could be bought from nearby Paul's Churchyard. Readers no longer had to rely on the closed circulation networks of the Inns to obtain thrilling visions of hot pursuit and beautiful – usually male – bodies. Thanks to a poetic lawyer in the 1560s, these stories were now available to buy. Like much in our story so far, it all goes back to Ovid.

Arthur Golding released the first four books of his translation of *Metamorphoses* in 1565 in advance of its full publication two years later. His 'pleasant and delectable' volume pleased almost everyone apart from Thomas Peend, a barrister and poet who – he claimed – had been hard at work on his own version of Ovid's classic. There wasn't much he could now do with his slightly plodding manuscript, although it seemed a shame to keep it locked away in his legal chambers on Chancery Lane. So later that year, Peend published *The Pleasant Fable of Hermaphroditus and Salmacis*, a single tale lifted from Book 4 of *Metamorphoses* and published as a standalone text, a neat and affordable package for those who couldn't stretch to Golding's more substantial work. Peend certainly didn't intend to come across as a libertine: the moral of

the story – laid out in ringingly misogynistic terms – concerned
the need for naïve young men to be wary of the 'mad desires of
women' (446). But in highlighting one of the more explicit stories
from *Metamorphoses*, and in radically restructuring the standard
dynamic of love poetry so the determined pursuer was a woman
and the bashful beloved a boy, Peend invented a new genre: the
lustful mini-epic with a focus on beautiful male bodies being
ravished by a divine lover.

Hermaphroditus – son of Mercury and Venus (otherwise
known as Hermes and Aphrodite) – is a beauty, as bright and fair
and shining as any romantic mistress and easily the equal, Peend
writes, of those other classical pin-ups like Narcissus and
Ganymede. He looks like a 'portraiture divine' (13), with a
god-like figure that 'far exceed[s] / The graces of all other' (9–10).
He is, in the world of Ovid, exceptionally vulnerable to seduction.

Resting during a journey, he spots an inviting pool, crystal
clear under the shade of circling trees. Before he can reach it, the
nymph Salmacis bursts out of the undergrowth, her heart
burning with 'smouldering heat' (103) and her body throbbing
with desire to fulfil her lust. She reaches for him, leans in for a
kiss, and the 'shamefast boy' (136) shies away, blushing 'as red as
blood' (138).

What Hermaphroditus really wants is a swim, and when he
disrobes and slips into the pool, Salmacis is unable to restrain
herself. Fired up and clothes off, she is after him like 'an eager
mastiff dog' (197), thoughts of persuasion fled and determin-
ation to possess now irresistible. Lust lends her power, and she
catches him as he tries to escape from the pool. They thrash
together in the water, Salmacis pressing her full body weight
against Hermaphroditus, consuming him with kisses as she
exalts in her success: 'Struggle on thy fill. / But now by force I
will obtain, / That shall content my will' (288–90). Salmacis's
desire is for endless pleasure, eternal propinquity, and Venus

– Hermaphroditus's oddly negligent mother – obliges, fusing into one body the forceful seducer and the resistant boy. 'Double-shaped' (328) Hermaphroditus steps out of the pool a different being, both male and female. But what Hermaphroditus loses in manhood they gain in kin, as the gods decree that all who enter the waters of Salmacis will emerge 'man and woman both' (311), new members of a unique community of intersex twinned souls.

Peend tried to frame his Ovidian fantasy as a cautionary tale with a moralising coda: Hermaphroditus represents all young men, like those at the Inns of Court, who set out into the world unprepared for the sinful women who will leap on them and drain their masculine spirits. But he could hardly hide the queer contours of a story that ends with a gender-fluid apotheosis and contains at its heart a vigorous domination fantasy in which the desired central figure is a beautiful youth, all lissom limbs and cheeks rosy with exertion (Salmacis's appearance barely gets a look-in). Whether his readers were men or women, the pleasure that Peend's pleasant fable promised was of a decidedly kinky nature.

When Shakespeare was contemplating his poetic moves in the plaguey summer of 1592, Peend's *Hermaphroditus and Salmacis* seems to have been on his mind. He might have been thinking about an Ovidian mini-epic for a while, ever since the Lincoln's Inn writer Thomas Lodge had revived the form in 1589 with his *Scylla's Metamorphosis* (dedicated to 'the gentlemen of the Inns of Court and Chancery'), another story featuring a reluctant male lover and a furiously passionate goddess. It's very possible Shakespeare had also read a manuscript version of Christopher Marlowe's *Hero and Leander*, a magnificent epyllion that was left unfinished at the time of Marlowe's death. The poem's theme – the athletic Leander's swim across the Hellespont to meet his lover Hero – gave Marlowe plenty of scope for lingering descriptions of his central male character. His Leander certainly has the physique of a champion swimmer: a body 'straight as Circe's wand' (1.61), a smooth chest and a broad back dinted by a 'heavenly path' between his shoulder blades (1.68). Leander is sufficiently dazzling to inflame Neptune, who nearly drowns the youth when he tugs him into his underwater lair for a spot of lovemaking.

But if Shakespeare had decided on an Ovidian epyllion, he needed to choose a topic. The repeated story of *Metamorphoses* – the transformation of a mortal into some symbolic alternative form as a result of rape or pursuit by the gods – gave him a lot of options, and plenty of variety in terms of transformer and transformee. He'd given the matter some thought already. In the opening scenes of *The Taming of the Shrew*, when down-and-out Sly is duped into thinking he's rich, his tricksters offer him erotic art inspired by famous scenes in Ovid. What would Sly prefer, they ask: Io facing rape by Jupiter, Daphne in flight from Apollo, or 'Adonis painted by a running brook, / And Cytherea [Venus] all in sedges hid' (Ind., 2.50–51)? In each case, a viewer like Sly would be expected to leer at the depiction or prospect of sexual assault, a central fantasy in early modern erotica whether the victim was male or female. Shakespeare evidently felt that the Venus and Adonis story – with its focus on a resistant youth fending off a determined lover – had merit as a source of high-end pornography.

Obviously, a poem about one of the most beautiful youths in history was going to have its attractions. Adonis features in Peend's epyllion as one of the pantheon of Ovidian studs to whom Hermaphroditus is compared, and he was already a popular subject in continental works of art. Titian's *Venus and Adonis*, which centres the composition around the bright bare skin of the goddess's back and Adonis's muscular right arm and pec, was dispatched from Spain to London in 1554 to join the picture collection of King Philip, then married to Mary I. But Shakespeare's chief source for the story remained *Metamorphoses*, and more specifically the particularly transgressive tenth book, a series of inter-nestled tales narrated by the iconic queer Orpheus – he of the male brothel on the plains of Thrace – about 'pretty boys / That were the darlings of the gods' and 'unlawful joys / That burned in the breasts of girls.' Orpheus tells the stories of 'prodigious lusts' such as those between Ganymede and Jupiter, or Hyacinth and Apollo (on the rebound after Daphne), or Pygmalion and his statue. Adonis is the result of a misbegotten union between the Cypriot princess Myrrha and her own father, born by a dramatic caesarean section that is also tree surgery: Myrrha is transformed into a myrrh tree to hide the shame of her incest, and her child is sliced out of her bark. Somehow, Adonis overcomes his difficult start in life to become the ancient world's sexiest boar-hunter, lusted after by the gods but doomed to embody the tragedy of desirable manhood cut down in its prime. His story had the requisite mix of beauty, sex and death to appeal to the overheated imaginations of the epyllia fans, especially in a time of anxious morbidity as the plague continued to rip through London, and so Shakespeare set about expanding one hundred lines of Ovid into more than a thousand lines of brand-new poetry.

Shakespeare's *Venus and Adonis* (1593) invites the reader to experience the seduction of a coyly resistant young man through the eyes of a 'bold-faced suitor' (6): the powerful, strapping figure of Venus, who is determined to sleep with her prey. He jumps right into the story, wasting no time on the boy's murky incestuous origins. His Adonis is a 'rose-cheeked' (3), hunting-obsessed teen, less hunky and more sulky than the Adonises of Renaissance painting and sculpture. He's 'more lovely than a man' (9), and even fairer than the smitten goddess of love, who hauls the gleaming youth off his horse and frogmarches him into a private glade:

Backward she pushed him, as she would be thrust,
And governed him in strength, though not in lust. (41–2)

Venus does her best (strokes his cheek, kisses him all over) and can't resist giving in to a little piqued pride – as she explains, Mars the god of war 'begged for that which thou unasked shalt have' (102) – but to no avail. Adonis won't be won. Enfolding him in a bear hug, Venus murmurs the ultimate come-on lines:

I'll be a park, and thou shalt be my deer;
Feed where thou wilt, on mountain or in dale;
Graze on my lips, and if those hills be dry,
Stray lower, where the pleasant fountains lie. (231–34)

If Adonis's perfect frame is like a work of art, vibrant with tints of white and red, the divine Venus has a confoundingly alluring body that contains enough 'round rising hillocks' and 'brakes [thickets] obscure and rough' (238) to keep a curious lover entertained for hours. But not Adonis. Even the enthusiastic mating of his horse with a frisky jennet fails to set an example to the youth, who explains he is 'unripe' (524) and too young to be 'plucked' (528).

By now night has fallen – Venus has been at her persuasions for a whole day – and she finally loses patience. Like Salmacis, whose passion produces a sort of enraged frottage, Venus gives in to a sexual 'blindfold fury' (554), overwhelming Adonis with foraging hands and hard, invasive kissing. Clumsy and stumbling, the pair end up in something approaching the missionary position, but 'he will not manage her, although he mount her' (598). Adonis breaks away from the flushed and sweating Venus and rushes off to prepare for the fatal boar hunt (he gives Venus's suggestion that he instead try the safer sport of hare coursing the short shrift it deserves).

In the end, it's the boar who achieves what Venus yearns for and yet cannot accomplish. In the fatal turmoil of the chase, the animal makes a 'foul [. . .] conquest' (1030) of Adonis, imagined by the grieving Venus as a deadly 'kiss' (1110) followed by a devastating penetration:

> And nuzzling in his flank, the loving swine
> Sheathed unaware the tusk in his soft groin. (1115–16)

Venus's wooing does, then, conclude with a consummation of a sort, as the triumphant boar stalks off, smeared with the emissions of conquest: a 'frothy mouth, bepainted all with red, / Like milk and blood being mingled both together' (901–2). Left alone, Venus watches as the corpse of the ravaged Adonis melts 'like a vapour from her sight' (1166) to leave behind an exquisite blood-red flower spotted with white.

In a time of pestilence and panic, Shakespeare produced one of the most explicitly erotic poems of the age for a readership in dire need of distraction. His riposte to the bleak preachers who blamed worldly pleasures for the descent of the plague was to find his inspiration in the single richest collection of queer mythology available to him, and expand tenfold Ovid's story of the beautiful Adonis's seduction. Far from drawing God's ire, Shakespeare hoped his poem would bring his readers some respite: as Venus murmurs to the boy, the plague-banishing breath that wafts from his lush lips has the power to 'drive infection from the dangerous year' (508). Shakespeare was writing for men and women (indeed, the only surviving copy of the first edition of the poem was owned by a seventeenth-century woman book collector), but he knew that his greatest concentration of readers in London was to be found among the educated young members of the Inns of Court, a thousand-strong or more, who were beginning to return to the capital as plague abated through 1593 and 1594. He anticipated that the Innsmen would understand the poem in its Ovidian context, with the story of Venus and Adonis folded into the polymorphous tales narrated by the queer poet Orpheus. In its origin, context, theme and allusions, *Venus and Adonis* was a golden treasury of same-sex fantasy, a song as hot as fire that foregrounded an irresistible male body and invited readers to imagine themselves in the role of rough seducer.

When Shakespeare's Stratford contemporary Richard Field printed the poem in May or June 1593, in a trim volume with appealingly large print and priced at about sixpence, it was instantly, overwhelmingly, name-makingly popular. If readers were looking for something to take their minds off the sickness and death still haunting the streets, then Shakespeare truly caught the mood with his lush, queerly angled fantasy. The poem went through six editions before the end of the century (with many more to follow), and it so captured the hearts of early readers that hardly any early copies survive, having been read and reread to tatters. It prompted immediate imitation and homage, with at least three poems that recast Venus's forceful wooing in other Ovidian guises appearing within the year: *Cephalus and Procris* and *Narcissus* by Thomas Edwards, and *Oenone and Paris*, probably by a young Thomas Heywood.

Venus and Adonis made Shakespeare's reputation, and cemented his renown as a writer of clever, erotic and intoxicatingly 'sweet' poetry – by which his fans meant verse that was sensual and alluring, not cute or saccharine. The Cambridge clergyman (clergyman!) William Covell praised 'sweet Shakespeare' and his 'wanton Adonis' in 1595, one of the earliest unambiguous references to his poetry in print. Gabriel Harvey noted that 'the younger sort takes much delight in Shakespeare's *Venus and Adonis.*' In fact, the younger sort, men and women, took to *Venus and Adonis* like wine. In a play written for performance by

Cambridge University students in about 1600, a foppishly absurd character pledges to hang a picture of 'sweet Master Shakespeare' on his study wall, and sleep with a copy of *Venus and Adonis* under his pillow. For Shakespeare fandom to be mocked like this suggests total cultural saturation. Few people outside the theatre profession or his hometown knew Shakespeare's name when the theatres closed in 1592; when they reopened two years later, he was a nationally famous poet. By the middle years of the decade, he was the undisputed master of sweetness, sex and Ovidian transgression. For the rest of his life, Shakespeare was to be known as the author of 'wanton pamphlets', responsible for poems that had a luridly arousing impact on their readers. In 1608, the playwright Thomas Middleton characterised *Venus and Adonis* and Marlowe's *Hero and Leander* (posthumously published in 1598) as 'two luscious marrow-bone pies', aphrodisiacal dishes with a delectable after-effect. Some knowledge of early modern patisserie is necessary to understand the simile; Middleton imagines the poems as sweet confections containing enough sugary candied fruits and rich meaty protein to keep a lover alert and vital all through the night.

Shakespeare's success had another result: it brought him into the orbit of a generous and highly attractive new patron. He wasn't to know that *Venus and Adonis* would be a smash, and in any case in an age before publishing royalties, there was no guarantee that a big-selling book would make its writer much money. So when he'd finished the final stanza of the poem, there was one more piece of inventive oratory he needed to pen: the dedication. Unlike other epyllion writers such as Thomas Lodge, Shakespeare didn't offer his first published words to the 'gentlemen of the Inns of Court'. He had his eye on a more valuable prize.

Dedications were a more pecuniary matter in the 1590s than they are today (this book is dedicated to my husband, but I don't expect him to pay me for the honour). A well-crafted dedication to a monied public figure could prompt the dedicatee to offer five or ten pounds – at least as much if not more than the fee Shakespeare would get for a full-length, singly authored play. Converting sixteenth-century sums to modern values is complex, as the buying power of sterling has fluctuated so much over the years. Ten pounds in 1593 is roughly equivalent to £1,500 or £2,000 today, but the same sum expressed as a multiplication of a daily salary implies a much greater reward. A tradesman would have to work for 200 days to earn £10; 200 days of earnings in modern terms suggests a value closer to £15,000 or £20,000. However one looks at it, these were significant sums of money. And no prior acquaintance was necessary, although a writer would do well to seek permission to print a dedication before the book went to press. Rich, well-known people – courtiers, the nobility, high-ranking churchmen – could expect to have appropriate books dedicated to them, and they understood that they played a key financial role in the diverse economy of publishing. If the text was at least half decent and not religiously or politically objectionable, the writer deserved a gratuity.

Shakespeare thought carefully about the right dedicatee for *Venus and Adonis*. It needed to be someone who would appreciate the sensual tone and queer point of view – and it was also important that the chosen candidate hadn't been too pestered by needy artists. That ruled out the two most obvious targets, the patrons of London's main theatre companies. Ferdinando Stanley, Lord Strange and Henry Herbert, Earl of Pembroke, had already paid out significant sums to their plague-struck troupes. The ideal choice would be young (like most of his readers), wealthy and up to speed with the latest literary fashions.

The man Shakespeare selected as patron for *Venus and Adonis* and his next long poem, *Lucrece*, was Henry Wriothesley (probably pronounced 'Rizley'), third Earl of Southampton. He was one of the most beautiful young men in Queen Elizabeth's court: luminous skin, dark auburn hair falling in a single love-lock over his shoulder, and a fondness for rich sable doublets set off by eye-wateringly expensive white lace collars. The young Southampton was so fine-featured that a painting of him aged about seventeen, attributed to the Flemish painter John de Critz, was until recently thought to be of a woman.

Rich and beautiful young noblemen tend to get noticed, and Southampton – aged nineteen when twenty-nine-year-old Shakespeare published *Venus and Adonis* in 1593 – had the add-itional burden of springing from intriguingly questionable stock. His Catholic parents had endured a cataclysmically unhappy marriage, and after the death of his father (long suspected of anti-Elizabeth plotting), the young Southampton had been educated in the household of the queen's chief minister William Cecil, Lord Burghley, part of whose sprawling portfolio of duties included raising as his own wards the children of nobles who had died, or fallen into bankruptcy, treason or lunacy. Among Burghley's perks as Master of the Court of Wards was the right to claim a portion of his wards' wealth, and determine their marriage prospects; any ward who refused Burghley's wedding orders was slapped with a hefty fine, to be taken out of their estates once they had come of age.

Southampton was gorgeous, strong-willed and rebellious. Although not yet of age, he was already several years into his campaign of passive resistance against Burghley's intention to marry him to his granddaughter, Elizabeth Vere, who was herself the result of an earlier act of Burghley's matchmaking, this time between his daughter Anne and his ward the Earl of Oxford. The Oxford marriage was enough to put anyone off – Oxford and Lady Anne were even more toxically ill-suited than Southampton's parents – and the young Southampton refused to give his consent to the arrangement. It wasn't just the fact that he didn't love Vere (no one thought about aristocratic marriages as romance). Saying no to Burghley, who extracted staggering sums from his hapless wards, was something Southampton did on principle.

It seems highly likely that Shakespeare knew something of Southampton's expected marriage to Elizabeth Vere. It's been a popular biographical game to posit a point in the early 1590s when Shakespeare and Southampton met – perhaps at the play-house, perhaps at some sort of aristocratic soirée where the playwright was the entertainment – and he learned about his future patron's nuptial troubles. No meeting would have been necessary, however, to bring Southampton into Shakespeare's view as a potential sponsor for his new book. Another writer with insider knowledge of Southampton's situation had already addressed him in a dedication that seemed to tell the world the young earl was ripe for attention from flattering poets.

In 1591, John Clapham published a Latin poem that trans-posed Ovid's story of Narcissus – a boy so beautiful and self-absorbed he falls for (and into) his own reflection in a pool, thus dying of self-love – to the English countryside. He dedicated it to 'clarissimo et nobilissimo domino Henrico Comiti Southamtoniae', 'the brightest and noblest lord Henry, Earl of Southampton'. The message of the poem was unmistakeable: beautiful young-sters should learn to shake off their adolescent wilfulness and relish the opportunity of becoming outward-looking married young noblemen. It so happened that John Clapham was Lord Burghley's secretary, so anyone in the know would have assumed that Narcissus was a text that came with tacit high-level approval from the powerful Master of the Court of Wards himself. In Narcissus, readers could see that an Ovidian story about a sexy, romance-resistant youth had been dedicated to Southampton by his guardian's own employee. But it's less likely Shakespeare would have recognised Narcissus for what it actually was: a salvo in a propaganda war being waged by Burghley against

Southampton's opposition to a seemingly sensible dynastic marriage. Instead, Shakespeare probably saw the earlier dedication as a precedent and a guide: Southampton appeared to be a good bet for metamorphic stories of seduction and pursuit. Shakespeare wasn't to know that Clapham had little hope of a five or ten pounds thank you from his dedicatee (the publication costs would have been borne by Lord Burghley, no doubt from the assets he creamed off from Southampton's estate). As far as he was concerned, Shakespeare had found his man, and he wrote him a letter.

The polite, slightly tentative epistle to Southampton that Shakespeare prefixed to *Venus and Adonis* was the very first printed text to bear the writer's own name:

Right Honourable,

I know not how I shall offend in dedicating my unpolished lines to your lordship, nor how the world will censure me for choosing so strong a prop to support so weak a burden; only, if your honour seem but pleased, I account myself highly praised, and vow to take advantage of all idle hours, till I have honoured you with some graver labour. But if the first heir of my invention prove deformed, I shall be sorry it had so noble a godfather, and never after ear so barren a land, for fear it yield me still so bad a harvest. I leave it to your honourable survey, and your honour to your heart's content; which I wish may always answer your own wish and the world's hopeful expectation.

Your honour's in all duty,

William Shakespeare.

It's the dedication of someone who's new to this sort of game, but these aren't bashful words – however deferential the tone (and at this point Shakespeare wasn't even a gentleman, a status he didn't achieve until 1596). The letter follows hard upon the volume's epigraph, a quotation in Latin from Ovid's *Amores*: '*Vilia miretur vulgus; mihi flavus Apollo / Pocula Castalia plena ministret aqua*' ('Let the masses wonder at cheap things: for me, let golden Apollo serve full cups straight from the Castalian spring'). It's a striking rejection of populist success for a man of the theatre, and a bid for elite literary fame; the Castalian spring was the ancient Greek source of poetic inspiration. *Venus and Adonis* might be the 'first heir' of his imagination – the first time he's appeared in print under his own name, not the first thing he's ever written – but Shakespeare doesn't apologise for the theme or content of the poem (only, self-deprecatingly, its style). This is rather steely artistic confidence, tactfully overwritten with social diffidence: as long as Southampton likes the poem, Shakespeare will immediately set himself the task of writing something 'graver' – not morbid or mournful, but serious, authoritative, consequential. Shakespeare is telling us – politely, self-effacingly – that he's just one step away from an instant classic.

If Shakespeare's dedication to Southampton was a gamble, it paid off. When the earl made his 'honourable survey' of the book, he evidently liked what he found. A lot. Every edition of *Venus and Adonis* printed in Shakespeare's lifetime bore the dedication; had Southampton objected, the epistle would have been excised from future printings (compare the experience of Thomas Nashe, who included a rather flippant dedication to Southampton in the first edition of his prose fiction *The Unfortunate Traveller* (1594) and had to pull it from all subsequent impressions).

Southampton's favour would have been accompanied by cash. Long-nurtured anecdotes suggest that it might have been considerably more than the typical handout. The seventeenth-century actor-manager William Davenant (who liked to claim he was Shakespeare's unacknowledged son and so may not be a reliable witness) swore that Southampton once gave the young poet £1,000 – an implausible sum equivalent to one third of the earl's annual revenue. Stories about his profligacy certainly abounded: a ballad of King James's time told a story of the earl wagering £7,000 on a jumping contest. Maybe 'thousands' just seemed a more fitting unit to attach to the glamorous Southampton than something humdrum like tens or hundreds. Southampton liked spending money that would otherwise have gone to Burghley, and so it's possible he gave Shakespeare an unusually generous fee, perhaps several times the standard. It was, after all, only a few years later – after a long period of plague lockdowns and disrupted theatrical seasons – that the Shakespeares were able to buy New Place, a sprawling Stratford-upon-Avon townhouse.

The sultry *Venus and Adonis* was Shakespeare's entrée to Southampton's world. Given his evident satisfaction with the poem and his pronounced disinclination to being told what to do, the earl can't have interpreted it, like Clapham's *Narcissus*, as an earnest treatise in favour of marriage. Shakespeare's version of the story doesn't imply that Adonis brings his death on himself by resisting Venus's approach; and Venus (already married to the god Vulcan) is hardly offering him a respectable future as man and wife. The pleasures of the poem lie instead in its lush eroticism (homo- and hetero-) and its lyrical, steamy language. Southampton responded enthusiastically to precisely the qualities that Shakespeare had been aiming for when he devised an Ovidian fantasy to appeal to the erotica-obsessed readers of the Inns of Court.

Southampton was something of an Innsman *deluxe*, after all. He'd been a member of Gray's Inn since 1588, and now in early adulthood he was starting to take a more active involvement in its activities; along with many other high-society figures, he took part in the Gray's Inn Christmas revels in 1594. Like the young men supposedly studying law at Gray's Inn, Southampton enjoyed expensive clothes: a portrait of the earl aged twenty-six shows him in a silver silk doublet, gold-flecked hose and embroidered gloves. He was an urbane, highly educated young man who liked literature (Nashe said he was 'a dear lover and cherisher' of both poets and 'the lovers of poets') and he had a weakness for the theatre: a courtier remarked disapprovingly in 1599 that Southampton and a friend 'pass the time in London merely in going to plays every day.' Shakespeare had made a good choice in his literary patron: here was someone who understood the worlds of poetry and theatre, who paid 'respect to those / Who had a name in Arts', as an admirer later put it, and who responded warmly to the queer overtones of *Venus and Adonis*.

Southampton was almost certainly sexually attracted to both men and women, and perhaps the sophisticated earl, like the Greco-Roman disputants in Lucian, enjoyed debating the relative attractions of Adonic twinky youths and handsome Venusian women. Just such a debate appears in another book dedicated to him, Achilles Tatius's *The Delectable History of Clitophon and Leucippe*, translated from the Greek by William Burton in 1597. This was the first English text to bring the homoerotic candour of the classical world to a general readership, some of whom may have been surprised by its conclusions: as is typical of late-antiquity erotic philosophy, the last word is granted to the boy-lovers.

In his own life Southampton was responsible for a good deal of emotional drama. He held out against Burghley's choice of wife, Elizabeth Vere, until after his guardian's death; with Burghley finally out of the picture, he secretly married one of the queen's ladies-in-waiting, Elizabeth Vernon, in 1598 (the bride was already pregnant). An irate Queen Elizabeth sent them both to the Fleet

Prison, where the new couple marked the birth of their daughter. Southampton, one way or another, spent a fair portion of his twenties in jail: he was committed to the Tower of London in 1601 for his part in a failed *coup d'état* by his friend Robert Devereux, second Earl of Essex. As part of the investigation into his involvement, the Privy Council received word from a paid informant that, in addition to his slippery political activities, Southampton had been known while on military campaign in Ireland to 'coll' (embrace), hug and 'play wantonly' with the man in charge of his cavalry.

Despite biographical speculation about Shakespeare's and Southampton's relationship, mostly driven by the earl's supposed involvement in the composition of the *Sonnets*, which we'll come to in the next chapter, it's very unlikely that the two men were ever anything other than a rather distant patron and client – let alone lovers. It seems instead that Shakespeare's special skill was in giving Southampton exactly what he wanted on the page. He'd scored a palpable hit with *Venus and Adonis*, and the many editions of the poem in Shakespeare's lifetime that included his flattering epistle took evidence of the earl's satisfaction into thousands of homes.

The next work of art that Shakespeare dedicated to Southampton was similarly engineered to please. This was *Lucrece* (published as *The Rape of Lucrece* only after Shakespeare's death), the 'graver labour' he had promised in *Venus and Adonis*: a magisterial, if ponderous, account of the shocking act of sexual violence that stimulated a republican revolution in ancient Rome. Lucrece, the wife of a high-ranking army officer, is raped by Tarquin, the son of the Roman king. In her trauma and grief, Lucrece takes her own life, and her devastated husband leads an uprising that exiles Tarquin and the disgraced Roman royal family.

If *Lucrece* and *Venus and Adonis* shared a certain thematic terrain – stories of uncontrolled lust lifted from classical sources – their purposes were quite different. *Lucrece* wasn't intended to excite: Gabriel Harvey concluded it was a poem for 'wiser' readers, unlike the giddy pleasures of *Venus and Adonis*. Instead, *Lucrece* spoke to the constitutional interests Southampton was developing with the Earl of Essex and his followers, who included Essex's sister Lady Penelope Rich. The Essex circle was fascinated by stories of Roman history, especially those that involved influential aristocrats seizing the reins of power from weak or corrupt monarchs. They were seeking political precedents for the rising that would become the Essex Revolt in 1601, when they attempted to 'free' the ageing Queen Elizabeth from a faction of their court enemies. In the 1590s, Southampton and Essex loved nothing more than researching the outcomes of successful patrician revolutions. Shakespeare struck gold a second time with his stately poem on the birth of Roman republicanism, a perfect fit for Southampton and his aristocratic friends, and well worth another payout of ten pounds or more to its increasingly popular writer.

The year 1594 – when the second flattering dedication to his lordship prefaced *Lucrece* – is the last point that the historical record lets us put Shakespeare and Southampton on the same page, metaphorically or literally. By the spring of that year, the terrible plague had finally burned itself out, and London's theatres could reopen with the expectation of remaining so for more than a few weeks. Shakespeare found himself in a newly constituted acting company established at the Theatre in Shoreditch and under the patronage of a different aristocrat, Henry Carey, the Lord Chamberlain – the authorities had taken advantage of all the disruption to stamp some order on the ever-shifting commercial theatre scene. Shakespeare's career swerve in 1592 and 1593, from drama to lyric poetry, took a reverse course in 1594, returning him to the playhouse – and away from the circle of the Earl of Southampton and his friends. He went back to work with crucial new insights into the tastes and preferences of his expanding audience. He had conclusively proved his mettle with two widely read works of high-end literature, and he'd acquired a print readership of mostly young people with an ear and eye for eroticism, queer desire and the stimulating proximity of sex and death. Shakespeare would make sure to convert his new readers into playgoers when he deployed precisely those tropes and emotional flashpoints in the three plays he wrote for the new theatrical season: *Richard II*, with its delicate hero worn down by brutal pursuit by a stronger antagonist, Henry Bolingbroke; *Romeo and Juliet*, in which the lovers' overheated sexual passion for each other tips over into 'death-marked' (Prologue, 9) obsession; and *A Midsummer Night's Dream*, Shakespeare's most Ovidian play, laden with transgressive and confusing desire and unsettling metamorphoses. But if he thought he was finished with lyric poetry for good, he was mistaken. The mid-1590s would see him make the acquaintance of a dazzling young poet who prompted him to explore queer desire with a thrilling new candour – and led him to the very brink of what his society was willing to accept.

PART III

Limits

6

The Queerest Year

28 December 1594. Frankly, it was getting embarrassing. Yes, he was the William Shakespeare who'd written Adonis. *No, he hadn't thought about making it into a stage play. Alas, the young lad who made such a handsome Tamora Queen of the Goths would not be giving his Venus any time soon. The questions had come thick and fast as William and his Chamberlain's Men fellows arrived at Gray's Inn.*

The actors made a tiring house in the buttery, heaping up costumes for The Comedy of Errors *in a corner. The noise from the Great Hall was a battlefield roar. The Innsmen seemed to be indulging, in one go, all of the Christmas festivities cancelled because of the pestilence. Three years of frustrated desire to mum, masque and sinfully revel was being released. William heard the sound of breaking glass and a series of drunken hoots. It was going to be a tough crowd.*

They'd come early, and the show would be going up late – if at all. William wandered out to the passage to investigate. He couldn't discover much. The members were absorbed in their own engrossingly exclusive merrymaking in the hall: something about a confected discourtesy on the part of their guests from the Inner Temple. It was all very hilarious, he was sure.

His way back was blocked by a Gray's Inn lawyer, his masquing costume already crumpled. A Master Knightley, William remembered; Northampton-shire gentry; liked a drink and a boy. Loved Adonis. *Knightley rested a velvet arm against the wall, a few inches from William's face.*

Was Master Shakespeare in the ingling mood this Christmastide night?

Ah, not while on the job.

Later, in my chambers?

Another time.

And tell me: had Master Shakespeare, like them all, not found the greatest contentment in Daphnis's poem The Affectionate Shepherd; *surely Ganymede was Adonis's twin?*

Knightley's hands were at William's chest, slipping a stab-stitched poetry book into his doublet.

New Year's gift, Knightley said.

The servants had brought the players beer and venison pasties, and word that the gentlemen in the hall were now throwing furniture. By midnight, Dick Burbage and Will Kemp, each an Antipholus and a Dromio, were swearing they'd never play the Inns of Court again. Half an hour later, when they finally got instruction that the play was expected, William put down the volume of Daphnis's poetry to change into his Duke Solinus costume.

Knightley might have been a drunk, but he was right. The verses in The Affectionate Shepherd *were fresh, with echoes of his own* Venus and Adonis, *the goddess swapped out for a passionate shepherd yearning for his young man, and much sweetness and pleasure in the lines. William played his opening scene with his mind still on the poetry book. The audience in the hall was inert, high spirits finally felled by barrels of sack and canary. William returned to the buttery. The night might have been a washout as far as his* Comedy of Errors *was concerned, but his discovery of Daphnis and Ganymede was a Christmas miracle.*

The commercial stage came roaring back to life. The Christmas season, from All Saint's Day (1 November 1594) until Candlemas (2 February 1595), was a blur of royal command performances and private entertainments for the Lord Chamberlain's Men.

High society grabbed the first chance in two years to let its hair down: the special performance of *The Comedy of Errors* at Gray's Inn was so memorably chaotic that a description of the carnage ('it was ever after called, "The Night of Errors" ') was published almost a century later. At thirty, Shakespeare was busier than he'd ever been with the demands of the professional stage. The new Lord Chamberlain's Men boasted the city's best comedian in William Kemp, and the country's most promising tragic leading man in Richard Burbage. Now Shakespeare took on a role that London's theatreland hadn't seen before: he became the company's house actor-dramatist, a shareholding player and playwright who deployed his staggering gifts in comedy, history and tragedy in the service of his increasingly profitable joint-stock troupe. And amid this era of astonishing dramatic productivity, Shakespeare started a new creative project. He began to work in earnest on a collection of pathbreaking sonnets of queer desire that would remain unpublished for more than a decade. In the years after 1595, Shakespeare had two canvases: the very visible realm of the playhouse, attended regularly by thousands of Londoners, and the far more exclusive world of lyric love poetry, where his new sonnets circulated as manuscript copies among a much smaller audience. But behind Shakespeare's private passion lay a series of published books by a new arrival on the London literary scene. A young poet called Richard Barnfield blazed into public consciousness in 1594 with the publication of *The Affectionate Shepherd*, swiftly followed by two more revolutionary works, including a sonnet sequence that spectacularly reinvented English homoerotic verse. It would be the queerest year England had ever seen, and it was to transform Shakespeare's approach to writing poetry.

The sonnet was the height of chic in the year the playhouses reopened. The short love poems – typically fourteen rhymed lines, concluding with a flourish in a couplet – followed a fashion set by the fourteenth-century Tuscan poet Francesco Petrarca, known in England as Petrarch. His collection *Il Canzoniere* ('The Songbook') told the story of his unrequited love for Laura and set the trend for sonnets that focused on agonised men and beautiful, remote heroines. The Petrarchan sonnet reached England through the courtier-poets of Henry VIII's time, especially Thomas Wyatt and Henry Howard, Earl of Surrey, whose poems were printed some years after their deaths in a popular miscellany edited by Richard Tottell called *Songs and Sonnets* (1557). Sonnets of various types and lengths appeared in collections by less aristocratic poets – including George Gascoigne, Barnaby Googe and George Turberville – through the 1560s and 1570s.

The sonnet was given a glamorous refurbishment in 1591, with the soldier-poet Philip Sidney's posthumously published collection, *Astrophil and Stella*. This was a long sequence of sonnets themed around a single narrative: the love of Astrophil (assumed to be Sidney himself) for the dazzling, but unobtainable, Stella – widely taken to be the Earl of Essex's sister Penelope Rich. Writers including Samuel Daniel, Edmund Spenser and Michael Drayton soon followed, with collections that grappled with the conflict between male desire and female disdain. No one saw fit to meddle with the essential dynamic of a 'goddess chaste', as Daniel put it in *Delia* (1592), shining beatifically beyond the reach of a desperate masculine speaker. Unlike Sidney's, most late-Elizabethan sonnet sequences weren't accounts of real affairs. It wasn't a coincidence that Daniel's Petrarchan beloved had a name that was an anagram of 'ideal': the point of the sonnet was for male poets to go into granular detail about the exquisite pain of their own frustrated passion, not waste too much time describing the specifics of the women by whom they were supposed to be obsessed.

Fourteen lines was a Goldilocks length for poets looking to riff on notions of courtly love. It wasn't so long that readers might lose the thread of a poem's premise, nor too short to prevent the writer having fun with extended metaphors and sophisticated imagery. The form's structural arrangement – broadly, three sets of four-line quatrains followed by a couplet – offered flexibility about where to place the emotional or intellectual twist, or *volta*. The *volta* gave a sonnet piquancy by allowing the writer to tack off in a contrasting direction, or suggest some new idea that enhanced the sonnet's basic theme. In one of Spenser's sonnets in *Amoretti* (1595), the speaker describes how the 'huge brightness' of his mistress robs him of the ability to speak or write – but his heart remains able to articulate 'the wonder that my wit cannot endite'. Poets liked the opportunity that an extended sonnet sequence seemed to present to reflect on the act of poetic composition. In writing dozens of sonnets to an idealised mistress, they could also talk at length about themselves.

It was perfectly possible to feel irritation with the earnestness and self-absorption of the sonnet. In the mid-1590s, the chief sonnet refusenik appeared, in fact, to be Shakespeare. Throughout the decade, he planted uncomplimentary references to the form in his plays. The ludicrous Abraham Slender in *The Merry Wives of Windsor* yearns for his copy of Tottell's *Songs and Sonnets* to furnish him with ready-made lines with which to woo Anne Page. Elsewhere, the sonnet is the blunt instrument of the fool: Thurio in *The Two Gentlemen of Verona*, Silvia's clod-hopping would-be seducer, is advised to:

> [T]angle her desires
> By wilful sonnets, whose composed rhymes
> Should be full-fraught with serviceable vows. (3.2.68–70)

If a sonnet wasn't crassly utilitarian – 'serviceable vows' are intended to get their subject into bed – then it was tiresomely over-stated. In *Love's Labour's Lost*, the king's friend Berowne says sonneteering 'makes flesh a deity, / A green goose a goddess' (4.3.72–73). Although he will go on to write one, Berowne nonetheless concludes that the form amounts to 'pure idolatry' (4.3.73): deifying mortal women isn't just in poor taste; it's unethical and possibly unhealthy. A sonneteering man usually spells trouble in Shakespeare's plays. In *Henry V*, the buffoonish French prince, the Dauphin, writes one in praise of his horse.

These characterisations of the sonnet as tacky cliché appear in plays that date (with the exception of the earlier *Two Gentlemen of Verona*) from the middle and end of the 1590s, when Shakespeare had already begun to write his own – and to share them in handwritten copies with what a contemporary observer in 1598 called a circle of his 'private friends'. Shakespeare the popular entertainer dismissed the sonnet with brusque unsentimentality; but Shakespeare the lyric poet was assiduously developing his craft. In the 1590s, he took care to keep his sonnets out of the public eye; two found their way into a pirated collection of modern poetry in 1599, but it wasn't until 1609 that the sequence as a whole made it through the press. The collection published as *Shakespeare's Sonnets* is in some respects a time capsule, capturing well after the fact (indeed, when the vogue for sonnet sequences had passed) a body of work written in part a decade before. We'll get on to the complexities of the poems' composition in due course; for now, let's consider the poems in the only significant format in which they survive: as a sequence published near the end of Shakespeare's career, when only a few final plays lay before him.

Shakespeare's Sonnets remains one of the longest collections of the form by a single author ever published in English, as well as the least transparently interpretable. Presented in an edition with only the most fleeting of editorial front matter, and without an authorial dedication, the framing of the volume gives the reader scant help in understanding its artistic or emotional purpose. But its content marks it out as extraordinary in the context of Shakespeare's contemporaries. His sonnets were nothing less than a wholesale rejection of the conventions of Petrarchan love poetry, with its perfect, unreachable female beloved, and a bold assertion of romantic cynicism in a form that had long competed with itself to manufacture the most reverent and sacralising metaphors for its subjects (Drayton's mistress in *Idea's Mirror* (1594) is, typically, a 'wonder of heaven' and a 'glass of divinity').

In the many overlapping narratives that make up *Shakespeare's Sonnets*, the speaker's inner torment doesn't lie in being rebuffed by a mistress, but in having sex with her repeatedly. And in the larger portion of Shakespeare's sequence, the unattainable beloved isn't a female ice-queen. He's an eye-delighting, Adonis-outshining 'lovely boy' (Sonnet 126.1), whose perfections possess the speaker's mind and provoke an obsessive love that tips him into near-madness – especially when the young man and the mistress appear to betray him by sleeping with each other. If other sonneteers fashioned their collections into lofty pedestals on which to mount implausibly perfect heroines – 'Erecting trophies to thy sacred eyes,' said Drayton – Shakespeare produced a testament to the artistic power of the queerly messy love triangle.

Because the 1609 edition lacks any kind of authorial positioning, and contains material written over a considerable period – one sonnet might date from the time of William and Anne's courtship; another appears to make reference to King James's coronation in 1603 – it's difficult to establish a singular throughline or narrative for the sequence as a whole. Unlike a play, *Shakespeare's Sonnets* doesn't have a straightforward plot. And nor is it always unambiguously clear whether the addressee of each poem is a 'lovely youth' (54.13) or a bewitching mistress, although the gatherings of thematically linked sonnets fashion a stable subject in the reader's mind's eye, even in poems without a giveaway pronoun or term of endearment. Instead, the sonnets exist as a collection of grouped poems and stand-alone singletons that captures the evolving nature of the speaker's desires and preoccupations.

Just as the poems' 'thou' shifts from male to female, it's possible that Shakespeare also imagined a number of different poetic 'I's; there's no reason to assume that all the sonnets are inherently autobiographical. One of Shakespeare's notable skills, after all, was in giving plausible human voices to a large cast of dramatic characters. But there's nothing random about the order in which the sonnets were published in 1609, and every indication that readers were expected to start at Sonnet 1 and work their way through to Sonnet 154.

As they did so, they would experience a series of interconnected scenarios. In Sonnets 1–17, the speaker addresses a youth whose beauty recalls the 'lovely April' (3.10) of his mother's young womanhood. He urges the boy to marry and produce an heir, thus preventing a slide into onanistic 'self-love' (3.8); he suspects the youth has been too much given to 'spend[ing] / Upon thyself thy beauty's legacy' (4.1–2), and he needs to start tilling an 'uneared womb' (3.5). There's a shift in mood towards the end of the 'procreation' sonnets, as the speaker introduces a theme to which he'll return: that the very poems the reader is holding in their hand also function – albeit imperfectly – as a memorial to the boy's perfections. This new concern heralds a wholly unexpected transition. From Sonnet 18 – in what has become the *sine qua non* of love poetry, 'Shall I compare thee to a summer's day?' – the speaker presents himself as the youth's beloved.

Sonnets 18–126 chart the ebb and flow of the affair between the two men, the speaker and the 'lord of my love' (26.1). Providing connective tissue through the 109 sonnets that treat of their romantic relationship (one more than the number of sonnets in Sidney's influential *Astrophil and Stella*) is the same notion of eroticised *amicitia perfecta* that motivated Marlowe's exploration of the affair between Edward II and Gaveston. These sonnets play with the idea that the speaker and his lover harbour a turbocharged version of Ciceronian perfect friendship, sharing a soul that is divided between two equally ardent bodies. The speaker preens himself on his handsome lover's 'seemly raiment' (attractive exterior), proud because it is also his: it's the body that encloses his own heart (22.6). He frets that praising his lover is a bit like blowing his own trumpet: 'O how thy worth with manners may I sing, / When thou art all the better part of me?' (39.1–2). When it becomes apparent that the young man has slept with the speaker's own mistress, the conceit of the two men's single shared soul offers a bittersweet consolation that, in having sex with the youth, the woman has in fact been sleeping with the speaker: '[H]ere's the joy, my friend and I are one; / Sweet flattery! Then she loves but me alone' (42.13–14).

The young man's perfections act on the speaker in powerful ways. His looks are a prompt to creativity, urging the speaker to put pen to paper and capture 'in these black lines' his 'sweet love's beauty' (63.12–13). But his androgynous appeal – part Adonis, part Helen of Troy (53.5–7) – is also confoundingly arousing, occupying the speaker's thoughts and banishing rest as his sleepless mind undertakes 'a zealous pilgrimage to thee' (27.6). Their dynamic is both entrancingly equalising ('"Tis thee (myself) that for myself I praise' (62.13)) and thrillingly masochistic ('Being your slave, what should I do but tend / Upon the hours and times of your desire?' (57.1–2)). The lovers thrive, endure separation, turn on each other, part, and reunite. The youth shines for the speaker as a beacon of loveliness in a debased world. He grouses that all he can do is churn out sonnets about the young man, and then complains that other writers are dedicating poems to him as well. A rival poet – a 'better spirit' (80.2) – appears on the scene and flings the speaker into despair.

Throughout, he is consoled by the thought that his poems will stand as testaments to the youth's beauty and worth, despite Time's 'cruel hand' (60.14). The corrupting passage of time – a unifying image for this section of the sonnets – is the theme of the final poem to his 'lovely boy' (126.1): a reflection that eventually even he and the speaker will be subject to its ravages. That Sonnet 126 brings the curtain down on the poems to the young man is indicated by its unusual twelve-line composition in which the missing couplet is marked by two sets of empty parentheses. They sit, a pair of cushions stacked on top of each other, at the foot of the poem, perhaps a graphic representation of 'Time's fickle glass' (126.2) that counts down the hours till the speaker and the youth must part for ever (they also look a bit like two bums in the left and right margins).

In Sonnet 127, the addressee is, for the first time, a 'mistress' (9). The final twenty-eight poems in *Shakespeare's Sonnets* usher in a very different tone to the preceding 126. Twenty-five of them concern a woman who excites the speaker with her unconventional looks and enthusiastic attitude to sex. But soon he turns against her for the very things that had initially attracted him, blaming her for his feelings of post-coital shame. Significantly for a form that typically praised the golden hair, fair skin and rosy cheeks of its idealised female subjects (*fair*, *gold* and *rose* are terms that cluster around the youth of Sonnets 1–126), Shakespeare chooses to present his mistress in terms that suggest she is a woman of colour: she has dark eyes and tightly curled black hair, and skin that looks 'dun' (130.3), or brown, compared to the snowy bosom of a Petrarchan heroine. In the racist terms of Renaissance beauty politics, she is 'coloured ill' (144.4) – and Shakespeare leans into a characterisation that figures her 'as black as hell, as dark as night' (147.14). She's sexually indiscriminate ('the bay where all men ride', or a harbour that welcomes all shipping (137.6)) and unbecomingly voracious (her 'will is large and spacious', a coarse observation about the size of her vagina (135.5)). She sleeps with the speaker's male lover, and there's an implication in Sonnet 144 that she is responsible for giving them both syphilis.

As we reach the end of the sequence, having been drawn into the relentless intensity of the speaker's feelings for the young man and the young woman, we might have the uncomfortable feeling that we've seen and heard things that not everyone would wish to be made public. As much as Shakespeare's sonnets articulate the pleasures of both queer and straight desire, they also display – in even more pitiless detail than that which he lavishes on the complex relationships in his plays – the cruel, obsessional and irrational sides of love. Petrarch this is not.

The sonnets that Shakespeare was composing, emending, improving, copying and sharing about amongst his 'private friends' through the 1590s and early 1600s could not have differed more from almost all of the printed lyric poetry he could buy in the bookstalls of Paul's Churchyard. The sonnet sequences by Sidney, Spenser, Daniel and Drayton cleaved closely to the 'golden' Petrarchan model in which a male speaker suffers pangs of hopeless love for a glittering mistress whose flawless beauty places her well out of his league. In 1593, Adonis had batted away the romancing Venus with the objection that her boilerplate endearments were an 'idle, overhandled theme' (770), and perhaps it was the sheer horror of cliché that provoked Shakespeare to diverge so staggeringly from the established conventions of love sonnets when he started writing his own (and, as we've seen, he maintained his condescending attitude to conventional sonnets in scathing remarks he scripted into his plays).

But inevitably, the sonnets' excoriatingly intimate tone has encouraged critics and biographers to look for real-life models for the 'fair youth' and 'dark lady' – neither of which are terms used by Shakespeare or any early readers, only becoming associated with the collection in the nineteenth century. There's not a lot to go on: suggestions for the original of the sonnets' mistress have included Mary Fritton, a brunette lady-in-waiting to the queen; the Anglo-Italian poet Emilia Lanier; and a Clerkenwell brothel-owner known as Lucy Morgan or 'Black Luce' – in all cases, the assertion has been made with no documentary hint that any of the women had direct acquaintance with Shakespeare. But seekers after a historical 'lovely boy' do have *something* to start with – the publisher Thomas Thorpe's dedication to the 1609 edition:

TO. THE. ONLY. BEGETTER. OF.
THESE. ENSUING. SONNETS.
M^r. W. H. ALL. HAPPINESS.
AND. THAT. ETERNITY.
PROMISED.
BY.
OUR. EVER-LIVING. POET.
WISHETH.
THE. WELL-WISHING.
ADVENTURER. IN.
SETTING.
FORTH.
T. T.

A discreetly anonymised 'Master W. H.' is given credit as the sole 'begetter' (or inspirer) of the sonnets, to whom the 'adventurer' (who must be the publishing entrepreneur Thorpe) sends his hopes for literary immortality. The poet – Shakespeare? – is 'ever-living' presumably because of the sonnets' invocation of verse that shall 'ever live young' (19.14). As dedications go, it's not the best-written of sentences, and made less clear by being set in tombstone-like capitals, each word separated off by a point.

Unlike other quotations in this book, I've replicated the original lineation and punctuation (although I've modernised the spelling) to show you quite how quirky the confetti-sprinkle of full stops looks on the page.

The identity of Master W. H. has been a biographical puzzle for centuries, not least because it's been generally assumed that the 'only begetter' was also the romantic subject of the 126 sonnets in the 'fair youth' sequence (*cherchez le jeune homme* . . .). Was he a boy actor called Willie Hughes, as Oscar Wilde argued? (No such person has ever been known to exist.) Or is it 'Wriothesley *comma* Henry', Shakespeare's previous patron, the Earl of Southampton, flying under cover? If so, the first seventeen 'procreation sonnets' would fall into the same category as John Clapham's nagging Latin epyllion *Narcissus*: a concerted attempt to get the dilatory earl to settle down.

Another marriage-resistant aristocrat has also been floated as the man behind W. H.: William Herbert, soon to be third Earl of Pembroke, future dedicatee of the First Folio of 1623, and son of the earl whose theatre company performed *Edward II* and Shakespeare's *Henry VI* plays in 1592. The young Herbert refused plausible matches with four different brides in the late 1590s, and his parents were getting twitchy. It's a neat thought that Herbert's poetic mother, Mary Sidney, brother of Philip, might have commissioned Shakespeare to write persuasive sonnets for her oat-sowing teenage son in about 1597, a useful extra gig that the playwright would have fitted around writing *The Merchant of Venice* and *Henry IV Parts 1* and *2*.

But even if he was a pen-for-hire in the 1590s for the families of either Herbert or Southampton, neither situation explains why Shakespeare took the conceit of a beautiful youth receiving life advice from a wise elder and transformed it into a love story between the two men; or why either high-born nobleman – and earls were exceptionally grand – should be referred to with breathtaking insolence in the 1609 dedication as 'Master W. H.'. It's just about possible that Shakespeare had a romantic or a sexual relationship with Southampton or Pembroke (although, unlike Southampton, there's no evidence that Pembroke had a queer bone in his body). It's almost inconceivable that Shakespeare or Thorpe would see fit to draw attention to it – however obliquely – in print. In social terms, Shakespeare was no different to the cavalry officer whom lewd rumour had charged with 'coll[ing]' and 'play[ing]' with the Earl of Southampton while on campaign in Ireland. As far as wider society was concerned, cross-class queer affairs like that were a matter for gossip and censure, not for celebration in poetry. It's difficult to imagine either Southampton (by then aged thirty-six) or Pembroke (twenty-nine, and married) willingly handing over five or ten pounds as thanks for T. T.'s convoluted dedication in 1609.

A more plausible but less dramatic interpretation is that 'Master W. H.' is simply a misprint for 'Master W. S.' (or 'W. Sh.'): that would make Shakespeare the 'only begetter', or author, of the ensuing sonnets, and the 'ever-living poet' (or 'ever-living Poet') is consequently God, maker of all things and provider of an eternal afterlife. Read like this, Thorpe's dedication – the only scrap of prefatory matter in the book – is a less exciting affair, but one more in line with other printed sonnet sequences. Spenser's *Amoretti* also contains a preface by the publisher on the author's behalf.

It seems unlikely we'll ever know if Shakespeare's sonnets were really *poèmes à clef* relaying a true story of passionate adoration and tempestuous sexual jealousy. It's difficult to believe he didn't find inspiration for his poems in the feelings he experienced throughout his life, but that part of Shakespeare's emotional biography is essentially unrecoverable. Any proposed real-life analogues for the fair youth and dark lady are so hedged about with implausibilities as to make the line of enquiry endlessly inconclusive: short of any documentary evidence beyond the sonnets themselves, identifying either figure is a parlour game with no hope of any proof. Not that that's stopped people trying. Whether or not our poet was 'ever-living', Master W. H. certainly shows no signs of dying. Shelves of books and entire provinces of the internet are given over to demonstrating his identity.

I want to direct your attention away from the much-discussed Southampton and Pembroke, because excitable theories about their involvement (or not) in the sonnets have obscured another crucial influence on Shakespeare in the 1590s: a young writer responsible for the single greatest effusion of queer literature that England had ever seen – or would see again until the twentieth century. In his publications between 1594 and 1595, Richard Barnfield did far more than join the ranks of English poets who riffed on classical homoeroticism for a Renaissance audience. He pioneered a new kind of poetry that placed queer desire centre stage, and brought a completely unprecedented candour to depictions of sexual feeling between men (while also, not unconnectedly, taking poetic misogyny to new heights). Barnfield's star was to blaze fiercely but briefly, but it shone at its brightest in the years that Shakespeare was fomenting his sequence of sonnets. If we're looking for a fair youth who inspired Shakespeare's urgent queer voice, we need to bring Barnfield into the story.

Richard Barnfield was baptised on 13 June 1574, born to self-regarding Midland landowners on both sides. The Barnfields were a Shropshire family with sprawling estates in Edgmond, twenty miles to the east of Shrewsbury, and a family crest that boasted a crowned lion. His mother's family, the Skrymshers, lived in a formidable moated grange just over the border in Staffordshire at Norbury. Legend had it that if the black-headed gulls that bred in the local swamp ever flew away, a Skrymsher would die. It wasn't a particularly bucolic place.

Barnfield's parents – Richard and Mary – were living at Norbury when their son was born, but then moved to the nearby market town of Newport, where more children – two boys, Robert and John, and a girl, Dorothy – joined their older brother. There would be no further children. There's evidence to suggest that two months after Dorothy's birth, and shortly before Richard's seventh birthday, Mary attacked her husband with a knife and then slit her own throat.

An uncorroborated contemporary account of the incident and its terrible aftermath exists in a transcript made by a Victorian antiquary and printed in a collection of Shropshire-related notes and queries:

> 1581. This year and in the month of May one Mistress Barnfield of Newport, being twelve miles from Shrewsbury, killed herself. The cause thereof was that not only she being jealous of her husband, and also not perfect in mind, one night being in bed with her said husband, and holding a naked knife in her hand, would have cut her husband's throat; and missing his weasand pipe [wind-pipe], [he] awaked upon the same and stayed her fury, and so called for help and locked her in a dark chamber, without any knife about her or anything else to hurt herself. But within a day or two she espied a rusty, broad arrowhead in a privy place and therewith cut her own throat most wickedly.

The judgemental tone of the report belies what may have been postpartum psychosis, another severe mental illness or a response to abuse. But whatever Mary was suffering from, for the Elizabethans, suicide was a terrible crime. If the account is true, Mary's final days must have been unspeakably wretched, left with her own demons in a dark room – the ordeal experienced by *Twelfth Night*'s Malvolio, and the standard 'treatment' for the mentally ill in the sixteenth century. Unlike Malvolio, Mary wasn't liberated from her captivity, and fear or despair overwhelmed her. If the Mistress Barnfield of the story is our Barnfield's mother, Richard Senior and the Skrymshers hushed up the scandal: Mary was buried with all due religious ceremony that May at Norbury.

The young Barnfield almost certainly remained with his mother's family in the damp, lowering manor house (when he matriculated at Brasenose College Oxford, he was identified as being from Staffordshire, not Shropshire, the county of his father's estates). Somehow, in the years after his mother's violent death, he put her loss behind him – or pushed it down and away from his everyday thoughts. There's no way to know Barnfield's feelings about his mother's suicide, or whether his later extreme poetic misogyny was in some sense an articulation of unresolved trauma. But it might be relevant that when he came to write a poem on the story of the Trojan princess Cassandra – cursed with unbelieved prophecy by Apollo and regarded as mad by those around her – he diverged from the established myth in which she was killed by Clytemnestra. Instead, his version of Clytemnestra locks her in a lightless tower, where Cassandra – tormented with grief – 'ends her fortune with a fatal knife' (459). Cassandra's 'purest soul' (465) is released from 'endless moan' (466) and transmigrates to Elysium, 'the place for wrongful death and martyrdom' (468).

Nothing is known of Barnfield's early education, although judging from his literary output it was, like Shakespeare's, thorough. There was plenty of family money to send him to university at fifteen, the standard age for a boy who'd attended a grammar school. Oxford initially suited him. He graduated in 1592, but swiftly abandoned plans for a Master of Arts (eighteen-hour days of theology, Aristotelian philosophy and logic weren't his thing). Instead, he cooled his heels until the plague was beginning to lift, and then made for London. By the time he was twenty, he was already a published poet: he wrote a short collection called *Greene's Funerals* (1594), which eulogised the contemporary crop of literary celebrities including Edmund Spenser and the late Robert Greene. The volume, which may have been issued contrary to his wishes, was dedicated to London's 'gentleman readers', code for the men of the Inns of Court, and probably a sign that he had joined an Inn of Court or Chancery himself. It's unlikely he intended to study or practise the law. Instead, the Inns of Court were an ideal place to absorb the queer poetry and drama that appeared in 1593 and 1594.

He was an early reader of Shakespeare's *Venus and Adonis*, which he devoured along with the other epyllia that followed in its wake. He got his hands on manuscript copies of Marlowe's *Hero and Leander*, and his wildly popular pastoral lyric poem that begins, 'Come live with me and be my love'. He also leapt on the two plays by Marlowe that appeared in print early in 1594, less than a year after the playwright's death, *Edward II* and *Dido Queen of Carthage*. All would find themselves echoed or quoted in the work Barnfield wrote at some speed and published in November 1594, a queer erotic fantasy that sensationally lifted the veil on the decorously classicised and Latinised conventions of pastoral romance.

This was the book published – anonymously at first – as *The Affectionate Shepherd*. It was a miscellany of a kind, but the surrounding material attracted much less attention than the substantial two-part pastoral poem at its heart, 'The Tears of an Affectionate Shepherd sick for love, or the Complaint of Daphnis for the love of Ganymede'. Readers expecting a familiar rehash of Virgil's second *Eclogue* were in for a surprise. This was Virgil supersized, sexualised and anglicised into something altogether new. It was in every respect bigger, longer and uncut.

The speaker Daphnis – a shepherd, but like all pastoral figures, intimately connected with lordly folk and divine creatures – adores the beautiful young Ganymede (another instance of that resoundingly queer name). But Ganymede is also beloved by Guendolen, Queen of the Nymphs – who is herself fending off advances from a geriatric suitor and mourning the loss of her first love.

Over two parts, or 'lamentations', an increasingly abject Daphnis goes all out to win over Ganymede, and entice him away from Guendolen, whose so-called love, Daphnis argues, is vapid and self-centred. Never before in English had a poet been so upfront about the bodily reality of queer male desire, a force which frames the poem from its first stanzas and propels the sequence of lures, promises and seductions that Daphnis places before Ganymede to persuade him to 'be my boy, or else my bride' (2.78).

In the opening lines, Daphnis describes – or perhaps imagines – an early-morning visit to Ganymede's chamber:

> Scarce had the morning star hid from the light
> Heaven's crimson canopy with stars bespangled,
> But I began to rue th'unhappy sight
> Of that fair boy that had my heart entangled.
> Cursing the time, the place, the sense, the sin,
> I came, I saw, I viewed, I slipped in.
>
> If it be sin to love a sweet-faced boy
> (Whose amber locks, trussed up in golden trammels,
> Dangle adown his lovely cheeks with joy,
> When pearl and flowers his fair hair enamels),
> If it be sin to love a lovely lad,
> Oh then sin I, for whom my soul is sad. (1.1–12)

The four 'sins' in two stanzas – and the Caesarean implications of conquest in 'I came, I saw, I viewed', to say nothing of the resonance of 'slipped in' – place Daphnis's desires and intentions well beyond anything that could possibly be understood as bloodlessly poetic yearning.

Part of the romantic deal that Daphnis proposes is transactional: he will reward Ganymede with a wealth of luxuries if the boy sleeps with him. Some are desirable consumer goods (a golden tennis racquet, or a fan made out of phoenix feathers). But other gifts are succulently edible – ripe-to-bursting cherries, oozing honey and strawberries 'bathed in a melting sugar-candy stream' (2.70). It's clear that Daphnis conflates the pleasure of these delicacies with the anticipated joy of Ganymede's body: 'O, would to God [. . .] My lips were honey, and thy mouth a bee,' he yearns:

> Then shoulds't thou suck my sweet and my fair flower
> That now is ripe and full of honey-berries.
> Then would I lead thee to my pleasant bower
> Filled full of grapes, of mulberries and cherries;
> Then shoulds't thou be my wasp or else my bee.
> I would thy hive, and thou my honey be. (1.95–102)

The flower-sucking and honey-depositing stays in Daphnis's imagination. In accordance with the traditions of Petrarchan love poetry or Virgilian pastoral, Ganymede remains unmoved. Daphnis threatens to exile himself to the Caucasus and let 'a vulture gnaw upon my heart' (2.30), but to no avail. He becomes resentful of Ganymede's shining ivory beauty, and his lazy assumption that everyone will fall at his feet in adoration. It's not just white boys, Daphnis hints, who can turn heads: 'We cannot choose, but needs we must confess: / Sable excels milk-white in more or less' (2.275–76). In a society such as Barnfield's, which was developing a growing awareness of racial difference, the possibility that Daphnis might seek love from a man of colour rather than the pale and disdainful Ganymede hovers at the margin of the poem.

As 'The Tears of an Affectionate Shepherd' comes to an end, the rueful Daphnis imagines that he has become not just older and wiser but 'age-withered' (2.414) and wrinkled, his very life force burnt up by his unrequited passion for Ganymede. He bids 'a thousand-thousand times farewell' to his 'love-hating boy' (2.421–22), and sadly gives up the field (although we never learn if the 'wantoniz[ing]' (1.161) competitor Guendolen ever gets her man).

The Affectionate Shepherd targeted the same post-plague readership, hungry for delight, that Shakespeare had served with *Venus and Adonis*. Barnfield was even more clear-sighted about what he understood his audience to want: an arousingly sexed-up version of the English pastorals that had proved such a hit since Spenser's *The Shepherd's Calendar* fifteen years before. Barnfield had no intention of sanitising the form's lush homoeroticism. He didn't want a reader like Spenser's annotator E. K. to delude themselves that Daphnis's feelings were free of 'disorderly love'. Orderly or otherwise, Daphnis's queer desires were very much the point of the poem, and they found instant 'friendly favour', as Barnfield later put it. *The Affectionate Shepherd*'s combination of queer sex appeal and misogynist exclusion (the vampish Guendolen is 'light' (1.158) and fickle) was calculated to please the young men of the Inns of Court.

The poem barely had a chance to astonish its readers before Barnfield exceeded it in imagination and innovation. He spent the Christmas holidays of 1594–95 – when, if he was in London, he may well have attended the infamous Gray's Inn festivities – rethinking the destiny he gave to Daphnis and Ganymede in the final pages of 'The Tears of an Affectionate Shepherd'. Barnfield decided to erase the shepherd's wizened, forlorn end and start his narrative again, reuniting his lovers in a numbered sequence of twenty sonnets. In moving Daphnis and Ganymede from the established classical setting of the pastoral romance to the as-yet-unqueered territory of the Petrarchan sonnet, he was breaking new ground. No one had ever cast two men in a published love sonnet before, let alone made them the stars of an entire collection. This was queer *terra incognita*.

He wrote quickly. By Easter, they were in print and on sale at the Paul's Churchyard bookshop of the up-and-coming publishing brothers Humphrey and Matthew Lownes. The volume – *Cynthia, with Certain Sonnets* – also included his legend of Cassandra and verses in lavish praise of the queen, and carried a poem in 'commendation of the author his work' by one 'T. T.', who may be the same Thomas Thorpe who would later publish *Shakespeare's Sonnets*. It was a classy publication, and it bore a sense of expectation that the same 'courteous gentlemen readers' who had lapped up *The Affectionate Shepherd* would return to buy Barnfield's next offering. In 'Certain Sonnets', Daphnis and Ganymede slotted easily into the roles of sonnet speaker and lusted-after love-object (they had, after all, rehearsed the parts extensively in *The Affectionate Shepherd*). Ganymede still has his 'sin-procuring' (17.13) body and an 'obdurate beauty' (19.4) that rebuffs all seductions; Daphnis vows he'll die unless Ganymede 'quench [his] thirst' (6.4) with kisses.

The mood is alternately keenly voyeuristic and chattily intimate. Daphnis imagines stealing a kiss from the sleeping Ganymede, and watches hungrily from the riverbank as his 'fairest fair' (7.6) swims in the Thames (there are echoes of Marlowe's *Hero and Leander* as Ganymede attracts aroused interest from Neptune). But he also settles down beside him for a revelatory heart-to-heart, and presents him with a pair of kid gloves – the traditional Elizabethan courtship gift.

Consummation arrives in the form of a vigorous wet dream, as Daphnis fantasises that Ganymede's 'sweet coral lips' (6.1) kiss him into a paroxysm of youthful energy, and he feels from his 'heart a spring of blood' that sends lusty strength coursing through his limbs. Daphnis recognises that 'in dreaming [. . .] [he] did speed' (6.13), or orgasm in his sleep, and wonders what it would be like to do so with Ganymede 'in deed' (6.14) – while wide awake.

He doesn't manage to sleep with him 'in deed', but Daphnis achieves something even more astonishing: a declaration to Ganymede that he is and always will be his beloved. In a culture that tried wherever possible to separate the intense romantic feelings of male friendship – *amicitia perfecta* – from erotic love, Barnfield collapsed the distinction in an utterly determined and unambiguous way. Placed in the very middle of the sequence, Daphnis's avowal (Sonnet 11) is worth quoting in full:

> Sighing and sadly sitting by my love,
> He asked the cause of my heart's sorrowing,
> Conjuring me by heaven's eternal king
> To tell the cause which me so much did move.
> 'Compelled,' quoth I, 'to thee I will confess.
> Love is the cause, and only Love it is
> That doth deprive me of my heavenly bliss:
> Love is the pain that doth my heart oppress.'
> 'And what is she,' quoth he, 'whom thou dost love?'
> 'Look in this glass,' quoth I, 'there shalt thou see
> The perfect form of my felicity.'
> When, thinking that it would strange magic prove,
> > He opened it; and taking off the cover
> > He straight perceived himself to be my lover.

This is queer drama in content and form: Ganymede's sudden realisation, delivered by means of a pocket mirror, that he is the cause of Daphnis's heartsickness comes as the *volta* in the sonnet's closing triplet. And although Barnfield's sonnets don't follow a chronological plot, this is a poem that gestures towards what might happen after such a declaration. What does Daphnis hope Ganymede will say?

Ganymede might well have struggled to find the words. Early modern English culture didn't have a language to describe an exclusive bond of erotic love between two men: there was no direct queer equivalent at this time of the romantic and sexual discourse of straight courtly love. In his sonnets, Barnfield was beginning to invent one. By lifting his love-lorn shepherds from classical pastoral and transplanting them into the English love sonnet, up to this point exclusively associated with poems in praise of a glacial Petrarchan mistress, he was giving a new vernacular voice to queer desire. This was Barnfield's – and English literature's – coming-out poem. Shakespeare, picking up a copy in Lownes's bookshop in 1595 and contemplating his own composition of love sonnets, had never seen anything like it.

But Barnfield's completely unparalleled queer artistic project wasn't over. In his third major publication within the year, he moved from the pastoral and the sonnet to the epyllion, the classical mini-epic that had proved so successful for Shakespeare and other young writers. Like *The Affectionate Shepherd*, Barnfield's epyllion gave him scope to explore the interface between ardent homoeroticism and its associated anti-women chauvinism. His theme was the tale of Orpheus and Eurydice from Book 10 of Ovid's *Metamorphoses* – in which Shakespeare had found the material for his *Venus and Adonis*. In *Orpheus His Journey to Hell* (1595), Barnfield told the story of the miraculously gifted Thracian musician – owner of 'a heavenly body and a soul divine' (36) – whose lyre and voice 'stilled the music of the bubbling springs' (39) and 'made the savage beasts forsake their prey' (41). On the day of his wedding, his bride Eurydice is killed by a snakebite, dying 'before she knew the pleasure of his bed' (120).

Thunderstruck by the unfairness of her death, and unjustly resentful of Eurydice for forsaking him at such an inopportune time, Orpheus descends into the depths of Hades, ruled by grim-faced Pluto, to fetch her back again. He plays and sings his way past scenes of torture where the damned 'fry and scorch' (351), their tender extremities cauterising in flashes of fire. His magical touch on the lyre strings lulls the inhabitants of hell into momentary release: the eternally labouring Sisyphus takes a breather, leaning upon his boulder; the bird ripping out Prometheus's innards looks up, heartstrings dangling from her beak. To everyone he meets, Orpheus relates the crashing injustice of his sudden loss and the collapse of his matrimonial hopes – an example, Orpheus explains with a phenomenal lack of gallantry, of women's notorious inconstancy.

His song persuades Pluto to release Eurydice, on the proviso that Orpheus lead his wife out of Hades without once turning back to look at her. Barnfield frames Orpheus's inability to comply with Pluto's rule as a result of his 'fond jealousy' (595), his lurking suspicion that even in the infernal depths, Eurydice is not to be trusted around other men. He looks behind him, Eurydice is snatched back to hell, and he stumbles into the land of the living to confront his future without her.

Orpheus's renewed loss tips him into fully fledged vituperative misogyny. He sings 'invective ditties' (655) against 'women's fawning fickle company' (662) in such persuasive tones that he soon attracts interest from other men, who leave their wives and join him in an anti-women, proto-queer commune: 'With which sweet life they seemed so well content, / As made them curse the former time they'd spent' (671–72). Unlike in *Metamorphoses*, Barnfield's Orpheus doesn't establish 'stews of males', or boy brothels, to entertain his new followers. The men are enough for one another.

The women of Thrace plot revenge. Gathering an arsenal of weapons, they ambush Orpheus and beat him to death, '[q]uenching their angry thirst with his warm blood' (692). Unrepentant, they confront the displeasure of the gods with their excuse: 'He was an enemy unto their gender' (696). The gods themselves, mourning the loss of a man so gifted in music and song, translate Orpheus's heavenly instrument to the skies as the constellation Lyra.

We might not be able to identify the real 'fair youth' of William Shakespeare's sonnets, but we can point to an influential portfolio of queerness produced in the year after autumn 1594 by a brilliant young poet new to the London literary scene. Barnfield's three major homoerotic works constituted the most overt canon of queer literature that had ever been published in English. 'The Tears of an Affectionate Shepherd' and 'Certain Sonnets' made male same-sex desire the central theme in the two most up-to-the-minute genres of late-Elizabethan love poetry, the pastoral lyric and the sonnet. In *Orpheus His Journey to Hell*, Barnfield had taken the heavily implied homoeroticism – and associated misogyny – of the fashionable epyllion and shaped those qualities into a mythic origin story for queer male desire predicated on sexist exclusion and conflict: Orpheus is reshaped into the martyred patron of men who turn away from their wives to cavort with one another in a utopic retreat.

If the twenty-one-year-old Barnfield was hoping to make his name with his publications, he succeeded. Barnfield's queer art was designed for the 'gentlemen readers' – the term with which he addressed his audience in all but one of his books – at the Inns of Court, where social life had recently revived after the disruptions caused by plague. He was soon being counted by the literati as among the best modern poets: the dramatist and pamphleteer Henry Chettle praised 'Daphnis' in print in 1595, and in 1598 the literary critic Francis Meres ranked him in dazzling company as the equal of Theocritus, Virgil and Mantuan – the exemplars of the pastoral form in Greek, classical Latin and modern Latin. *Cynthia, with Certain Sonnets* went into a second edition within a year.

In 1595 and the years afterwards, as Shakespeare was beginning to think about his private sonnets to the 'fair youth' and the 'dark lady', he faced a literary field that had been transformed, newly sown by Barnfield. The younger poet had radically expanded what English letters could do and pushed at the edges of the acceptable in the expression of queer desire. Barnfield had reached into the classical past, and drawn on contemporary literary fashions, to create a new queer poetic sensibility that was engineered to appeal to young men. In doing so, he'd broken the homoerotic *omertá* by which educated Englishmen were expected to abide: the understanding that candid discussions of queer male desire must remain locked away in Latin, a language accessible only to the privileged few. Barnfield's work didn't carry the anxious content warnings of Philemon Holland's translation of Plutarch's 'Dialogue on Love'. It was overt, unapologetic, *proud* – and available in affordable, pocket-sized editions from the bookstalls of Paul's Churchyard.

Barnfield's was an exclusionary, chauvinistic queerness marked by an elevated celebration of both male beauty and patriarchal privilege, but it was also uncompromising in its honesty and candour about sexual love between men. Most importantly, Barnfield showed Shakespeare what the love sonnet – that hackneyed vehicle for crass 'idolatry' – could be. He stimulated an astonishing artistic response in Shakespeare that was to play out over the next decade as the older man developed – and undercut – the twin helix of lush homoeroticism and biting misogyny that Barnfield had established in his queerest year of literary productivity. But even as Shakespeare began his project of response to and expansion of Barnfield's queer artistic vision, it became evident that the younger poet had overstepped the mark. His breach of decorum and convention would have consequences, for both Barnfield and Shakespeare.

Private Friends

Early 1596. *The young man's back wasn't the most stable of surfaces, but it was pleasingly broad enough for the half-folio sheet. He lay on his front, propping himself on his arms, and craned his head round to look at the writer straddling his body.*

What are you doing?

Ruling lines; lie down.

He laughed. Lying full length, his shoulder muscles relaxed and the paper settled on his bare skin. That tickles, he said, as the stylus moved back and forth, grooving fourteen indentations on the creamy paper. The writer gave him another handwritten sheet. The young man could feel the weight of him tilt forward, his body pressing warmly into the small of his back.

Here's the original. You read aloud and I'll write.

On me?

Why not?

The man set the original against the headboard and squinted at the unfamiliar handwriting.

Sometimes I wish that I his pillow were . . . Is that really the first line?

The writer swapped the stylus for a quill: Sometimes I wish, he wrote. The nib caught in a crease of paper. The young man shifted, adjusting himself on the bed. The writer dipped his quill in the ink pot.

So might I steal a kiss and yet not seen, the man recited as the writer wrote. Is that what we're going to do?

Would you like to?

Only if I'm awake for it. Hang on, you take the original. I want to see if I can tell what you're writing.

The writer formed his letters carefully: So might I gaze upon his sleeping eyne . . .

It's no good, the paper's too thick.

The writer lifted the page from the man's back and, with the tip of his finger, drew a slow, snaking 'S' on the warm skin. And then an 'O', wide enough to stroke the tender part near his underarm. He could feel the man shiver.

Is it so . . .?

It is so.

The man suddenly flipped himself over. The copy slid onto the bedsheets.

Who's the poem for, anyway?

You, if you want it.

For well over a decade before 1609, the nationally famous lyric poet William Shakespeare – beloved author of the widely read *Venus and Adonis* and *Lucrece* – chose to forego the significant financial reward that would come with a published volume of sonnets dedicated to a rich aristocrat. Instead, his growing collection found an audience through the closed network of manuscript circulation: individual pages or slender sheaves of verses hand-copied by readers and shared with like-minded friends. The intimate, first-person tone of lyric poetry – the romantic 'I' of the speaker, the 'thou' of the subject – made it ideal material for private exchange motivated by literary interest or amorous desire: each poem a letter between lover and beloved, every sonnet an encapsulation of a particular moment in a relationship. Without the fixative effect of publication, Shakespeare's sonnets continued to evolve as he tinkered with them over a dozen years, inspired above all by the body of queer verse that Barnfield had sensationally published in 1594 and 1595. But Shakespeare was to have reason to be grateful that his queer sonnets remained in the discreet space of private collection when Barnfield's printed poetry caused a storm of controversy that cut him off from his family, and silenced his artistic voice for good.

The book-reading world first heard about Shakespeare's sonnets in 1598, three years after the publication of Barnfield's 'Certain Sonnets'. The news was carried by the same man who had praised Barnfield as a modern-day Virgil. Francis Meres's *Palladis Tamia: Wit's Treasury* was a 600-page collection of godly adages that contained almost as an afterthought a 'comparative discourse of our English poets', with their Greek, Latin and Italian forebears. Meres conducted his analysis of modern literature through analogy between famous classical authors, and contemporary writers who had taken up their mantle. Along with twelve of Shakespeare's plays, Meres also commended his poetry:

> As the soul of Euphorbus was thought to live in Pythagoras, so the sweet witty soul of Ovid lives in mellifluous and honey-tongued Shakespeare; witness his *Venus and Adonis*, his *Lucrece*, his sugared sonnets among his private friends, etc.

Meres takes an example from *Metamorphoses* itself – Ovid wrote that the Greek philosopher Pythagoras, who placed great stress on the transmigration of souls, claimed to be the reincarnation of Euphorbus, a Trojan war hero – to illustrate the conceit that Shakespeare was an Elizabethan Ovid, seducing his readers with steamy tales of classical love tricks. The seeming tautology of 'mellifluous and honey-tongued' (the second phrase translating the Latin of the first word: 'flowing with honey') emphasises quite how clearly Meres wants us to register that Shakespeare's writing is oozingly sweet. As we have seen, 'sweet' was an early modern code word for sexy, and things get no less syrupy when Meres mentions the sonnets, 'sugared' treats that delighted those lucky enough to taste them.

The manuscript circulation that Meres points to with his reference to a readership of 'private friends' might have involved just a small coterie, or the broadcasting of Shakespeare's sonnets could have been a more substantial operation. Meres is, after all, inviting his readers to 'witness' the spread of Shakespeare's work. Some handwritten Elizabethan and Jacobean poems can be found in scores of copies in dozens of different archives (although the earliest manuscript copies of Shakespeare's sonnets to survive today date from the 1620s). A single sonnet copied and distributed just twice by each reader would soon find itself multiplied exponentially; it was possible for manuscript texts to exist in numbers almost as large as printed editions.

But in general, writers chose to keep their work out of print in order to limit its distribution. Manuscript circulation had a social cachet that the indiscriminate multiplication of print didn't: not everyone had the time, penmanship or social connections to obtain a beautifully hand-copied poem. And it was free of the state censorship that was conducted on behalf of the government by the Stationers' Company, the trade body for publishers and booksellers: every printed book had to be authorised by the Stationers' wardens, who were on the lookout for politically, religiously or culturally contentious subjects (although much slipped through their net). Manuscript essays or poems could more easily touch on things that were forbidden to be discussed publicly: the management of the Church of England, the plans for the queen's succession, or the candid erotic desires of their authors.

Beyond the cultural capital or political security that came with manuscript circulation, it allowed for a very hands-on process of selection, collation and editing on the part of the reader. A person could copy out what they liked best, in whatever order or arrangement they pleased. If the spirit moved them to change a word here or there, then that's what they did. And readers didn't just collect manuscript texts. They magpie-ed from printed sources, too. In an era before the institutions of literary civic society (art periodicals, academic journals and learned societies were all to come in the following century), engaging in the creation, duplication and swapping of manuscript poetry was a way to stay involved in the ebb and flow of literary fashion.

Whatever the identity of the 'private friends' who were the first readers of Shakespeare's sonnets in manuscript, they were participants in this active, well-connected culture. It's almost certain that those early readers would have known about, and read, Barnfield's 'Certain Sonnets' and 'The Tears of an Affectionate Shepherd' too: in the late 1590s, Barnfield's and Shakespeare's sonnets constituted an entirely novel queer literary movement, poems by a pair of male writers who took as their subject a beautiful young man. Francis Meres was surely part of this readerly circle. He was familiar enough with Shakespeare's unpublished sonnets to describe them as 'sugared' (so he knew they were erotic rather than, say, religious or satirical), although whether that makes him a 'private friend' is open to question. But he was certainly close to 'my friend Master Richard Barnfield', as he called him in *Palladis Tamia*. As for Barnfield, he put his admiration for Shakespeare in print, in his own version of Meres's analytical 'discourse of our English poets'. In 'A Remembrance of some English Poets', published in 1598, Barnfield praised Spenser, Daniel and Drayton before devoting his longest stanza to Shakespeare:

And Shakespeare thou, whose honey-flowing vein,
Pleasing the world, thy praises doth contain;
Whose *Venus* and whose *Lucrece* (sweet, and chaste)

Thy name in Fame's immortal book have placed.
Live ever you! At least, in Fame live ever:
Well may the body die, but Fame die never.

Barnfield was a much better sonneteer than he was an encomiast (that final couplet is appalling, although the invocation to 'live ever' might have provided Thomas Thorpe with his epithet 'ever-living' in the dedication to the 1609 edition of *Shakespeare's Sonnets*).

And Shakespeare most certainly knew Barnfield's published work, lifting ideas and imagery from 'Certain Sonnets' and 'The Tears of an Affectionate Shepherd' in a process of influence, exchange and dialogue that must have been noticed by readers of both men's poetry. Given the difficulty of dating Shakespeare's sonnets, it's just possible that the inspiration was the other way around: that Barnfield, as part of his early immersion in queer literature, saw a version of Shakespeare's 'fair youth' poems before he embarked on his own 'Certain Sonnets'. But most recent scholarly opinion points to the great majority of Shakespeare's sonnets being written after 1595, the year Barnfield's sequence was published. It seems safe to assume that the echoes and quotations that readers would have detected between the two collections travelled from Barnfield to Shakespeare.

It was Barnfield's earlier collection that originated the idea, so important to Shakespeare's sonnets, of a male speaker ravished with desire for an exquisite, disdainful young man. In both cases, the youth has been handcrafted by the gods for beauty and virtue, and his unattainability compels the speaker to indulge in fantasies of sexual possession. The speaker endures a period of separation from his beloved, and comes to realise that the boy is not just coolly uninterested but actively resistant to him. Barnfield's speaker's creative energies wilt by the final sonnet, and he acknowledges that 'these lines, the sons of tears and dole' (20.8)

– his poems, in other words – will have to stand as witness to his love for the youth, the 'essence' of his soul. As Shakespeare puts it, his 'verse in time to come' (17.1) will 'give life' (18.14) to the youth's beauty. Although some of the themes in Barnfield's collection – the pain of unrequited love, the perfection and unreachability of the lover – are conventional in Petrarchan love poetry, his particular arrangement of homoerotic desire, queer bodily yearning and poetic immortality was not merely strikingly unconventional, but unprecedented in English verse.

Shakespeare didn't just echo the principal motifs of Barnfield's sequence. He also reworked specific conceits he found in the younger man's sonnets. Barnfield's Sonnet 1 presents Ganymede as a thief who has stolen the speaker's heart. But a judging panel of the speaker's Conscience and Reason accuses him of negligence in allowing Ganymede's beauty free access through 'the body's 'fensive wall' (1.6) and finds the boy 'not guilty' (1.8), instead sentencing the speaker to be drowned in tears. Shakespeare's Sonnet 46 repeated the legal metaphor of the speaker's mind sitting as an inquest in judgement on his senses, to assess whether his eyes or heart are entitled to possession of the youth's beauty:

> To 'cide this title is empanelled
> A quest of thoughts, all tenants to the heart,
> And by their verdict is determined
> The clear eyes' moiety, and the dear heart's part. (46.9–12)

Shakespeare took the structure of Sonnet 46 from Barnfield, too: the outline of the 'case' occupies the first quatrain; the second quatrain explains the ambiguous vulnerability of the speaker's heart, which can be reached without anyone piercing the body's outer covering; the metaphysical courtroom is summoned in the third quatrain; and the verdict is given in the final couplet.

Barnfield's characterisation of Ganymede also seems to lie behind one of the most daring and provocative of Shakespeare's sonnets, number 20. Readers have been shocked by this poem for centuries: an early commentator damned it as a 'fulsome panegyric addressed to a male object' ('fulsome' here meant 'repugnant' rather than just 'abundant'). The outrage lay in the speaker's teasing account of the fair youth's intoxicatingly fluid allure:

> A woman's face with Nature's own hand painted
> Hast thou, the master-mistress of my passion;
> A woman's gentle heart, but not acquainted
> With shifting change, as is false woman's fashion;
> An eye more bright than theirs, less false in rolling,
> Gilding the object whereupon it gazeth;
> A man in hue, all hues in his controlling,
> Which steals men's eyes and women's souls amazeth;
> And for a woman wert thou first created,
> Till Nature as she wrought thee fell a-doting,
> And by addition me of thee defeated,
> By adding one thing to my purpose nothing.
>> But since she pricked thee out for women's pleasure,
>> Mine by thy love, and thy love's use their treasure.

Sonnet 20 has provoked a good deal of debate and disagreement, not just from readers like the frothing commentator who objected to its 'fulsome' subject. Few critics can agree about whether the sonnet advertises or denies a sexual relationship between the youth and the speaker – not least because its ostensible meaning seems to be undercut by the implications of its language. The lovely boy's beauty equals that of a woman, and indeed exceeds it in worth because, unlike women (the poem is as misogynist as it is queer), the young man is upright and loyal, and not fickle and changeable. The young man, therefore, has both men and women fall at his feet; and indeed Mother Nature herself initially set out to fashion a woman, but finding herself besotted with her creation, she added 'one thing' – a penis, punned as 'prick' in the next line – to the gestating frame, producing the epicene male who so dazzles all onlookers.

And here's where the meanings multiply. The final lines of the sonnet can be read to mean that the fair youth's penis has put him out of the picture for the speaker's own sexual purposes, with the men's love remaining in the chastely romantic realm while the youth has sex with women. But the suppleness of Elizabethan slang stops us settling conclusively on this rather vanilla interpretation. The crux starts at line 12: Nature added to the fair youth 'one thing to my purpose nothing', an apparently straightforward statement that gains complexity when we realise that 'nothing' could, in the 1590s, also mean 'female genitalia'; a vagina joke in line twelve would fit with the prick gag in line thirteen. The added prick is a 'nothing' as far as the speaker is concerned: a sexual part designed to entice and excite other men. The double meaning of 'nothing' opens up a reading of the sonnet which sees the speaker and the boy enjoying the full physical range of 'love' (which the youth takes like 'women's pleasure'), while the fair youth discharges his procreative duty – 'love's use' – by fathering a child with a woman.

The poem is ambiguous by design, its multiple meanings doing double duty as plausible deniability even as they give pleasure to readers alert to their queer implications. But it has a precedent in Barnfield's Sonnets 9 and 10, a linked pairing which forms an account of Ganymede's divine creation. Diana, chaste goddess of the hunt, fashions the boy's essence from her own blood and mountain snow. The formless creature is taken to the temple of Venus, where the goddess of love creates his face and 'delicately frame[s]' his limbs and every 'member' (10.6). But because his 'pure, spotless, virtuous mind' (10.9) springs from Diana's blood, Ganymede remains devoted to chastity and 'loves to be beloved, but not to love' (10.14): his is a body ready for sex, and a brain that always says no.

As with the connection between Sonnets 1 and 46, we can detect a sort of structural rhyming across Barnfield's 10 and Shakespeare's 20: in each, the manner and the consequences of the goddesses' acts of creation occupy the first three quatrains, with the couplet providing the apparently last word on the impossibility of the speaker and the beloved having sex (although, as we've seen, Shakespeare makes his final line – 'Mine be thy love, and thy love's use their treasure' – wide open to the contrary interpretation). In both, the speaker grapples with the deranging effects of loving a youth whose extreme sexual provocativeness – his 'sin-procuring' body as Barnfield puts it – is matched by an apparent resistance to seduction.

We see other Barnfield borrowings in Shakespeare's Sonnet 20, too. He seems to have taken the sentiment and the 'pleasure / treasure' rhyme of his concluding couplet from 'The Tears of an Affectionate Shepherd', when Daphnis encourages Ganymede to contrast his ardent and selfless love with Guendolen's crudely acquisitive desire:

> I love thee for thy gifts, she for her pleasure;
> I for thy virtue, she for beauty's treasure. (1.209–10)

At the level of language and content, Barnfield's work demonstrated to Shakespeare the possibilities of the queer Petrarchan sonnet. If Shakespeare's responses to Barnfield are anything to go by, the younger poet's innovations reclaimed and revivified the tired sonnet form for him, showing him that the poems needn't contain the vacuous clichés he had mocked (and was to mock again) in his plays.

In the vibrantly productive years of the mid- and late-1590s, Barnfield helped Shakespeare to see the stimulating potential of a sonnet that teased its reader with the possibility of sexual consummation, a tantric pleasure that was particularly acute when the imagined sexual act was homoerotic. If Barnfield was bolder when it came to the realities of sex between men – in his sonnets, the reader imagines sucking honey from Ganymede's 'coral lips', and thinks about the orgasmic effects of Daphnis's wet dream – Shakespeare's sequence was a much more substantial examination of the emotional reality of queer desire for early modern men. It's Shakespeare's poems that excavate the implications of a same-sex love that finds its articulation in the ideologies of classical *amicitia perfecta*, and think about the challenges of loving someone who is not only a social superior but also younger and better-looking. His sonnets are wittier than Barnfield's, and also more anguished; his poetic speaker is elevated but petty, self-denying and selfish. And part of his achievement was in responding to, but then calling into question, the misogyny that Barnfield had entwined into his queer poetic vision.

Shakespeare certainly didn't need to look to Barnfield to find a prompt for sexist literature. He lived in a patriarchal society that took every opportunity to castigate women for any form of sexual feeling that deviated from the model of chaste femininity laid down by religion and culture. But his sonnets present a vision of female sexuality that is so bleak and hostile – and so different to the more nuanced picture in his plays, where heroines such as Rosalind in *As You Like It* or Beatrice in *Much Ado About Nothing* are granted a worldly awareness of desire – that it's tempting to see Barnfield's particularly savage attitude in 'The Tears of an Affectionate Shepherd' and *Orpheus His Journey to Hell* as his model.

Shakespeare's sonnets to his 'dark lady' are, in truth, difficult to enjoy for a modern reader. The few from the sequence that are widely read today enjoy their popularity precisely because they are atypically positive in their presentation of the relationship between the man and the woman: in Sonnet 130, the wittily realistic confession that begins 'My mistress' eyes are nothing like the sun', the speaker sets out to demonstrate that his lover possesses none of the hackneyed attributes of the subjects of love poetry. More characteristic is Sonnet 147, which takes the Petrarchan conceit of sexual passion as a raging fever and makes it depressingly, insultingly literal:

> My love is as a fever, longing still
> For that which longer nurseth the disease,
> Feeding on that which doth preserve the ill,
> Th'uncertain sickly appetite to please.
> My reason, the physician to my love,
> Angry that his prescriptions are not kept,
> Hath left me, and I, desperate, now approve
> Desire is death, which physic did except.
> Past cure I am, now reason is past care,
> And frantic-mad with ever more unrest;
> My thoughts and my discourse as madmen's are,
> At random from the truth vainly expressed:
>> For I have sworn thee fair, and thought thee bright,
>> Who art as black as hell, as dark as night.

The speaker reflects on the perversity that keeps him returning to his mistress, whom he understands to be a toxic influence on his health and sanity. His 'reason' – the intellectual force that in Sonnet 46 had summoned an inquest of 'thoughts' to mediate constructively on the speaker's desire for the fair youth – has, in this sonnet, packed up and departed, disgusted that his guidance has been ignored. The speaker is left 'frantic-mad' with self-loathing desire, as he comes to realise that he has deluded himself that his mistress is anything other than a dark malignity. It is in every respect an unsalvageably hateful poem, filled with racist and misogynist invective against the individual who has spurred the sexual desire that the speaker resents so keenly.

Not all of the twenty-eight sonnets in the 'dark lady' section are as unpleasant as 147, although many of them are pretty vile. Throughout the sequence the speaker blames the woman for her sexual appetite, for her infidelities (the speaker too is unfaithful), for her unwelcome knack for provoking his lust, and for her disingenuity and deceit. Taken as a whole, the 126 sonnets in the 'fair youth' sequence are a bewitching act of seduction and a testament to deeply felt adoration. Read through in one go, Shakespeare's 'dark lady' poems are a bleak account of the psychological and physical cost of heteroerotic sexual obsession. If a real person lay behind the characterisation of the dark lady, she would have been devastated beyond measure at the cruelty and lack of respect on show in many of sonnets 127 to 154.

But *Shakespeare's Sonnets* – the 1609 volume – doesn't end with the final 'dark lady' sonnet. The edition concludes with a longer lyric poem called 'A Lover's Complaint', which does something (not enough, perhaps) to mitigate the brutal misogyny of most of the poems addressed to a woman. Although it's rarely read or studied, Shakespeare's 'A Lover's Complaint' deserves to be considered alongside the sonnets as part of the same artistic endeavour. The poem – voiced by an unnamed male observer but largely narrated by a woman – tells the story of a 'gentle maid' (177) deflowered and abandoned by a beautiful, smooth-talking young man, who – significantly – writes her romantic sonnets as part of his seduction technique. The youth 'preached pure maid and praised cold chastity' (315) – talked like a virgin and said how much he valued sexual restraint – in order to get her into bed. After this, he ditches her and moves on to other girls. The poem argues forcefully that inexperienced young women aren't to be blamed for giving in to this sort of devilish persuasion, which acts like a contagion on its innocent victims, infecting them with venery and leaving them ruined and disgraced.

The consequences for the abandoned lover are grim – not only the loss of her sexual reputation but also, the poem implies in its final lines, a dangerously permanent receptivity to her seducer's sexual wiles. The young woman fears that were she to meet the man again, his attractions:

> Would yet again betray the fore-betrayed,
> And new pervert a reconciled maid. (328–9)

It's a gruesome couplet with which to conclude a volume of love poetry, conjuring in the mind a future of repeated sexual exploitation and consequent despair for the victim, and proof of the man's brutally effective techniques. As we close *Shakespeare's Sonnets*, we're left unsure of the ultimate tone of 'A Lover's Complaint' (and by extension, the tone of the collection as a whole): are we being encouraged to condemn the sexual double standard that damns the woman and lets the man off scot-free, or salaciously anticipate a forthcoming sequel that continues the story of erotic conquest? The ambiguity may be the point: Shakespeare is inviting us to reflect on the ethical purpose of the poetry we've been reading, to think about the reality of sexual infatuation of all kinds, and to acknowledge the distance between a conventional Petrarchan lover on the page, and the flesh-and-blood real deal.

In his tragedy *King Lear* (1606), the declining king is mistreated by his unkind daughters, and in his confusion and despair he vows to 'anatomise Regan', to open up and disjoint her body to discover the source of her unfilial cruelty (3.6.76). We might use the word 'anatomise' for Shakespeare's sonnets, too, although in this case the subject of the living autopsy is the rich psychosexual terrain of his culture's attitude to sex, both queer and straight. He followed Barnfield in making a good proportion of his poems queer, but he also queered the form, if a modern literary critical term can do service: unlike his era's fashion for idealising, conformist, bloodlessly romantic sonnets, his sequence is sexually dissident, questioning, unconventional and frequently disturbing.

It is also, in every respect, better and more substantial than Barnfield's 'Certain Sonnets'. But Barnfield's signal achievement was in emphatically clearing space in his literary culture for the overt and unapologetic expression of queer desire. His verse has been praised for its 'unlaboured fluency and grace', and he put those skills to a specific purpose, writing love poems that used an easy, accessible style to celebrate sexual love between men. As Shakespeare took up Barnfield's baton, he must have been aware that they were both doing something unprecedented. No other male English writer before them had published an extended collection of sonnets addressed to a man – and none would for centuries afterwards. Although Shakespeare's sequence registers an interest in the idea of literary competitiveness, in more than one 'worthier pen' (79.6) who excels him in hymning the praises of the beautiful youth, in actual fact there weren't any such quills other than Barnfield's: they were the only two poets of their era to queer the sonnet in this way. Perhaps for Shakespeare, Barnfield *was* the competition. The theme of artistic rivalry was a common enough literary trope – Barnfield deployed it too, imagining notable poets Edmund Spenser ('chief of shepherds all' (20.9)) and Michael Drayton excelling him in their praise of Ganymede – but thirty-something Shakespeare might well have felt a little put in the shade by his younger colleague. At barely twenty-one, Barnfield had published four books that spanned an impressive variety of genres and styles, and had made himself the talk of the town.

But Barnfield's new fame brought with it censure, and called into question the future of the queer project that included his poems and Shakespeare's sonnets. Barnfield's queer year of productivity had devastating consequences for the young poet's relationship with his family, and marked a change in Shakespeare's prospects as well. By 1598, Barnfield was already beginning to suffer the effects of a negative reaction to his poetry. To understand precisely how he had offended against his society's expectations, we need to go back to the buzz that surrounded the publication of *The Affectionate Shepherd* in autumn 1594, and *Cynthia, with Certain Sonnets* at Eastertime 1595.

The Affectionate Shepherd – the volume that had been such a hit with the 'courteous gentlemen' of the Inns of Court – had been published without an author's name on the title page. But it had carried a dedication: to Penelope Rich, the Earl of Essex's politically active sister and the rumoured muse for Philip Sidney's *Astrophil and Stella*. In the 1590s, Lady Rich was also famous for her openly adulterous relationship with the handsome Charles Blount, Baron Mountjoy – a distinct improvement on her desiccated husband Richard, third Baron Rich. Barnfield was presumably successful in his anticipated financial payout from the well-connected Lady Rich; perhaps he had targeted her for patronage on the logic that she would be sympathetic to a sexually adventurous narrative in which Daphnis and Queen Guendolen compete for the attentions of a beautiful youth (one hopes she was able to look past the poisonous misogyny). Barnfield signed the dedicatory poem to the 'fair lovely lady' Penelope with the name of his poetic hero: Daphnis. In the prefatory matter to his published homoerotic pastoral, Barnfield was firmly associating his writerly self with the poem's queerly desiring shepherd, the Daphnis who yearns for kisses and more from the sultry and sulky Ganymede.

He dropped the fiction of anonymity a few months later in the two prefaces to *Cynthia, with Certain Sonnets*. This volume too bore a short cash-eliciting dedication to an aristocrat (to William Stanley, sixth Earl of Derby, a middle-aged courtier who had recently married Elizabeth Vere, the bride rejected by Shakespeare's previous patron, the Earl of Southampton). But the more interesting prefatory epistle to *Cynthia, with Certain Sonnets* was that addressed to the 'gentlemen readers' of the Inns of Court, which Barnfield signed with his own name: '[L]ast term there came forth a little toy of mine, entitled *The Affectionate Shepherd*'. In setting the scene for his new book, Barnfield was looking back to his earlier, wave-making publication, and stepping into the light as its author. In doing so, he was also owning up to his identity as 'Daphnis'.

He acknowledged *The Affectionate Shepherd* as his first 'fruits', and identified *Cynthia, with Certain Sonnets* as a sequel, linked in theme and intention. Perhaps to make as much as possible of the connection between the two works, he also used the epistle to the gentlemen readers to deny responsibility for other recently published books ascribed to him, despite the fact that the inoffensive *Greene's Funerals* has since been identified by stylistic analysis as his own (it's not clear why he disowned it: but as the earlier work, ascribed on the title page to 'R. B.', included a printer's dedication claiming it was published 'contrary to the author's expectation', perhaps the discourtesy of a pirated volume still grated on Barnfield).

But the main purpose of the epistle was to make clear his artistic aims in both the previous *The Affectionate Shepherd* and the ensuing 'Certain Sonnets', and to respond to what he regarded as misguided chatter about the first outing of Daphnis and Ganymede:

Some there were, that did interpret *The Affectionate Shepherd* otherwise than (in truth) I meant, touching the subject thereof:

to wit, the love of a shepherd for a boy, a fault the which I will not excuse, because I never made. Only this: I will unshadow my conceit, being nothing else but an imitation of Virgil, in the second *Eclogue* of Alexis.

London had evidently talked after the publication of *The Affectionate Shepherd* in autumn 1594. But about what? Had the dripping fruit, sucking bees and oozing honey that surrounded Ganymede and Daphnis been interpreted for what they were: an overt invocation of queer male sex set within the world of Virgilian pastoral fantasy?

Although Barnfield might appear to be enacting a damage-limitation exercise – 'it's not obscene, it's just Roman' – his excuse isn't quite what it seems. This is very different to the sanitising glossings by E. K. of *The Shepherd's Calendar*, another 'imitation of Virgil'. For a start, Barnfield is deliberately obscure about where, precisely, the misinterpretation lies. Does he mean some people misunderstood 'The Tears of An Affectionate Shepherd' if they thought it was about the love of a shepherd for a boy? That's hardly credible, given that the relationship is the centre of the poem. It's possible he was drawing a distinction between different kinds of boy-love: if some readers assumed he meant the 'faulty', or sinful, kind, well then – they were very mistaken. But this, too, faces a valid charge of disingenuity. Barnfield had admitted in *The Affectionate Shepherd* that Daphnis's desire for Ganymede was a 'sin', and the reader was about to discover in 'Certain Sonnets' that the lovelorn shepherd had unabashedly carnal feelings towards the boy.

In the context of *The Affectionate Shepherd* and 'Certain Sonnets', appealing to the classy Latinity of the second *Eclogue* was no cover whatsoever. It's certainly true that Barnfield used the *Eclogue* as his inspiration, recasting Corydon as Daphnis and Alexis as Ganymede. But in his explicit depiction of homoerotic love – naturalised and domesticated into an English rural setting – Barnfield demolished the myth that a literary affair like that of Corydon and his beloved Alexis had nothing to do with sex. Far from excusing his poetry with an appeal to chaste Roman principle, Barnfield tugged the classical heritage of queer male desire into the light, and compelled his English readership to see it.

It was an astonishingly bold move. Barnfield was drawing attention to a potential homoerotic scandal in his earlier work, while owning up to writing it – and just before his readers were to encounter an even more overt presentation of same-sex desire in his revolutionary queer 'Certain Sonnets'. The crux of his epistle seems to lie in his qualification of The Affectionate Shepherd's main character, Daphnis, the boy-loving shepherd (with whom Barnfield had associated himself in that book's dedication): the character's presentation was, Barnfield writes, 'a fault the which I will not excuse, because I never made'. This was more than a non-apology. It was a statement of principle: the only thing Barnfield claims not to have done in presenting two men in love was commit a 'fault'. The writer who signed himself 'Daphnis' was celebrating his own queer desires, and firmly rejecting the idea that a poem in praise of homoeroticism could be considered a sin.

It turned out to be a reckless decision. Early modern English society wasn't willing to incorporate candid and upfront male homoeroticism into its vernacular poetic culture without the cover provided by the classical tradition. In demanding that his peers see and acknowledge his queerness, Barnfield was met with disinheritance, obscurity and poverty. It was a disaster that Shakespeare – whose sonnets circulating among 'private friends' were part of the queer literary movement of 1590s London – must have noted with dread.

★

The years after 1595 are not easy to piece together for Barnfield, but the evidence strongly suggests that he suffered a calamitous decline in his fortunes. His impressive rate of productivity – four books in little more than a year – slowed down markedly. He didn't publish another collection until 1598, when a motley assortment of pieces, many about the difficulty of making an income, was published under the title *The Encomium of Lady Pecunia, or The Praise of Money*. He chose a line from Horace's *Epistles* as his epigraph: '*Quaerenda pecunia primum est, / Virtus post nummos*' ('You must first seek wealth; virtue follows cash'). Barnfield's concern for his financial standing in these pieces seems keen. In 'The Complaint of Poetry for the Death of Liberality', he mourns the disappearance of patronage: 'Bounty is dead, and with her died my joy' (6). Alongside a professional decline, he was also struggling with a crisis closer to home.

At the start of 1598, Richard Barnfield's father – then aged about sixty – decided to make a significant alteration to his estate. He'd changed his mind about his legacy, and he didn't want his wishes to be challenged after his death in a contested will. The widowed Barnfield Senior was a rich man, with good lands in the farming country of Shropshire on both sides of the River Severn. The estate of Wilderley, in rolling hills south of the river, came with over a hundred acres, a dovecote perched on spindly brick pillars, and twelve tenanted cottages. The more developed lands at Edgmond, twenty miles to the north-east, were richer still: forty cottages brought in ten pounds annual rent, and a watermill – grinding neighbouring farmers' wheat – made money with every lazy turn of its wheel. The near-unbreakable rule of primogeniture said that all this would descend on his death to his eldest son, Richard. Barnfield Senior was about to break that rule.

His course of action required an exhausting journey from Edgmond to London, a 300-mile round trip, and the expenditure of the considerable sum of twelve pounds at the Alienation Office, down a poky lane off Fleet Street. Licences of alienation were required to pass on land that had been appropriated during the Reformation, and most of Barnfield Senior's estate had been carved out of the old Haughmond Abbey. If he wanted to make absolutely sure that his property was passed on as he wished, he needed to attend to the transaction while he was still alive.

The first strike came on 2 March. Barnfield Senior purchased a licence to redirect his estate away from Richard and settle it on his younger son, Robert, not yet of age (he appointed three other men to act as guarantors). Under the terms of the new licence, Richard would only inherit if Robert died before him or left no heirs. If Barnfield Senior made some other arrangements to compensate Richard, no evidence of this has survived. Flying in the face of long-established custom, it seems that he disinherited his eldest son.

Primogeniture was more than just tradition. It was regarded as a fundamental social process that maintained the stability of a patriarchal world. Primogeniture allowed expectant young men to live on the credit of their future inheritances, giving them the means to make their way in the world before the deaths of their parents. It ensured eldest sons of the gentry could live in the style to which their state entitled them, thereby confirming the rightness of the social divisions that held the classes in their place. Primogeniture kept the rich rich: 'God hath appointed it,' wrote William Gouge in his conduct manual *Of Domestical Duties* (1622). Disinheritance was unthinkable, unless the heir was 'notoriously wicked' or in other ways patently unfit to succeed. In John Fletcher's play *The Elder Brother* (c. 1620s), a wealthy father tries to persuade his hopeless son to sign away his birthright 'to pass the land [. . .] unto your younger brother.' Perhaps similar pressure was put on Richard, whose name appears on the licence of

2 March 1598. But he was nowhere to be seen on the second document that sealed his fate. Four years later, Barnfield Senior and Robert made another strike, with a final visit to the Alienation Office. This time Barnfield Senior sold up entirely. He settled a new estate on Robert, who had recently married, and re-established himself at Darlaston, twenty miles from his old home of Edgmond. As he anticipated grandchildren through Robert's line, there was now no need to retain Richard as residual legatee. By 1602, the firstborn Richard Barnfield had been cut off without a shilling. With no prospect of future wealth, he lost all ability to live on the credit that underlay so much of early modern society. The taps had been turned off. Shorn of his status as heir, he would have had few resources to maintain himself in an expensive city like London. Unlike Shakespeare, he didn't have a generous and growing income from playwriting and theatrical share-owning. It's hard to avoid the conclusion that his father's actions impoverished him.

The alienation document of 1602 marked Barnfield's retreat into obscurity. At some point he left London, probably very soon after his disinheritance. He may have been responsible for a new edition of *The Encomium of Lady Pecunia* that appeared with minor changes in 1605, but beyond that date he slips almost entirely from the historical record. If he tried to maintain himself through writing, nothing more has survived. His estranged family lived fruitful and comfortable lives as Shropshire gentlefolk. Barnfield Senior survived well into his ninth decade, an extraordinary achievement at the time, and bequeathed to his relations the bricolage of gold rings, gilt spoons and *memento mori* proper to a country squire. His eldest son seems to have died before him, laid to rest in a Shropshire parish some distance from Darlaston; burials of men called Richard Barnfield are recorded in 1620 and 1626. There is no evidence he was ever reconciled with his father and brother.

It used to be assumed by scholars that the aged Barnfield Senior's will, signed in 1627, was that of the poet. The document appeared to reassure posterity that, although Barnfield had come dangerously close to endorsing unspeakable vice with his imitations of Virgil, he had drawn back. He abandoned his youthful folly and settled down as a married country gentleman in easy circumstances, where he brought his poetic career to a close by writing an amusingly ironic collection about being short of money. Though his initial 'choice of subject was not happy', said an early twentieth-century critic, it was at least a relief that he hadn't actually meant any of that repellent Ganymede business. As the Victorian editor Edward Arber put it, Barnfield wrote 'skilful poetry, *not* expressing any personal feelings' (the italics were Arber's own).

In reality, Barnfield's story was more turbulent. His journey took him from the stability and privilege of a gentry upbringing to Oxford, London and literary celebrity. But he didn't coast into a peaceful retirement. His career was cut short by a catastrophic breakdown in relations with his family that removed, at a stroke, his ability to borrow on credit, and therefore his financial security. The last two decades of his life passed in precarity, and perhaps in want. His father's punishment explains Barnfield's absence from any of the historical documents that speak of security or standing: he left no will that has been discovered, and no one paid tribute to his poetry at his death.

The reason for Barnfield's ostracism could, in truth, have been anything. But nothing suggests that he was a drunk, or mentally ill, or that he had married beneath him or converted to Catholicism (all sins that a Protestant patriarch might consider merited the 'unnatural, injurious and ungodly' step of disinheritance). His only known trespass is the 'fault' he both admitted and denied in the epistle to *Cynthia, with Certain Sonnets*: 'the love of a shepherd for a boy'. With his open acknowledgement of authorship and queer intent, Barnfield made his name, and lost his fortune.

He had reached – and breached – the extent of early modern England's tolerance for queer desire. There was a fine line between conventional neoclassical homoeroticism and illicit sodomitical lust, and he had crossed it. Barnfield's error was threefold: he had boldly shed the Latinate literary veil that protected exploration of male homoeroticism in print, and he had married that candour with a poetic misogyny that was excessive even by early modern standards. Perhaps most daringly, he had openly associated himself with his queerly desiring poetic character. His particular combination of unapologetically explicit queer sex and anti-women sentiment made it virtually impossible to interpret his work as anything other than an expression of preference. Barnfield's poetry made visible what the law and the church said was 'detestable and abominable', and what he himself had boldly characterised as a sin ('If it be sin to love a lovely lad . . .'). He had revealed all too publicly that he was a young man determined to go his own way, and his bravery cost him his inheritance, security and future literary reputation. As he put it in a defiant quotation from the second *Eclogue*, which he appended to *The Encomium of Lady Pecunia*: '*Trahit sua quemque voluptas*' ('Each man is dragged by his own desire').

It's important to note that Barnfield published his poetry openly, with the support of established printers and booksellers. His manuscripts would have been read and approved by officers of the Stationers' Company, whose monopoly over the English press was contingent on them acting as the government's censors. Studied piecemeal, and examined page by page by an overburdened Stationer, Barnfield's work appeared to sit – just – within the realm of allowable literary eroticism. But once his identification with Daphnis became apparent, *The Affectionate Shepherd* and 'Certain Sonnets' took on another hue. The public could read a new meaning back into the existing poems, and the evidence suggests that some readers – including Barnfield's family – were appalled by what they saw. Barnfield's reputation, so dazzling for a few years in the 1590s, collapsed. His poetry was forgotten, and when it wasn't forgotten it was deplored in the strongest possible terms. An editor of 1841, justifying his decision to omit *The Affectionate Shepherd* and 'Certain Sonnets' from a facsimile of Barnfield's work for an antiquarian press (in a run of just sixteen copies), explained:

Such is our observance of external propriety, and so strong the principles of a general decorum, that a writer of the present age who was to print love-verses in this style, would be severely reproached and universally proscribed.

With Barnfield's withdrawal from late-Elizabethan London literary life, the queer poetic circle, of which he and Shakespeare had been a part, dissolved. No other early modern English poet was to publish love sonnets between men, or homoerotic pastoral that was as steamily explicit as Barnfield's. More importantly, Shakespeare's sonnets – inspired by and in conversation with Barnfield's – remained for most of his life in their closed manuscript network. Possibly they stayed in a cupboard; almost nothing was heard of them in the decade after Meres's tempting description of their circulation. Two poems from the 'dark lady' sequence appeared in a pirated collection of modern poetry called *The Passionate Pilgrim* in 1599, suggesting that individual sonnets were still to be found by those who knew where to look. But his 'fair youth' sonnets escaped further notice until the publication of the entire sequence, with 'A Lover's Complaint', as *Shakespeare's Sonnets* in 1609. The volume was met by the reading public with a conspicuous and loaded silence, despite Shakespeare's considerable fame as a playwright and lyric poet: the ninth edition of *Venus and Adonis* had been published the previous year, with the tenth to follow in 1610. Sonnets weren't the fashionable novelties they had been in 1595, and Shakespeare's had an air of something unpalatable to those readers who didn't simply ignore them. 'What a heap of wretched infidel stuff,' scrawled one early annotator at the end of the sequence. No one saw fit to praise them in print, unlike the approving notices that greeted *Venus and Adonis* and *Lucrece*.

Scholarly doubt has traditionally hung over the authenticity of the 1609 volume. Was it published with Shakespeare's consent and involvement, or does the lack of any authorial preface imply that – like *The Passionate Pilgrim* – it was an unethical publisher's tilt at the main chance, an attempt to exploit a famous writer's name recognition? (If so, the low-impact book must have signally failed to bring much profit.) To imagine *Shakespeare's Sonnets* as pirated raises questions about the status of the poems, the order in which they appear, and the authorship of some or all of its contents. In the nineteenth and twentieth centuries, distaste at and dismay about the sonnets' homoerotic and misogynist character could be expressed through bibliographic scrupulousness about whether they were truly what Shakespeare intended to write.

Recent research suggests that the published volume does reflect the author's wishes. Thomas Thorpe was a reputable businessman without a history of piracy. The order of the sonnets and 'A Lover's Complaint' might be impressionistic and at times non-sequential, but it's evidently intentional. Quite when in the preceding decade and a half the structure of the collection took its ultimate shape remains a matter of conjecture. But perhaps something beyond a preference for manuscript circulation (if indeed the poems were doing much circling after the 1590s) motivated Shakespeare to keep his extensive sequence of sonnets private, despite his publishing triumphs with *Venus and Adonis* and *Lucrece*. Surely Shakespeare baulked at the idea of his first-person poems – brimming with homoerotic desire and straight sexual shame – being passed hand-to-hand among casual readers, particularly so soon after Barnfield's ill-fated acknowledgement of his queer identity as 'Daphnis'. Whether or not the poems reflected his own experiences and feelings, it wouldn't be unreasonable for readers to take the autobiographical tone at face value.

Perhaps it was only the passage of time that gave Shakespeare the confidence to release his sonnets to a wider reading public – a hope that their relationship to Barnfield's 'Certain Sonnets' would be much less evident after fourteen years. Shakespeare was not looking to challenge sexual orthodoxy in the way Barnfield had done. The younger man's ostracism must have been a profound shock. If Shakespeare was taking something of a risk in publishing his queer sonnets – with their 'infidel' sensibility and revealingly homoerotic 'I' – then it's possible he greeted their failure with something like relief. By 1609, Shakespeare's queer world, and his attitude to it, had been transformed.

Epilogue

His Verse in Time to Come

June 1599. The young Stationers' Company clerk – arms like twigs, face the colour of milk posset – struggled with the pile of books on the cart. Many of them were bound and tooled, having been seized from the binders the day before, when the pronouncement by the bishops had been cried from Paul's Cross. The clerk's job was to rip the pages from their leather bindings. The drama of the moment required he do it in one go, separating contents and cover in an incontestable act of holy purgation. But he was too feeble. He had to go gathering by gathering, thin fingers feeling along the gutters of every volume to find the edges of each stitched segment. As he tugged the books apart, he dropped the pages onto the pyre in the middle of the courtyard. The unbound ones were easier. He could fling those whole onto the flames, the fire roaring as it consumed the paper like the bundles of brushwood under a convicted heretic.

William stood among a small crowd, watching as books by Tom Nashe, John Marston and poor dead Kit Marlowe went up in smoke in the courtyard of Stationers' Hall. The titles had barely had a chance to offend. Marston's lusty Pygmalion story had only been out a year. John had tempted retribution: his wanton muse had lasciviously sung of sportive love, as he put it. Wanton and lascivious in the same sentence was asking for trouble. But it all seemed a strangely unthorough punishment to William, a lackadaisical blow against a handful of recent books that were easy to find in the shops of Paul's Churchyard. He had a dozen just as obscene or intemperate at home. The fire was a message, not a purification ritual: the men in charge were finally losing patience with the satires and love poems that sold so well in post-plague London. William had cause, he reflected, to heed the warning.

Since his intolerable loss at home – Hamnet, dead at eleven – he could feel the axis of life tilting. Posterity didn't dwell with his family any longer. After Barnfield's decline and with the bishops' clampdown, it was a question whether even his verse offered him life in time to come. Instead, his legacy was taking shape across the river on Bankside, where the new Globe Theatre was set to open on Maiden Lane, walls limewashed a dazzling white and the stage inside nearly ready to present its first play. His name and credit were locked into the building like the joists of the very timbers themselves: William's money had helped raise the thatched roof, and his reputation would entice spectators through the doors. His future was in the oak and lath and plaster of his company's new playhouse.

The bonfire of books at Stationers' Hall followed an edict issued by Richard Bancroft, the Bishop of London, and John Whitgift, the Archbishop of Canterbury, on 1 June 1599. The bishops' order was both sweepingly capacious and oddly specific. It outlawed completely the printing of 'satires or epigrams', made all English history books subject to Privy Council approval, and banned for good everything ever written by the professional provocateurs Thomas Nashe and Gabriel Harvey. In addition, the bishops ordered the Stationers' Company to burn copies of nine recent books by some of the city's best-known satirists and erotic poets, among them John Marston's *Pygmalion, with Certain Other Satires* (1598) and his *The Scourge of Villainy* (1598), Thomas Middleton's *Microcynicon: Six Snarling Satires* (1599) and Christopher Marlowe's translation of Ovid's *Amores*, published together with the *Epigrams* of John Davies (1599).

It wasn't an unprecedented clampdown – although the book-burning was an unexpectedly dramatic addition. The Church and state had many tools at their disposal for controlling and suppressing the press: as recently as 1596, the authorities had launched a campaign to stamp out pamphlets of 'ribaldry [. . .] superstition [. . .] and flat heresy'. The conflation of sexuality with political and religious subversion indicated how intertwined Elizabeth's government thought those issues were.

What the country's rulers really hated was the idea that writers were pushing the limits of obedience and decorum at a time of great political uncertainty. The queen was sixty-five years old in the summer of 1599, declining in body and mind. Her favourite, the Earl of Essex, was jockeying to be kingmaker ahead of the next reign, and as part of his tilt for glory he had recently departed with a massive army for Ireland, where he hoped to subdue the Spanish-sponsored Gaelic clans who were fighting for freedom from England. His mission was soon mired in disaster, and statesmen fretted about what an angry, resentful nobleman with 15,000 troops under his command might do next (in the event, his palace coup was an unsupported failure). At home, years of poor harvests had sent the cost of living sky-rocketing. All in all, the late 1590s was a testy, anxious and ill-humoured time. Government censors had a low tolerance for satires that mocked public figures, or lubricious epigrams that seemed to encourage immoral behaviour.

Like most book-burnings, the Bishops' Ban of 1599 wasn't particularly effective. The targeted books had already been printed and sold en masse, and the affected writers turned their hands to other forms of slyly satirical literature, such as the city comedies that were flourishing in the playhouses. Pornographic poetry in the style of Marston's epyllion 'The Metamorphosis of Pygmalion's Image' – in which the living statue's 'arms, eyes, hands, tongue, lips and wanton thigh / Were willing agents in Love's luxury' – was soon available to buy again in the bookstalls of Paul's Churchyard.

But the incineration of edgy, fashionable writing that June day in 1599 – much of it by men Shakespeare knew, or had known, very well – seemed to augur ill for his future as a lyric poet, for all that his own publications had escaped the fire. It compounded a sense of unease at the earlier controversy around Barnfield's *The Affectionate Shepherd* and 'Certain Sonnets' that the public's taste for 'honey-flowing' verse was coming under suspicion. Perhaps, as he watched the ashy remnants of his friends' work ascend above Ludgate Hill, he thought with relief of his own candid and erotic sonnets, tucked away out of sight in the chests and cabinets of friends and friends-of-friends. The Bishops' Ban didn't do much in the end to bring London's press to heel, but it was a vivid symbol for a change of mood, a newly sour atmosphere as the country worried about food prices, the succession and the war in Ireland.

It's possible that, by the end of the decade, Shakespeare was himself less inclined to live up to his reputation as the nation's chief purveyor of sweet and succulent poetry. His poetic voice must have been deeply affected by the death of his and Anne's only son Hamnet in August 1596, although scholars have debated for centuries the impact of the loss on the tragedies and bittersweet comedies – often culminating in scenes of miraculous reunion between father and child – that followed in the years after the boy's burial. The connection, if there is one, between Shakespeare's son and his greatest tragedy, *Hamlet*, remains intriguingly obscure.

The most painful and ill-timed part of the wretched autumn after Hamnet's death was the visit Shakespeare made to the College of Arms in London, on 20 October 1596, to collect a document on behalf of his father John. The Letters Patent he picked up that day made his father, his brothers and himself gentlemen, thanks to the prosperity and status William had accrued for the family through playwriting, patronage and business dealings. Their new gentility descended on all male 'children, issue, and posterity'. But William would be the last gentle Shakespeare of his line and name. At forty, Anne was probably beyond safe childbearing. His brothers Gilbert, Richard and Edmund were to die unmarried. His daughters Susanna and Judith would form new families with their future husbands John Hall and Thomas Quiney. William's posterity, in the patriarchal logic of early modern England, was stopped. If the 'procreation sonnets' addressed to the fair youth were written after Hamnet's death, they must have brought as much agony to their writer as they have brought pleasure to readers.

But if Shakespeare was dealing with personal loss, and the apparent closure of an artistic door as the state turned on the sexual and satirical avant-garde, his profession as a dramatist and company man was advancing in leaps and bounds in June 1599. He was an investor and shareholder in the Lord Chamberlain's Men, whose brand-new playhouse – with three floors of lavishly painted audience galleries, a gilt and decorated ceiling that spanned the stage, and an absorbent thatched roof that prevented sheets of rainwater dripping onto the audience standing in the yard below – would open that summer. The name they had chosen for their new home – the Globe – blazed the company's confidence in their ability to attract all comers.

The Globe would be the crucible for Shakespeare's most extraordinary achievements in tragedy – *Hamlet*, *Othello*, *Macbeth*, *King Lear*, *Antony and Cleopatra*. It was from its Bankside base that the Chamberlain's Men received a giddying social escalation in 1603, on the death of the old queen and the accession of her successor. They became the new King James's servants, the most rewarded theatre troupe in the land. As a member of the King's Men, the middle-aged Master Shakespeare wore royal livery when he attended Court or toured to other towns and country houses throughout England.

The arrival in London of the Scottish King James VI – now England's James I – might have been expected to bring a new queer sensibility to English cultural life: this was the same monarch who, as a teenager, had poured his heart into a poem in memory of his beloved favourite, Esmé Stewart, Seigneur d'Aubigny. But it seemed for the time being that the grown-up James had learned to manage his queer affairs in a way that didn't interfere with his duties of kingship: since Aubigny, he had made every effort to avoid a Gaveston-like crisis between an indulged favourite and the country's piqued nobles.

James's young male favourites still shared his bed, received royal gifts and usually ended up with a title, but he didn't try to leverage them into high political office any more. Before his marriage to Anna of Denmark in 1589, James's constant companion – his 'only minion and conceit' – had been Alexander Lindsay, later Lord Spynie. When he made the journey south to claim the English crown, the role of king's minion was occupied by John Ramsay, soon ennobled as Viscount Haddington. Soon after his arrival in London, James's roving royal eye landed on nineteen-year-old Philip Herbert, brother of the William who has sometimes been identified as the sonnets' 'Master W. H.' (Philip was rewarded with the earldom of Montgomery). Queen Anna lived apart from her husband, and soon developed her residences at Greenwich Palace and Somerset House on the Strand (renamed Denmark House) into cultural salons that rivalled the king's court as centres of artistic and political patronage.

The king's queer identity was taken for granted by most observers as an aspect of his kingly privilege (although after his death people were more open about their disapproval: the Civil War memoirist Lucy Hutchinson castigated the 'fools and bawds, mimics and catamites' who had brought debauchery to the Jacobean court). But that didn't translate into a change in attitude towards the queer desires of the population at large. In theory, sodomy was still punishable by death – not that the rate of prosecution went up. Law and society continued to count it as one of the worst, most chillingly unnatural offences a man could commit. Sodomy, said James in his treatise *Basilikon Doron* ('The King's Gift', 1599), was among the crimes a monarch was 'bound in conscience never to forgive'. The king could allow himself to appear unbending in his refusal to pardon sodomy. There were barely any occasions when he would be called upon to do so.

But James's reign did affect the lives of queer people in England. In presenting such a visible example of same-sex desire, James and his minions gave identifiable shape to the scarcely believable crime of sodomy – vanishingly rare in prosecution, yet an everyday activity in practice. Sodomy had been thought of as something so cataclysmic that it belonged in the stories of the Old Testament, or in tales of godless societies in other parts of the world – and nothing like the everyday pleasures to be found with willing bedfellows or persuadable servingmen. Now there were rumours of it in the heart of government, where the monarch's passions were soon a matter for public comment.

The king's ability to separate his queer love from his political ambitions didn't last. The Aubigny situation played itself out again – twice. First there was the handsome, athletic Robert Carr, twenty-three when he was first noticed by the king in 1607. Carr was the undisputed social hub of the royal court. Before long, James was loading him with state duties too: membership of the Privy Council, Lord Privy Seal, Warden of the Cinque Ports and finally Lord Chamberlain, head of the king's entire household. With the offices came titles: Viscount Rochester, then Earl of Somerset. For those who remembered James's intemperate adoration of Esmé Stewart, it was all depressingly familiar.

Carr – now Somerset – was the instrument of his own fall. He fell in love with the married Countess of Essex, provoking a

lurid divorce trial in which accusations of impotence, witchcraft and adultery flew. His extravagance was legion: it was said
he blew through £90,000 in one year. Most damagingly, he
couldn't bear competition. When James, in the summer of
1614, met twenty-one-year-old George Villiers ('the handsomest-
bodied [man] in England' according to one courtier), it was all
over for Somerset.

Somerset raged about his eclipse, shocking observers with
public discourtesy to the king and – what was worse, as far as
James was concerned – refusing to sleep with him (the king
deplored his 'long creeping back and withdrawing yourself from
lying in my chamber, notwithstanding my many hundred times
earnest soliciting you to the contrary'). Meanwhile, Villiers was
being polished, decked and primped by Somerset's political
enemies to draw the king's eye. It worked: by August 1615,
Villiers was sharing the king's bed, and the predictable shower of
high offices followed: Master of the Horse, Order of the Garter,
Privy Councillor; a baronetcy, an earldom and finally elevation as
Duke of Buckingham, the second most senior peer in the land.
James's love for Buckingham spilled out in public and private
declarations of devotion. The duke's star soared and stayed high:
the ambitious and strategic Buckingham was the centre of
political power for the remainder of James's reign, and continued
so into Charles I's (until he was assassinated by an army officer in
1628). Somerset – an altogether messier minion – ended up
implicated in the murder of his former friend Thomas Overbury
and died a largely forgotten figure in 1645.

Few people were unaware of how the king liked to live and
govern. In 1615, a Latin satire detailed James's daisy chain of
lovers (Ramsay, Herbert, Carr, Villiers) and asked – disingenuously – whether anything was wrong with 'advancing the
beautiful'. Simonds D'Ewes, the lawyer who had reflected on his
education at Middle Temple, huffed in his diary how widespread

sodomy had become 'in this wicked city', a sin – he added daringly – 'of the prince [i.e., 'ruler'] as well as the people'.

The king's queer relationships increased the pressure on those lower down the social scale. Far from leading by example, James gave a new language to moral crusaders who charged others with that which they dared not indict the king. During James's reign, the accusation of sodomy became a powerful political tool, hurled at overreaching public figures whether or not they had queer relationships. Francis Bacon – the philosopher and statesman who very much did enjoy same-sex lovers – was libelled in 1621 during his impeachment for corruption with a placard nailed to his house: 'Within this sty a hog doth lie / That must be hanged for sodomy.'

Shakespeare's new royal patron was no queer hero. The Jacobean age was, if anything, a more dangerous one for sexually nonconforming people than the previous reign. Shakespeare had fewer avenues to explore queer desire when he became a king's servant in 1603; the awkward silence that attended his sonnets on their eventual publication spoke volumes about the new suspicions faced by men who loved men, despite the queer monarch who was at that moment adorning Robert Carr with land, jewels and titles (in January 1609, James gave the recently knighted Carr the West Country estates he had seized from the imprisoned Walter Raleigh).

That isn't to say that Shakespeare shied away from exploring queerness in the later part of his career. The institutional bases for homoeroticism in early modern England – the schoolroom, the playhouses, the Inns of Court and the universities, the life of the streets – continued their enthusiastic and sometimes problematic fostering of queer male desire. Playwrights developed ever more nuanced and compelling ways to objectify the boy actors at their disposal. Some of Shakespeare's most subtle explorations of sexuality and gender can be found in Jacobean-era plays: consider Imogen's performance as the sexually vulnerable page Fidele in *Cymbeline*, or Cleopatra's astonishing acknowledgement of her character's embodiment by a young man when she reflects on her future mockery on stage by a 'squeaking' adolescent. The queer themes and relationships that had proved so compelling in his younger years continued to inspire Shakespeare's writing.

In what was probably his very last play, Shakespeare returned to the topic of intense *amicitia perfecta* pitted against straight desire, one of the most generative and dramatically rewarding of all early modern stage conflicts. This time, he wrote with a collaborator: John Fletcher, the playwright whose prodigious intimacy with Francis Beaumont was noted by contemporaries. By 1613 he was the new King's Men house dramatist, groomed to replace Shakespeare. The two men dramatised Geoffrey Chaucer's 'The Knight's Tale', already a venerable classic in the early seventeenth century. In *The Two Noble Kinsmen*, cousins and devoted friends Palamon and Arcite wind up in an Athenian prison for life after being taken captive on the battlefield. Little daunted, Arcite embraces the prospect of knowing 'nothing here but one another' (2.2.41):

> We are an endless mine to one another;
> We are one another's wife, ever begetting
> New births of love; we are father, friends, acquaintance;
> We are, in one another, families. (2.2.79–82)

Palamon, made 'almost wanton / With [his] captivity' (96–97), is delirious: 'Is there record of any two that loved / Better than we do, Arcite?' (112–13). The friends' splendid hyperbole lasts approximately six seconds, which is the time between Palamon's rhetorical question and the entrance of Emilia, who is seen walking in the garden below their prison cell, first by Palamon and then by Arcite. The two men come to bitter recriminations and threats of murderous violence as love and kinship dissolve in the face of the sublime Emilia. *Amicitia perfecta* is remembered only as a crafty trick to gull the other into renouncing his prior claim:

> ARCITE. Let me deal coldly with you. Am not I
> Part of your blood, part of your soul? You have told me
> That I was Palamon, and you were Arcite.
> PALAMON.   Yes.
> ARCITE. Am not I liable to those affections,
> Those joys, griefs, angers, fears my friend shall suffer?
> PALAMON. Ye may be.
> ARCITE.   Why then would you deal so cunningly,
> So strangely, so unlike a noble kinsman,
> To love alone? (2.2.184–191)

Arcite's appeal to the sort of sexual open-handedness practised by heroic friends like Titus and Gisippus, who share one wife between them, does not go down well.

Eventually, the friends, having clawed back some of their virtue and dignity, are put to a knightly tournament to decide which of them shall claim Emilia, and which shall die for flouting the chivalric codes of Athens. Emilia finds herself unable to choose (or perhaps distinguish) between '[t]wo fair gauds of equal sweetness' (4.2.53). Arcite wins the tournament, but Palamon's execution is stayed at the last moment by the news that his competitor has been thrown from his horse and is near death, although he rallies long enough to seek forgiveness from Palamon and bequeath Emilia to him with the devastatingly laconic '[t]ake her. I die' (5.4.95). The elegiac mood of the last scene of the play is confirmed by Palamon's final words to the dead Arcite:

That we should things desire which do cost us
The loss of our desire! That nought could buy
Dear love but loss of dear love! (5.4.110–12)

Palamon realises not merely that his love for Arcite and Emilia
are equally weighted, but that the one has been achieved at the
cost of the other. Forty years after his first exposure to the
Ciceronian celebration of *amicitia perfecta*, Shakespeare was still
probing the ambivalences of a love between men that passes
understanding, especially when placed in competition with desire
for the same woman.

And in *The Two Noble Kinsmen*, Shakespeare and Fletcher
finally achieved a compelling portrait of female queer desire.
Intimate female friends in the Ciceronian mould (for all that
Cicero's misogynist rules precluded women from experiencing
'perfect' friendship) had long been a feature of Shakespeare's
plays. Helena and Hermia in *A Midsummer Night's Dream* share
'two seeming bodies but one heart' (3.2.212), a spiritual and
bodily 'incorporat[ion]' (208) that makes the apparent betrayal
of their love in the chaos caused by Puck's sex-magic all the
harder to bear. In *As You Like It*, Rosalind and Celia must endure
the splitting of their own exclusively intimate life – 'wheresoe'er
we went, like Juno's swans / Still we went coupled and inseparable' (1.3.75–6) – to facilitate their straight marriages to Orlando
and Oliver (although Rosalind goes about her seduction of
Orlando in a decidedly queer way).

But Emilia is granted a past queer life that lives in her memory
as an irreplaceable experience of emotional and erotic intimacy. As
she confesses to her sister Hippolyta, she loved her girlhood friend
Flavina 'like the elements' (1.3.61), each of them acting in powerful and transformative ways on the other. They gloried in a
harmony of tastes and desires, and although Flavina died in adolescence, when the girls' breasts were 'but beginning / To swell', she

leaves in Emilia's soul a fast 'faith' that 'the true love 'tween maid and maid may be / More than in sex dividual' (i.e., between the two sexes) (1.3.67–68, 98, 81–2). As Hippolyta notes observantly, Emilia is out of breath when she talks of Flavina, a true sign that she 'shall never [. . .] Love any that's called man' (1.3.84–85). Emilia's highly equivocal acceptance of Palamon – and her disinclination to be treated like a chivalric prize – suggests she doesn't waver in her faith. It might have taken him an entire career to properly address female homoeroticism – but Shakespeare got there in the end (with Fletcher's help).

Not long after the premiere of *The Two Noble Kinsmen* – probably at the King's Men's sophisticated new indoor playhouse in the former Blackfriars monastery – Shakespeare went home for good. He might have sold his lucrative shares in the company he'd helped run for nearly twenty years; certainly, he vacated his writer's seat in favour of Fletcher. At New Place in Stratford-upon-Avon, he rejoined Anne and Judith (Susanna had married in 1607). The house held a population of servants and staff and hangers-on, sustaining the trading, brewing and land-management businesses that Anne had run so well for three decades. It was a satisfying and substantial home for a man of means. Shakespeare died there, in April 1616, on or close to his fifty-second birthday.

   That's where our story ends, too. Our final sight of Shakespeare is as he takes his leave of his family, last will and testament signed and bequests endorsed ('second best bed' for Anne and all). Perhaps that seems an oddly conventional end for an account of Shakespeare's queer lives: despite my best intentions, I appear to have spanned cradle to grave after all. But examining Shakespeare's queer life and art doesn't mean erasing his wife or his children, just as their existence doesn't disprove his queerness. Early modern queer lives weren't lived with the doctrinaire clarity of today. But as we're re-examining promises I made in the Prologue, let's circle back to that reductive 'Was he or wasn't he?' question. I said then that the issue of sexual identity wasn't the be-all and end-all of this topic, and I still believe that, seven chapters later. But for what it's worth, I think Shakespeare's passionate interest in queer desire is its own answer, although his personal queerness must have been bi rather than gold-star gay.

Straight Acting has been an invitation to think honestly about Shakespeare's evolution as a queer artist, to examine the factors that helped and hindered his growth, and to consider the ways his culture both endorsed and suppressed queer desire. My approach produces a different sort of Shakespeare to the one many of us are used to: a writer more responsive to his predecessors and contemporaries, perhaps; a dramatist alert to the meaning that lay in the bodies of his actors, sexed and gendered as they were in creative and expansive ways; and a poet alive to his participation in a unique and unrepeated queer artistic movement in the 1590s.

The years in which Shakespeare launched himself on his career in theatre and poetry emerge in these pages as something of a queer oasis, when early modern queer cultural life enjoyed a flowering on page and stage despite religious and social hostility. The fashions for honeyed erotic verse, neoclassical homoeroticism and artful boy actor performances combined in the last decades of the sixteenth century to create a briefly supportive space for artists like Shakespeare who wanted to explore same-sex desire. But those conditions didn't last. Would-be Shakespeares or Barnfields in the following decades – men desperate to express their queer love in plays, lyric poetry or sonnets – faced the most violent of opposition from a straight establishment newly primed to detect transgressions of gender presentation and sexual behaviour. Frightening new institutions – societies for the reformation and protection of 'manners', a popular press keen to fashion sodomites and 'mollies' as public enemies, and a conservative social elite giddy with the proceeds of imperial plunder – filled the vacuum of surveillance that had once kept early modern English queer desire thriving as a cultural force. Barnfield and Shakespeare may be the only early modern Englishmen to have published queer sonnets. But we can be sure they weren't the only ones to write them. The queer dramatists and sonneteers of the seventeenth and eighteenth centuries – and beyond – wrote in secret and in fear. Our hidden canon of queer love still awaits recovery. All the more important, then, that we treasure Shakespeare for the queer artist he was. His genius blazed out on the light-drenched open stages of early modern London, and captivated readers in bold, clear print. Shakespeare looked to the future, to the time beyond, when 'in black ink my love may still shine bright' (65.14). It's a testament to him, and to the other queer artists of his age, that it does.

Acknowledgements

Juliet Brooke, editor extraordinaire and Shakespeare devotee, made this book happen and I can't thank her enough. Her successor at Sceptre, Charlotte Humphery, wrangled the manuscript with wisdom and a wicked sense of humour. Holly Knox has been a guiding voice from the start. I'm grateful to copy-editor Sophie Bristow for staging an intervention when she saw my addiction to hyphens. My thanks to Louise Court, Olivia French and the tireless publicity department for their work in spreading the word. The team at Basic Books in New York were patience itself: thank you Claire Potter and Marissa Koors, both now thriving in pastures new. The estimable Michael Kaler made the book so much better. An especially ardent thank you to Chin-Yee Lai and colleagues for the gorgeous cover. Nothing at all would have been written without the advice, advocacy and energy of my agent Eleanor Birne of PEW Literary.

More than twenty years ago, Tiffany Stern took me down a research rabbit hole when she supervised an essay on early modern boy actors; if this book has a point of origin, that is it. I've been so fortunate in my scholarly mentors and friends. I remain indebted to Warren Boutcher, David Colclough and the late Lisa Jardine. Four people I admire more than I can say read the manuscript at an early stage and saved me from scores of glaring errors: bless you Stephen Guy-Bray, Robert Stagg, Emma Smith and Alan Stewart (all remaining mistakes are my own). I'm grateful to Hailey Bachrach, Robin Craig, Julie Crawford, Ari Friedlander, Daniel Gosling, Evey Reidy, Nate Szymanski and several cohorts of Shakespeare's Globe/King's College London MA students for helpful conversations. In 2022, I was lucky enough to work alongside Karen Ann Daniels, Malik Work and Devin E. Haqq as they developed a new play, *Our Verse in Time to Come*, commissioned by the Folger Shakespeare Library. I took inspiration from their title – a riff on Shakespeare's Sonnet 17 – for my Epilogue.

Thank you to truly spectacular colleagues (past and present) at Shakespeare's Globe: Joe Atkins, Hanh Bui, Mel Chetwood, Neil Constable, Claudia Conway, Eli Court, Lucy Cuthbertson, George Dennis, Jane Fowler, Lucy Hurst, Pollyanna Jenkins, Stella Kanu, Richard Knowles, Victoria Lane, Pete Le May, Sharni Lockwood, Jo Luck, James Maloney, Cleo Maynard, Philip Milnes-Smith, Zoë Morrall, Kate Peters, Josiah O'Brien, Daniel L. Rabinowitz, Craig Ritchie, Patrick Spottiswoode, Michelle Terry and Rob Thorpe-Woods. It's hard to express sufficient thanks to Farah Karim-Cooper for enabling the work that went into this book. I'm so grateful for her support and friendship.

I've never been able to write at home, so it's lucky I could impose on other people. Adam Smyth and Eliane Glaser opened their Oxfordshire house to friends with books on the go: ever so many thanks to them and my fellow guests Eleanor Birne, Dennis Duncan, Chloë Houston, Abigail Reynolds, Olivia Smith, Siobhan Templeton, Tom Templeton and an ostentation of peacocks. Alexander Duma has been a consummate host and friend for many years. Staff at the British Library and the London Library made their reading rooms a home-away-from-home. The Royal Hotel in Deal, Kent, isn't a writing retreat, but I think we should all go back and turn it into one: the sea air makes you write like a demon.

For insights, hospitality and good cheer (often all three), I thank Christopher Adams, Stefan Adegbola, Timothy Allsop,

Samuel Aremu, Sally Barnden, Mark Belcher, Jack Bootle, Paul Edmondson, Jennifer Edwards, Andrew Fallaize, Ben Higgins, Johnnie Johnson, Andy Kesson, Daniel Mallory, Kate Maltby, Andy McDowell, Blanche McIntyre, Clare McManus, Lucy Munro, Alistair Pegg, Martin Prendergast, Emily Rowe, David Salcedo, Gyuri Sarossy, Erman Sozudogru, Daniel Starza Smith, Annalisa Thomas, Emma Whipday, Ed Whiting, Tom Wicker, Ben Wosskow, Beth Wosskow and Thomas Wynn.

Finally, family. Kate Davies, Victoria Fitzpatrick and Felix Davies-Fitzpatrick have enriched my life in numberless ways. Julianne Chaloux, Norma Clarke, Barbara Taylor, Clare Torday, Jane Torday, Nick Torday, John Tosh, Nick Tosh and Caroline White give love and bring joy. And to Piers Torday: I offer you this book with all my heart.

Bibliographic Essay

Prologue: Was He or Wasn't He?

This essay continues my litany of thanks in the Acknowledgements. I've been pondering a version of this book for two decades, and along the way I have read, heard and spoken to a large number of scholars whose research has shaped the way I think about the topic of queer Shakespeare. *Straight Acting* contains the ideas of many people, and it's an honour to account for my journey through the rich scholarship on late-sixteenth-century literature, Shakespeare's life and work, and early modern sexualities.

First, the biographies that give shape to my own queer version of the form. I leaned on S. Schoenbaum, *William Shakespeare: A Compact Documentary Life* (Oxford, 1977, 1987); Park Honan, *Shakespeare: A Life* (Oxford, 1999); Katherine Duncan-Jones, *Shakespeare: An Ungentle Life* (London, 2001, 2010); and Peter Ackroyd, *Shakespeare: The Biography* (London, 2005). I took occasional dips into Jonathan Bate, *The Genius of Shakespeare* (London, 1997); and Stephen Greenblatt, *Will in the World: How Shakespeare Became Shakespeare* (London, 2004). By far the most useful was Lois Potter, *The Life of William Shakespeare: A Critical Biography* (Malden, MA, 2012): Potter shares new information, or newly resonant echoes in Shakespeare's work, on nearly every page. *Straight Acting* has two 'hero books': James Shapiro, *1599: A Year in the Life of William Shakespeare* (London, 2006) – for all that my story stops more or less when his begins – and Emma Smith, *This Is Shakespeare* (London, 2019), a masterclass in accessible literary criticism.

Readers may be interested in the key developments of queer scholarship that I cite in passing in the Prologue. Among the first post-war contributions to queer history were Noel I. Garde, *Jonathan to Gide: The Homosexual in History* (New York, 1964); and H. Montgomery Hyde, *The Love That Dared Not Speak Its Name: A Candid History of Homosexuality in Britain* (Boston, 1970). The era's dedication to uncovering hidden queer histories (although that wasn't the term used) was exemplified in John Boswell, *Christianity, Social Tolerance and Homosexuality: Gay People in Western Europe from the Beginning of the Christian Era to the Fourteenth Century* (Chicago, 1980). This period of gay scholarship has been studied in its turn: see Alan Stewart, 'Homosexuals in History: A. L. Rowse and the Queer Archive', in Katherine O'Donnell and Michael O'Rourke (eds), *Love, Sex, Intimacy, and Friendship Between Men, 1550–1800* (Basingstoke, 2003), pp. 53–69; and Will Fisher, 'A Hundred Years of Queering the Renaissance', in Vin Nardizzi, Stephen Guy-Bray and Will Stockton (eds), *Queer Renaissance Historiography: Backward Gaze* (Farnham, 2009), pp. 13–40.

The first (slim) volume of Michel Foucault's uncompleted *History of Sexuality – The Will To Knowledge* – was translated from the French into English in 1978. His influence was seismic, not merely in the important works by Bray and Sedgwick I mentioned in the Prologue. Foucault's challenge to sexual categorisation appeared to do away with the 'dreary labelling' of historical persons as homosexual, as the classics scholar David M. Halperin put it (*One Hundred Years of Homosexuality and other essays on Greek Love* (New York, 1990), p. 7). Work in the 1980s, 1990s and early 2000s expanded the field of 'gay and lesbian history' in dynamic ways, creating the disciplines of queer theory and queer early modern studies, and finding new ways to analyse queer experience. Important contributions of that time that are still much read include Jonathan Goldberg, *Sodometries: Renaissance Texts, Modern Sexualities* (Stanford, 1992) and his edited collection *Queering the Renaissance* (Durham, NC, 1994); Louise Fradenburg and Carla Freccero (eds), *Premodern Sexualities* (New York, 1996); Valerie Traub's revelatory *The Renaissance of Lesbianism in Early Modern England* (Cambridge, 2002); and Rebecca Ann Bach, *Renaissance Literature Before Heterosexuality* (New York, 2007).

In the past two decades, scholars have, to an extent, returned to an assumption that forms of sexual identity have an observable history: see Halperin's various models of premodern homoerotic identity in 'How to do the history of male homosexuality', *GLQ: A Journal of Lesbian and Gay Studies* 6 (2000), pp. 87–123; and a critique that his distinctions are over-rigid by George E. Haggerty, 'Male Love and Friendship in the Eighteenth Century', in O'Donnell and O'Rourke (eds), *Love, Sex, Intimacy, and Friendship*, pp. 70–81. Other scholars have embraced a literary theory-led 'presentist' approach that rejects the overwhelmingly historicist nature of much early modern criticism. Both sides have endeavoured to explore the seemingly paradoxical association between the grave sin of sodomy, and the obvious – indeed flagrant – homoeroticism of early modern culture (see Tom Betteridge, 'Introduction', in Betteridge (ed.), *Sodomy in Early Modern Europe* (Manchester, 2002)).

Some of the most exciting recent work has been from scholars who are thinking ambitiously and intersectionally about sexuality, gender and race: I've learned from Urvashi Chakravarty, 'More Than Kin, Less Than Kind: Similitude, Strangeness, and Early Modern English Homonationalisms', *Shakespeare Quarterly* 67.1 (2016), pp. 14–29. A recent special issue of the *Journal for Early Modern Cultural Studies* on 'Early Modern Trans Studies', 19.4

(2019), edited by Simone Chess, Colby Gordon and Will Fisher, was rightly hailed as a watershed moment in the field. Joseph Gamble, *Sex Lives of the Early Moderns: Intimate Infrastructures in Early Modernity* (Philadelphia, 2023) provides a marvellous account of sexual knowledge in Shakespeare's time.

Edited collections offer an excellent entry point for those keen to understand the extent of the field: I recommend James M. Bromley and Will Stockton (eds), *Sex Before Sex: Figuring the Act in Early Modern England* (Minneapolis, 2013); and Goran Stanivukovic (ed.), *Queer Shakespeare: Desire and Sexuality* (London, 2017). Melissa E. Sanchez's handbook *Shakespeare and Queer Theory* (London, 2019) is a model of clarity and synthesis.

Chapter 1: Lady Birch

For my account of an early modern middle-class male upbringing, I consulted Elizabeth A. Foyster, *Manhood in Early Modern England: Honour, Sex and Marriage* (London, 1999) and Alexandra Shepard, *Meanings of Manhood in Early Modern England* (Oxford, 2003). On Galenic medicine and the 'one sex' model, see Thomas Laqueur, *Making Sex: Body and Gender from the Greeks to Freud* (Cambridge, MA, 1990, 1992), and the important critique of Laqueur, which centres female experience, in Laura Gowing, 'Women's Bodies and the Making of Sex in Seventeenth-Century England', *Signs: Journal of Women in Culture and Society* 37.4 (2012), pp. 813–22. For more on the rituals of catechism and confirmation, see Ian Green, '"For Children in Yeeres and Children in Understanding": The Emergence of the English Catechism under Elizabeth and the Early Stuarts', *Journal of Ecclesiastical History* 37.3 (1986), pp. 397–425.

The Elizabethan grammar school is a well-researched topic, and I enjoyed three excellent older works: J. Howard Brown, *Elizabethan Schooldays: An Account of the English Grammar Schools in the Second Half of the Sixteenth Century* (Oxford, 1933); Kenneth

Charlton, *Education in Renaissance England* (London, 1965); and Joan Simon, *Education and Society in Tudor England* (Cambridge, 1966). The standard work on the grammar school syllabus is T. W. Baldwin's two-volume *William Shakspere's Small Latine and Lesse Greeke* (Urbana, IL, 1944), which is still useful if one can get past the eccentrically spelled title.

I benefited enormously from Elizabeth Pittenger, 'Dispatch Quickly: The Mechanical Reproduction of Pages', *Shakespeare Quarterly* 42.4 (1991), pp. 389–408; and Wendy Wall, ' "Household Stuff": The Sexual Politics of Domesticity and the Advent of English Comedy', *ELH* 65.1 (1998), pp. 1–45, both of which explore the masculinising effect of a grammar school education.

On Cicero's significance in the early modern period, see Howard Jones, *Master Tully: Cicero in Tudor England* (Nieuwkoop, 1998). On the potency of *amicitia perfecta*, see Laurens J. Mills, *One Soul in Bodies Twain: Friendship in Tudor Literature and Stuart Drama* (Bloomington, IN, 1937); Gregory Chaplin, ' "One flesh, one heart, one soul": Renaissance Friendship and Miltonic Marriage', *Modern Philology* 99.2 (2001), pp. 266–92; and Laurie Shannon, *Sovereign Amity: Figures of Friendship in Shakespearean Contexts* (Chicago, 2002). I address the topic in my own *Male Friendship and Testimonies of Love in Shakespeare's England* (London, 2016). For more on Shakespeare's devotion to Ovid, you can't do better than Jonathan Bate, *Shakespeare and Ovid* (Oxford, 1993).

The grim consequences of early modern corporal punishment were first explored in Walter Ong, 'Latin Language Study as a Renaissance Puberty Rite', *Studies in Philology* 56 (1959), pp. 103–24. Ong steered clear of thinking about sex and gender, an omission rectified by Elizabeth Pittenger, ' "To Serve the Queere": Nicholas Udall, Master of Revels', in Jonathan Goldberg (ed.), *Queering the Renaissance* (Durham, NC, 1994), pp. 162–89; Alan Stewart, *Close Readers: Humanism and Sodomy in Early Modern England* (Princeton, 1997); and Lynn Enterline, *Shakespeare's*

Schoolroom: Rhetoric, Discipline, Emotion (Philadelphia, 2012). Alan Stewart will be a recurring guest star in this bibliographic essay, and I want to acknowledge his abiding influence on this book, and my gratitude for his intellectual inspiration.

My reading of *The Merchant of Venice* – especially its closing moments – has been hugely influenced by Arthur L. Little, Jr., 'The Rites of Queer Marriage in *The Merchant of Venice*', in Madhavi Menon (ed.) *Shakesqueer: A Queer Companion to the Complete Works of Shakespeare* (Durham, NC, 2011), pp. 216–24; and Edward J. Geiseidt, 'Antonio's Claim: Triangulated Desire and Queer Kinship in Shakespeare's *The Merchant of Venice*', *Shakespeare* 5.4 (2009), pp. 338–54. I was helped in my thinking about *The Two Gentlemen of Verona* by J. L. Simmons, 'Coming Out in Shakespeare's *Two Gentlemen of Verona*', in *ELH* 60.4 (1993), pp. 857–77; and David L. Orvis, ' "Which is worthiest love" in *The Two Gentlemen of Verona?*', in Stanivukovic (ed.), *Queer Shakespeare*, pp. 33–49.

Chapter 2: The Third University

Anne Shakespeare is well served by Germaine Greer, *Shakespeare's Wife* (London, 2007). Lena Cowen Orlin, *The Private Life of William Shakespeare* (Oxford, 2021) reminds us about the contingent and ambiguous documentary record that undergirds our narratives about Shakespeare's family. Questions remain over Anne Shakespeare's date of birth and her lineage, for instance, for all that the balance of probability maintains received opinion that she was Anne Hathaway, daughter of Richard, and born in about 1556.

My sense of early modern London has been built from Peter Clark, *The English Alehouse: A Social History 1200–1830* (London, 1983); John L. McMullan, *The Canting Crew: London's Criminal Underworld 1550–1700* (New Brunswick, 1984); Vanessa Harding,

'The Population of London, 1550–1700: A Review of the Published Evidence', *London Journal* 15 (1990), pp. 111–28; and Paul Griffiths, *Lost Londons. Change, Crime and Control in the Capital City (1550–1660)* (Cambridge, 2008). Shakespeare's neighbourhoods of Shoreditch and Bishopsgate can be explored in James Bird and Philip Norman (eds), *London County Council Survey of London. Vol 8: The Parish of St Leonard, Shoreditch* (London, 1922); and Geoffrey Marsh, *Living with Shakespeare: Saint Helen's Parish, London, 1593–1598* (Edinburgh, 2021).

The queer implications of early modern bedsharing are unveiled by David L. Orvis in his excellent chapter '"Good sweet bedfellows" and same-sex marriages on the early modern stage', in 'Queer Subjectivities in Early Modern England', PhD dissertation (University of Arizona, 2008). Jeffrey Masten's work on bedsharing and co-authorship in *Textual Intercourse: Collaboration, Authorship, and Sexualities in Renaissance Drama* (Cambridge, 1997) lies behind my account of Beaumont and Fletcher. For more on the culture of bedsharing, bisected sleep and the night-time worlds in general, see A. Roger Ekirch, 'Sleep We Have Lost: Pre-Industrial Slumber in the British Isles', *American Historical Review* 106.2 (2001), pp. 343–86; and Sasha Handley, *Sleep in Early Modern England* (New Haven, 2016).

My understanding of male sex-work is built upon Jennifer Panek, '"This Base Stallion Trade": He-Whores and Male Sexuality on the Early Modern Stage', *English Literary Renaissance* 40.3 (2010), pp. 357–92; and Dimitris Savvidis, 'Male prostitution and the homoerotic sex-market in Early Modern England', PhD dissertation (University of Sussex, 2011). For more on Protestant England's horror of sodomy, I recommend H. G. Cocks, *Visions of Sodom: Religion, Homoerotic Desire and the End of the World in England, c.1550–1850* (Chicago, 2017).

The scholarship on St Paul's Walk and Churchyard is capacious and fascinating. I urge you to visit the marvel that is the 'Virtual

St Paul's Cathedral Project: A Digital Recreation of Worship and Preaching at St Paul's Cathedral in Early Modern London', https://vpcathedral.chass.ncsu.edu. While taking in the artful digital rendering of the medieval, pre-Christopher Wren cathedral, you should read Thomas Dekker's delightful satire, 'How a gallant should behave himself in Paul's Walks', in *The Gull's Horn-book* (1609) (ed. by E. D. Pendry, Cambridge, MA, 1968). For more on the significance of Paul's Walk, see Mary Bly, 'Carnal Geographies: Mocking and Mapping the Religious Body', in Roze Hentschell and Amanda Bailey (eds), *Masculinity and the Metropolis of Vice, 1550–1650* (New York, 2010), pp. 89–113. The standard work on London's book quarter is Peter W. M. Blayney, *The Bookshops in Paul's Cross Churchyard* (London, 1990). See also Benjamin King-Cox and Daniel Starza Smith, 'Buying and Selling Books Around St Paul's Cathedral: "Be Dishonest, and Tell Lies"', in Shanyn Altman and Jonathan Buckner (eds), *Old St Paul's and Culture* (Milton Keynes, 2021), pp. 269–92; and Adam G. Hooks, 'Shakespeare at the White Greyhound', *Shakespeare Survey* 64 (2011), pp. 260–75.

Shakespeare's engagement with the classics is a thriving field. I started with Colin Burrow, *Shakespeare and Classical Antiquity* (Oxford, 2013) and Jonathan Bate, *How the Classics Made Shakespeare* (Princeton, 2019), but much of my understanding of the queer literature of the Greco-Roman world is thanks to Bruce R. Smith, *Homosexual Desire in Shakespeare's England: A Cultural Poetics* (Chicago, 1991, 1994). I found the following very useful on the *Eclogues*: Robert Cummings, 'Abraham Fleming's Eclogues', *Translation and Literature* 19.2 (2010), pp. 147–69; Andrew Wallace, *Virgil's Schoolboys: The Poetics of Pedagogy in Renaissance England* (Oxford, 2010); and Erik Fredericksen, 'Finding another Alexis: pastoral tradition and the reception of Vergil's second eclogue', *Classical Receptions Journal* 7.3 (2015), pp. 422–41. Heaven only knows what early modern people thought of

Catullus: Julia Haig Glaisser, *Catullus and His Renaissance Readers* (Oxford, 1993) tries to explain. I consulted the English-language essays in Hugh Roberts, Guillaume Peureux and Lise Wajeman (eds), *Obscénités Renaissantes* (Geneva, 2011) for more prurient detail.

Talking of prurience, I enjoyed finding out more about Pietro Aretino from Celia R. Daileader, 'Back-Door Sex: Renaissance Gynosodomy, Aretino, and the Exotic', *ELH* 69.2 (2002), pp. 303–34; and Eric Langley, 'Postured like a whore? Misreading Hermione's statue', *Renaissance Studies* 27.3 (2013), pp. 318–40. The ten of Aretino's 'Lustful Sonnets' that fly the flag for anal sex are Sonnets 2, 3, 7, 8, 9, 10, 11, 13, 16 (and probably 12).

I based my reading of Sebastian and Antonio in *Twelfth Night* on Emma Smith's essay in *This Is Shakespeare*, pp. 177–92; as well as Joseph Pequigney, 'The Two Antonios and Same-Sex Love in *Twelfth Night* and *The Merchant of Venice*', *English Literary Renaissance* 22.2 (1992), pp. 201–221.

Chapter 3: Galatea's Children

The (now ageing) standard work on Paul's Playhouse is Reavley Gair, *The Children of Paul's: The Story of a Theatre Company, 1553–1608* (Cambridge, 1982). I augmented it with useful additions from Herbert Berry, 'Where Was the Playhouse in which the Boy Choristers of St Paul's Cathedral Performed Plays?', *Medieval and Renaissance Drama in England* 13 (2001), pp. 101–16; José A. Pérez Díez, 'The "Playhouse" at St Paul's: What We Know of the Theatre in the Almonry', in Altman and Buckner (eds), *Old St Paul's and Culture*, pp. 197–220; and Roze Hentschell, *St Paul's Cathedral Precinct in Early Modern Literature and Culture: Spatial Practices* (Oxford, 2020).

For more on Paul's and the other children's companies of early modern London, see Mary Bly, *Queer Virgins and Virgin Queans on the Early Modern Stage* (Oxford, 2000); Lucy Munro, *Children of the Queen's Revels: A Jacobean Theatre Repertory* (Cambridge, 2005); Edel Lamb, *Performing Childhood in the Early Modern Theatre: The Children's Playing Companies (1599–1613)* (Basingstoke, 2009); and Jeanne H. McCarthy, *The Children's Troupes and the Transformation of English Theater 1509–1608: Pedagogue Playwrights, Playbooks, and Play-boys* (Abingdon, 2017). I found David Kathman, 'How Old Were Shakespeare's Boy Actors?', *Shakespeare Survey* 58 (2005), pp. 220–46; Evelyn Tribble, 'Marlowe's Boy Actors', *Shakespeare Bulletin* 27.1 (2009), pp. 5–17; and Harry R. McCarthy, *Boy Actors in Early Modern England: Skill and Stagecraft in the Theatre* (Cambridge, 2022) invaluable in recreating the professional lives of these child and adolescent performers.

For the relationship between the Corporation of London and the burgeoning theatre industry, see Andrew Gurr, *The Shakespearean Stage, 1574–1642* (Cambridge, 1970, 2009). On courtly performances, see John C. Astington, *English Court Theatre 1558–1642* (Cambridge, 1999).

John Lyly deserves a good new biography. For now, make do with G. K. Hunter, *John Lyly: The Humanist as Courtier* (Cambridge, MA, 1962); and the very useful biographical and critical context in Andy Kesson, *John Lyly and Early Modern Authorship* (Manchester, 2014).

Scholarship on the dramatic purpose and erotic effect of early modern boy actors is legion. I started with Peter Stallybrass, 'Transvestism and the "Body Beneath": Speculating on the Boy Actor', in Susan Zimmerman (ed.), *Erotic Politics: Desire on the Renaissance Stage* (London, 1992), pp. 64–83; and Michael Shapiro, *Gender in Play on the Shakespearean Stage: Boy Heroines and Female Pages* (Ann Arbor, 1996). Nothing dates more quickly than gender studies, though, as Roberta Barker explains: "'Not One Thing Exactly": Gender, Performance and Critical Debates over the Early Modern Boy-Actress', *Literature Compass* 6.2 (2009), pp. 460–81.

Recent excellent work has been done by David L. Orvis, 'Cross-Dressing, Queerness, and the Early Modern Stage', in E. L. Maccallum and Mikko Tuhkanen (eds.), *The Cambridge History of Gay and Lesbian Literature* (Cambridge, 2014), pp. 197–217; Simone Chess, 'Or whatever you be: Crossdressing, Sex, and Gender Labor in John Lyly's *Gallathea*', *Renaissance and Reformation* 38.4 (2015), pp. 145–66; as well as her 'Queer Residue: Boy Actors' Adult Careers in Early Modern England', *Journal for Early Modern Cultural Studies* 19.4 (2019), pp. 242–64. You'd be well-advised to read Jeffrey Masten's *Queer Philologies: Sex, Language, and Affect in Shakespeare's Time* (Philadelphia, 2016), particularly 'Lexicon 2: Boy-Desire'; and Ezra Horbury's 'Transgender Reassessments of the Cross-Dressed Page in Shakespeare, *Philaster*, and *The Honest Man's Fortune*', *Shakespeare Quarterly* 73. 1–2 (2022), pp. 100–20. I also consulted Michael Witmore, *Pretty Creatures: Children and Fiction in the English Renaissance* (Ithaca, 2007); and Scott A. Trudell, *Unwritten Poetry: Song, Performance, and Media in Early Modern England* (Oxford, 2019) – I recommend his chapter 'Child Singers' Mediated Bodies', pp. 79–111. For detail about the cosmetics that transformed boys into stage heroines, I relied on Farah Karim-Cooper, *Cosmetics in Shakespearean and Renaissance Drama* (Edinburgh, 2006, 2019).

An excellent account of the life and notoriety of Moll Frith is to be found in Kit Heyam, *Before We Were Trans: A New History of Gender* (London, 2022). The Thomas Clifton case is explored in James H. Forse, 'Extortion in the name of art in Elizabethan England: The impressment of Thomas Clifton for the Queen's Chapel Boys', *Theatre Survey 31* (1990), pp. 165–76; and Lucy Munro, 'Living by Others' Pleasure: Marston, *The Dutch Courtesan*, and Theatrical Profit', *Early Theatre* 23.1 (2020), pp. 109–26.

My understanding of *As You Like It* was transformed by Mario DiGangi, 'Queering the Shakespearean Family', *Shakespeare Quarterly* 47.3 (1996), pp. 269–90.

Chapter 4: Kings And Minions

Biographies of Christopher Marlowe stretch from the sexless to the salacious: exemplifying the former is Constance Brown Kuriyama, *Christopher Marlowe: A Renaissance Life* (Ithaca, 2002); for an example of the latter, try Charles Nicholl, *The Reckoning: The Murder of Christopher Marlowe* (London, 1992, 2002), although Nicholl's salaciousness lies in his dramatising attitude to the archive rather than any interest in Marlowe's queerness. Biographical debunking of Marlowe's wild life has been performed by Stephen Orgel, 'Tobacco and Boys: How Queer Was Marlowe?', *GLQ: A Journal of Lesbian and Gay Studies* 6.4 (2000), pp. 555–76; and Lukas Erne, 'Biography, Mythography, and Criticism: The Life and Works of Christopher Marlowe', *Modern Philology* 103.1 (2005), pp. 28–50. I also consulted A. L. Rowse, *Christopher Marlowe: A Biography* (London, 1964, 1981); and James Shapiro, *Rival Playwrights: Marlowe, Jonson, Shakespeare* (New York, 1991).

For establishing the chronology of Marlowe's plays, I relied on Martin Wiggins, 'Marlowe's chronology and canon', in Emily C. Bartels and Emma Smith (eds), *Christopher Marlowe in Context* (Cambridge, 2013), pp. 7–14.

On the work of Pembroke's Men, see G. M. Pinciss, 'Shakespeare, Her Majesty's Players and Pembroke's Men', *Shakespeare Survey* 27 (1974), pp. 129–36; David George, 'Shakespeare and Pembroke's Men', *Shakespeare Quarterly* 32.3 (1981), pp. 305–23; and Roslyn L. Knutson, 'Pembroke's Men in 1592–3, Their Repertory and Touring Schedule', *Early Theatre* 4 (2001), pp. 129–38.

Marlowe's traceable influence on Shakespeare is charted by Robert A. Logan, *Shakespeare's Marlowe: The Influence of Christopher Marlowe on Shakespeare's Artistry* (Ashgate, 2007; London, 2016).

My account of King James's affair with Aubigny is based on Alan Stewart, *The Cradle King: A Life of James VI and I* (London,

2003). I also made use of John Guy, *Queen of Scots: The True Life of Mary Stuart* (Boston, 2004); and Paulina Kewes, 'Marlowe, history, and politics', in Bartels and Smith (eds), *Christopher Marlowe in Context*, pp. 138–54. For more on James's 'Phoenix' and his other poetic writings, see Sebastian Verweij, '"Booke, go thy ways": The Publication, Reading and Reception of James VI/I's Early Poetic Works', *Huntington Library Quarterly* 77.2 (2014), pp. 111–31.

The dangerously messy world of France's Henri III is revealed in Andrew M. Kirk, *The Mirror of Confusion: The Representation of French History in English Renaissance Drama* (New York, 1996); Katherine B. Crawford, 'Love, Sodomy, and Scandal: Controlling the Sexual Reputation of Henry III', *Journal of the History of Sexuality* 12 (2003), pp. 513–42; Gary Ferguson, *Queer Re(Readings) in the French Renaissance: Homosexuality, Gender, Culture* (Aldershot, 2008); Jeffrey Rufo, 'Marlowe's Minions: Sodomitical Politics in *Edward II* and *The Massacre at Paris*', in *Marlowe Studies: An Annual* 1 (2011), pp. 5–23; Una McIlvenna, *Scandal and Reputation at the Court of Catherine de Medici* (London, 2016); and Alan Stewart, 'Edouard et Gaverston: New Ways of Looking at an English History Play', in Kirk Melnikoff (ed.), *Edward II: A Critical Reader* (London, 2017), pp. 97–117.

My reading of *Edward II* owes a great deal to Christopher Shirley, 'Sodomy and Stage Directions in Christopher Marlowe's *Edward(s) II*', *Studies in English Literature 1500–1900* 54.2 (2014), pp. 279–96. For more on *Dido Queen of Carthage*, see Jackson I. Cope, 'Marlowe's *Dido* and the Titillating Children', *English Literary Renaissance* 4.3 (1974), pp. 315–25; and Ruth Lunney, '*Dido, Queen of Carthage*', in Sara Munson Deats and Robert A. Logan (eds), *Christopher Marlowe at 450* (Farnham, 2015), pp. 13–49. I recommend Julia Briggs, 'Marlowe's *Massacre at Paris*: A Reconsideration', *The Review of English Studies* 34.135 (1983), pp. 257–78 for a defence of the merits of Marlowe's likely final play.

Chapter 5: Toys for the Inns of Court Boys

For my description of the plague-struck city, I plundered Thomas Nashe's vivid accounts in *The Unfortunate Traveller* (1594) and *Have With You to Saffron Waldon* (1596), both printed in Ronald B. McKerrow (ed.), *The Works of Thomas Nashe*, 3 vols (Oxford, 1958). The standard work on the pestilence in Shakespeare's time is Paul Slack, *The Impact of Plague in Tudor and Stuart England* (Oxford, 1985). Although it recounts a different outbreak, I found Keith Wrightson, *Ralph Tailor's Summer: A Scrivener, his City and the Plague* (New Haven, 2011) an unforgettable read.

On the topic of reading: my understanding of the literary marketplace in early modern England was shaped by the essays in Andy Kesson and Emma Smith (eds), *The Elizabethan Top Ten: Defining Print Popularity in Early Modern England* (London, 2013), in particular Alan B. Farmer and Zachary Lesser, 'What Is Print Popularity? A Map of the Elizabethan Book Trade', pp. 19–54.

For more on the epyllion, see Clark Hulse, *Metamorphic Verse: The Elizabethan Minor Epic* (Princeton, 1981); Jonathan Bate, 'Sexual Perversity in *Venus and Adonis*', *The Yearbook in English Studies* 23 (1993), pp. 80–92; William Weaver, *Untutored Lines: The Making of the English Epyllion* (Edinburgh, 2012); and Sophie Chiari's 'General Introduction' in her *Renaissance Tales of Desire* (Newcastle-upon-Tyne, 2012). Stephen Guy-Bray, *Shakespeare and Queer Representation* (Abingdon, 2021) advanced my thinking about *Venus and Adonis* considerably.

Two recent essays have shown how much more there is to say about Ovidian stories of sexuality and seduction: Hilary Ball, ' "A Fair Boy, Certain, but a Fool to Love Himself": Queer Reflections of the Myth of Narcissus in Shakespeare and Fletcher's *The Two Noble Kinsmen*', *Shakespeare* 16.1 (2020), pp. 1–13; and Abdulhamit Arvas, 'Leander in the Ottoman Mediterranean: The Homoerotics of Abduction in the Global Renaissance', *English Literary Renaissance*

51.1 (2020), pp. 31–62. Both have influenced the way I read Shakespeare's *Venus and Adonis*. The essays in John Garrison and Goran Stanivukovic (eds), *Ovid and Masculinity in English Renaissance Literature* (Montreal, 2021) also look set to revivify the topic.

I took much of my visual portrait of the Inns of Court from Francis Cowper, *A Prospect of Gray's Inn* (London, 1951, 1985). Details about the culture of the societies are to be found in Philip J. Finkelpearl, *John Marston of the Middle Temple: An Elizabethan Dramatist in His Social Setting* (Cambridge, MA, 1969); Wilfrid R. Prest, *The Inns of Court under Elizabeth I and the Early Stuarts, 1590–1640* (London, 1972); and the many excellent essays in Jayne Elisabeth Archer, Elizabeth Goldring and Sarah Knight (eds), *The Intellectual and Cultural World of the Early Modern Inns of Court* (Manchester, 2011).

See Arthur F. Marotti, *Manuscript, Print, and the English Renaissance Lyric* (Ithaca, 1995) for a thorough study of manuscript circulation within the Inns. The liveliest recent account of John Donne's cultural milieu is Katherine Rundell, *Super-Infinite: The Transformations of John Donne* (London, 2022). The Innsmen's obsession with penis jokes is well demonstrated in Robert Parker Sorlien (ed.), *The Diary of John Manningham of the Middle Temple 1602–1603* (Hanover, NH, 1976).

Henry Wriothesley, third Earl of Southampton, is crying out for a good new biography. The current standard work is G. P. V. Akrigg, *Shakespeare and the Earl of Southampton* (London, 1968). I also made use of Margot Heinemann, 'Rebel Lords, Popular Playwrights, and Political Culture: Notes on the Jacobean Patronage of the Earl of Southampton', *The Yearbook of English Studies* 21 (1991), pp. 63–86; and Lara M. Crowley, 'Was Southampton a Poet? A Verse Letter to Queen Elizabeth', *English Literary Renaissance* 41.1 (2011), pp. 111–45.

For my conversion of early modern sums of money, I used The National Archives Currency Converter, https://www.nationalarchives.gov.uk/currency-converter/. Robert Bearman,

Shakespeare's Money: How much did he make and what did this mean? (Oxford, 2016) is a useful book to have to hand.

On the Essex circle, I relied on Paul E. J. Hammer, *The Polarisation of Elizabethan Politics: The Political Career of Robert Devereux, 2nd Earl of Essex, 1585–1597* (Cambridge, 1999); Alan Stewart, 'Instigating Treason: The Life and Death of Henry Cuffe, Secretary', in Erica Sheen and Lorna Hutson (eds), *Literature, Politics and Law in Renaissance England* (Basingstoke, 2005), pp. 50–70; and Alexandra Gajda, *The Earl of Essex and Late Elizabethan Political Culture* (Oxford, 2012).

Chapter 6: The Queerest Year

The performance of *The Comedy of Errors* during a chaotic entertainment at Gray's Inn is entertainingly relayed by the anonymous author of *Gesta Grayorum, or the History of the High and Mighty Prince Henry of Purpoole Anno Domini 1594*, ed. by Desmond Bland (Liverpool, 1968).

Much of the scholarship on *Shakespeare's Sonnets* divides into three camps: historicist studies of the genre that place his poems in conversation with the Elizabethan sonnet craze; formalist analyses of the sonnets; and slightly kooky biographical approaches that seek the real-life inspirations for the 'fair youth' and 'dark lady'. Among the examples of the first on which I relied was Sasha Roberts, 'Shakespeare's Sonnets and English Sonnet Sequences', in Patrick Cheney, Andrew Hadfield and Garrett A. Sullivan (eds), *Early Modern English Poetry: A Critical Companion* (New York, 2007), pp. 172–83. You can't hope for a better formalist literary critical reading of the sonnets than Helen Vendler, *The Art of Shakespeare's Sonnets* (Cambridge, MA, 1997) – how can one resist a scholar who 'found it necessary to learn the Sonnets by heart' (p. 11) in order to produce her commentaries? I'd love to hear her recite them.

Biographical studies of the sonnets were more common in past generations than now. See Frank Harris, *The Man Shakespeare and his Tragic Life Story* (London, 1909) for an argument in favour of Mary Fritton as the woman behind the 'dark lady'; and A. L. Rowse (ed.), *The Poems of Shakespeare's Dark Lady* (London, 1978), his edition of Emilia Lanier's *Salve Deus Rex Judaeorum* (1611). A more recent, and much more subtle, attempt to link the 'dark lady' to a Clerkenwell brothel-owner known as 'Lucy Negro' or 'Black Luce' is Duncan Salkeld, *Shakespeare Among the Courtesans: Prostitution, Literature, and Drama, 1500–1600* (Farnham, 2012). Salkeld's work has inspired a collection of verse by Caroline Randall Williams, *Lucy Negro, Redux: The Bard, a Book, and a Ballet* (Nashville, 2019).

Cheerleaders for Southampton as the 'fair youth' are also more thin on the ground now than they used to be (although alive in authorship-conspiracist circles); for the older establishment view, see J. A. Fort, 'Thorpe's Text of *Shakespeare's Sonnets*', *The Review of English Studies* 2.8 (1926), pp. 439–45. A more popular candidate these days is William Herbert: see Brian O'Farrell, *Shakespeare's Patron William Herbert Third Earl of Pembroke 1580–1630: Politics, Patronage and Power* (London, 2011). Oscar Wilde's 'The Portrait of Mr W. H.', originally printed in *Blackwood's Edinburgh Magazine* in July 1889, is widely available: *The Complete Works of Oscar Wilde* (London, 1966), pp. 1150–201. For the argument that the dedication to *Shakespeare's Sonnets* has been misread and 'Mr W. H.' simply refers to the author, 'Master W. Sh.', see Donald Foster, 'Master W. H., R.I.P.', *PMLA* 102 (1987), pp. 42–54; and Lynne Magnusson, 'Thomas Thorpe's Shakespeare: "The Only Begetter"', in Hannah Crawforth, Elizabeth Scott-Baumann and Clare Whitehead (eds), *The Sonnets: The State of Play* (London, 2017), pp. 33–54.

I have learned a good deal from studies of the sonnets that consider their queerness, and their engagement with racial politics. Joseph Pequigney, *Such Is My Love: A Study of Shakespeare's Sonnets* (Chicago, 1985) was a landmark work, the first to take the queer narrative(s) in the sonnets seriously. James Schiffer (ed.), *Shakespeare's Sonnets: Critical Essays* (New York, 2000) brings together some important articles, including Margreta de Grazia's ground-breaking essay 'The Scandal of *Shakespeare's Sonnets*', originally published in *Shakespeare Survey* 46 (1993), as well as Bruce R. Smith's, 'I, You, He, She, and We: On the Sexual Politics of *Shakespeare's Sonnets*'. My thinking was helped by William Nelles, 'Sexing *Shakespeare's Sonnets*: Reading Beyond Sonnet 20', *ELR* 39.1 (2009), pp. 128–40; and Robert Matz, 'The Scandals of *Shakespeare's Sonnets*', *ELH* 77.2 (2010), pp. 477–508. Any complacency about the dating of the sonnets is helpfully challenged by Paul Edmondson and Stanley Wells (eds), *All the Sonnets of Shakespeare* (Cambridge, 2020).

My understanding of the racial (and racist) characterisations in the sonnets was shaped by Kim F. Hall, *Things of Darkness: Economies of Race and Gender in Early Modern England* (Ithaca, 1995), in particular her second chapter, 'Fair Texts/Dark Ladies: Renaissance Lyric and the Poetics of Color', pp. 62–122; Marvin Hunt, ' "Be Dark, but Not Too Dark": Shakespeare's Dark Lady as a Sign of Color', in Schiffer (ed.), *Shakespeare's Sonnets*, pp. 369–90; and Imtiaz Habib, ' "Two Loves I Have of Comfort and Despair": The Circle of Whiteness in the *Sonnets*', in Arthur L. Little, Jr. (ed.), *White People in Shakespeare: Essays on Race, Culture and the Elite* (London, 2023), pp. 29–43. The best accessible account of early modern racialising language is Farah Karim-Cooper, *The Great White Bard: Shakespeare, Race and the Future* (London, 2023).

There's not a lot of scholarship on Richard Barnfield, but what there is has been of extraordinary value to this book. Barnfield's biography was sensationally rewritten by Andrew Worrall following intrepid archival sleuthing: his 'Biographical Introduction:

Barnfield's Feast of "all Varietie"', in Kenneth Borris and George Klawitter (eds), *The Affectionate Shepherd: Celebrating Richard Barnfield* (Selinsgrove, 2001), pp. 25–40, is a treasure trove and I've depended on it. All the essays in Borris and Klawitter's collection are estimable and do a great deal to recover the significance of this neglected poet.

My readings of Barnfield's poems have also been aided by Scott Giantvalley, 'Barnfield, Drayton, and Marlowe: Homoeroticism and Homosexuality in Elizabethan Literature', *Pacific Coast Philology* 16 (1981), pp. 9–24; A. Leigh DeNeef, 'The Poetics of Orpheus: The Text and a Study of *Orpheus His Journey to Hell* (1595)', *Studies in Philology* (1992), pp. 20–70; Clinton E. Hammock, 'Hope, Despair and the Voicing of Renaissance Homoeroticism in Richard Barnfield's "Certaine Sonnets"', *Cahiers Élisabéthains* 79 (2011), pp. 11–18; and Andrew Hadfield, 'Richard Barnfield, John Weever, William Basse and Other Encomiasts', in Paul Edmondson and Stanley Wells (eds.), *The Shakespeare Circle: An Alternate Biography* (Cambridge, 2015), pp. 199–212.

The only full-length critical study of Barnfield's poetry is Harry Morris, *Richard Barnfield: Colin's Child* (Tampa, FL, 1963), which signally fails to engage with the central homoerotic themes in his work. Leo Daugherty, *William Shakespeare, Richard Barnfield, and the Sixth Earl of Derby* (Amherst, NY, 2010) puts over an eccentric reading of Barnfield's oeuvre that uses his 'Affectionate Shepherd' to argue that William Stanley, Earl of Derby, is Shakespeare's 'fair youth'.

I can't fail at this point to mention one of my most loved possessions, a limited-edition volume of *Richard Barnfield's Sonnets* exquisitely illustrated by Clive Hicks-Jenkins and printed by Nicolas McDowall (Llandogo, 2001). This breathtaking volume almost makes up for the continuing lack of scholarly attention paid to his poetry.

Chapter 7: Private Friends

For a slightly more serious-minded take on manuscript circulation than the one I hint at in my opening vignette, see Noah Millstone, *Manuscript Circulation and the Invention of Politics in Early Stuart England* (Cambridge, 2016); and Arthur F. Marotti, *The Circulation of Poetry in Manuscript in Early Modern England* (Abingdon, 2021). I learned a great deal from Rebecca Yearling, 'Homoerotic Desire and Renaissance Lyric Verse', *Studies in English Literature, 1500–1900* 53.1 (2013), pp. 53–71. My unnamed writer and his lover are in the act of copying out Barnfield's Sonnet 8, by the way.

My analysis of the influence on Shakespeare by Barnfield is drawn from Paul Hammond, *Figuring Sex Between Men from Shakespeare to Rochester* (Oxford, 2002), especially his second chapter, 'Shakespearian Figures', pp. 62–116. I also made use of Charles Crawford, 'Richard Barnfield, Marlowe, and Shakespeare', in his *Collectanea* (Stratford-upon-Avon, 1906), pp. 1–16.

My understanding of Barnfield – and my approach to this book – was transformed by Sam See, 'Richard Barnfield and the Limits of Homoerotic Literary History', *GLQ: A Journal of Lesbian and Gay Studies* 13.1 (2006), pp. 63–91. I've presented See's reading of Barnfield's 'non-apology' in the preface to *Cynthia, with Certain Sonnets*. The world lost an exceptional Barnfield scholar when See died, at a tragically young age, in 2013.

To understand the actions undertaken by Richard Barnfield Senior, I consulted W. J. Jones, *The Elizabethan Court of Chancery* (Oxford, 1967); Edith G. Henderson, 'Legal Rights to Land in the Early Chancery', *The American Journal of Legal History* 26.2 (1982), pp. 97–122; Susan T. Moore, *Family Feuds: An Introduction to Chancery Proceedings* (The Federation of Family History Societies, 2003); and John Baker, *The Oxford History of the Laws of England: Vol VI 1483–1558* (Oxford, 2003). The details of the poet's disinheritance are to be found in Simon R. Neal and Christine

Leighton (eds), *Calendar of Patent Rolls 39 Elizabeth I* (List and Index Society, 2008), Part VIII: C 66/1465, item 515; and *Calendar of Patent Rolls 44 Elizabeth I* (List and Index Society, 2013), Part XX: C66/1589, item 984.

Epilogue: His Verse in Time to Come

On the Bishops' Ban and the bonfire of June 1599, see Richard McCabe, 'Satire and the Bishops' Ban of 1599', *The Yearbook of English Studies* 11 (1981), pp. 188–93; and Adam Hansen, 'Writing, London, and the Bishops' Ban of 1599', *The London Journal* 43.2 (2018), pp. 102–19.

On the activities of Scotland's James VI once he became James I of England, I returned to the ever-essential Alan Stewart, *The Cradle King*, as well as the invigorating chapter on the monarch in Ben Miller and Huw Lemmy, *Bad Gays: A Homosexual History* (London, 2022). The standard work on James's relationships with his male favourites is David M. Bergeron, *King James and Letters of Homoerotic Desire* (Iowa City, 1999).

Notes

A word on spelling, punctuation and dating.

As Shakespeare is always read in modernised spelling editions, I've taken the liberty of updating the spelling and punctuation for all the early modern material I cite (unpredictable sixteenth-century orthography is an absolute joy, but if we don't recognise *A Midsommer Nights Dreame* then we don't deserve *The Dvtchesse of Malfy*).

I date plays by Shakespeare and his contemporaries according to their composition or first performance (estimated if necessary), rather than first printing.

All references to Shakespeare's plays and poems are taken from the second edition of *The Riverside Shakespeare*, ed. by G. Blakemore Evans and J. J. M. Tobin (Boston, 1997), although I haven't always adhered to the Riverside punctuation.

I include in-text act, scene and line references for plays, and line references for poems, whenever I cite Shakespeare, as well as the following writers whose work is available in modern editions:

Ben Jonson, *Poetaster*, ed. by Henry S. Turner, in Jeremy Lopez (ed.), *The Routledge Anthology of Early Modern Drama* (Abingdon, 2020); and *Volpone*, ed. by Brian Parker and David Bevington (Manchester, 1999)

John Lyly, *Galatea*, ed. by George K. Hunter and David Bevington (Manchester, 2000)

Christopher Marlowe, *Dido Queen of Carthage, Doctor Faustus,*

Edward II, The Jew of Malta, Tamburlaine the Great Parts 1 and
2 and *Hero and Leander* in *The Complete Works of Christopher
Marlowe*, ed. by Fredson Bowers, 2 vols (Cambridge, 1973)
Thomas Peend, *Hermaphroditus and Salmacis*, in Sophie Chiari
(ed.), *Renaissance Tales of Desire* (Newcastle-upon-Tyne, 2012)
John Webster, *The Duchess of Malfi*, ed. by Leah S. Marcus
(London, 2009)

Richard Barnfield is – as ever – a special case. His work remains
bewilderingly hard to find. A good critical edition (*Richard
Barnfield: The Complete Poems*, ed. by George Klawitter, Selinsgrove,
PA, 1990) is now out of print, but it is possible to obtain a print-
on-demand collection (without glosses or notes but with a short
introduction), from which I have taken the lineation for all my
references: *Poems of Richard Barnfield*, ed. by George Klawitter
(New York, 2005).

I cite a good deal of prefatory matter from Shakespeare's and
Barnfield's poetry (dedications, epistles and so forth). These
come in the foregoing pages without line or page references, but
are to be found in the editions mentioned above.

1   **minds / Admit impediments**: 'Sonnet 116 personalised wool throw'
     is available for £90 from www.etsy.com (accessed 17 November 2023).
1   **together in matrimony**: 'The form of the solemnization of matri-
     mony', *The Book of Common Prayer* (1559), consulted at www.justus.
     anglican.org (accessed 17 November 2023).
2   **turning in his grave**: Richard Spillett, ' "Shakespeare would be turn-
     ing in his grave!"': Outrage after BBC's PC adaptation of a *Midsummer
     Night's Dream* airs – including gay trysts AND a lesbian kiss', *Mail
     Online*, 31 May 2016 (https://www.dailymail.co.uk/news/arti-
     cle-3618284/Outrage-BBC-s-PC-adaptation-Midsummer-Night-s-
     Dream-airs.html, accessed 23 October 2023).
3   **own sexual preferences**: uncatalogued correspondence of Michelle
     Terry, to be archived in Shakespeare's Globe's Research and Collections
     Centre at the end of her tenure as artistic director.

3   **don't say gay**: Martin Pengelly, 'Florida schools plan to use only excerpts from Shakespeare to avoid "raunchiness"', *Guardian*, 8 August 2023 (https://www.theguardian.com/us-news/2023/aug/08/florida-schools-shakespeare-sexual-material, accessed 23 October 2023).

6   **sweet love**: John Benson (ed.), *Poems, written by Wil. Shakespeare, Gent* (London, 1640), sig. F6v.

6   **praise of his mistress**: Bernard Lintott (ed.), *A Collection of Poems in Two Volumes, Being all the Miscellanies of Mr William Shakespeare* (London, 1711), title page.

6   **heart's heart chaste**: Coleridge, *Marginalia* (2 November 1803), cited in Graham Robb, *Strangers: Homosexual Love in the Nineteenth Century* (New York, 2003), p. 112.

6   **any unworthy alloy**: Shelley, 'Discourse on the Manners of the Ancient Greeks Relative to the Subject of Love' (1818), cited in ibid., p. 113.

6   **had never written [them]**: cited in Robert Matz, 'The Scandals of Shakespeare's Sonnets', *ELH* 77.2 (2010), pp. 477–508, p. 490.

7   **put upon Shakespeare**: cited in Lawrence Danson, 'Oscar Wilde, W. H., and the Unspoken Name of Love', *ELH* 58.4 (1991), pp. 979–1000, p. 979.

8   **Socrates, Michelangelo and Shakespeare**: cited in Gregory Woods, *Homintern: How Gay Culture Liberated the Modern World* (New Haven, 2016), p. 141.

8   **their own peculiarity**: Hesketh Pearson, *A Life of Shakespeare: With an Anthology of Shakespeare's Poetry* (1949), pp. 37–38.

8   **of the Homintern; just yet**: cited in Joseph Pequigney, *Such Is My Love: A Study of Shakespeare's Sonnets* (Chicago, 1985), pp. 79–80.

8   **than normally heterosexual**: A. L. Rowse, *Homosexuals in History: A Study of Ambivalence in Society, Literature and the Arts* (London, 1977), p. 46 (and pp. 29, 104–5, 165 and 211).

8   **homosexual idealism**: G. Wilson Knight, *The Mutual Flame: On Shakespeare's Sonnets and 'The Phoenix and the Turtle'* (London, 1955), pp. 24–25.

9   **frankly lustful**: Hallett Smith, 'Sonnets', in *The Riverside Shakespeare*, p. 1840.

9   **hint of homosexual passion**: Peter Ackroyd, *Shakespeare: The Biography* (London, 2005), p. 293.

10   **sodomitess**: cited in Alan Bray, *Homosexuality in Renaissance England* (London, 1982; New York, 1992), p. 14.

10   **homosocial; ideological homosexuality**: Eve Kosofsky Sedgwick, *Between Men: English Literature and Male Homosocial Desire* (New York, 1985), p. 25.

10 **'bro' culture**: Jane Ward, *Not Gay: Sex Between Straight White Men* (New York, 2015), p. 4.

11 **suffused**: the term is used in a literary context by both Alan Bray, 'Homosexuality and the Signs of Male Friendship in Elizabethan England', *History Workshop Journal* 29 (1990), pp. 1–19, p. 5; and Jenny C. Mann, *The Trials of Orpheus: Poetry, Science, and the Early Modern Sublime* (Princeton, 2021), p. 131.

12 **of *course* he was**: Don Paterson, *Reading Shakespeare's Sonnets* (London, 2010), p. xiii.

21 **by reason or force**: Thomas Smith, *De republica anglorum* (1583), cited in Elizabeth A. Foyster, *Manhood in Early Modern England: Honour, Sex and Marriage* (London, 1999), p. 29.

23 **second degree of age**: Anon., *The Office of Christian Parents* (Cambridge, 1616), sig. L1r.

25 **all [their] betters**: 'The Order of Confirmation', *The Book of Common Prayer* (1559), consulted at www.justus.anglican.org (accessed 17 November 2023), and cited in Lois Potter, *The Life of William Shakespeare: A Critical Biography* (Malden, MA, 2012), p. 18.

25 **their own house**: *Office of Christian Parents*, sig. O4v.

26 **and less Greek**: Ben Jonson, 'To the memory of my beloved, the author Master William Shakespeare, and what he has left us', in *Master William Shakespeare's Comedies, Histories, & Tragedies* (London, 1623), sig. πA4r.

27 **principles of grammar**: cited in Levi Fox, *The Early History of King Edward VI School Stratford-upon-Avon*, Dugdale Society Occasional Papers 29 (Oxford, 1984), p. 9.

28 **of things learned**: cited in Kenneth Charlton, *Education in Renaissance England* (London, 1965), p. 110.

28 **for them both**: cited in J. Howard Brown, *Elizabethan Schooldays: An Account of the English Grammar Schools in the Second Half of the Sixteenth Century* (Oxford, 1933), p. 70.

31 **other human concerns; divine and human; humanity than friendship; another self**: Marcus Tullius Cicero, *How To Be A Friend: An Ancient Guide to True Friendship*, trans. Philip Freeman (Princeton, 2018), pp. 35, 39, 41 and 139.

32 **established and confirmed; both men can't have**: ibid., pp. 129 and 67.

34 **faithful friends**: the title of an anonymous play addressing this topic, written in 1614 and surviving in manuscript: G. M. Pinciss (ed.), *The Faithful Friends*, Malone Society (Oxford, 1970).

34 **confederated**: Thomas Elyot, *The Book Named the Governor* (1531) (ed. by S. E. Lehmberg, London, 1962), p. 136.

38 **in pieces drag**: Ovid, *Metamorphoses*, trans. Arthur Golding (1565–67) (ed. by Madeleine Forey, London, 2002), p. 102.

38–39 **of the gods; white as milk; wholesome examples**: ibid, pp. 179, 52 and 3.

39 **once Will Shakespeare's**: cited in Jonathan Bate, *Shakespeare and Ovid* (Oxford, 1993), p. 28.

40 **man and lad; trim young men; fresh and fair**: Ovid, *Metamorphoses*, pp. 105 and 106.

41 **pleasure for to take**: ibid, p. 297.

41 **sometime man; man no more; double-shaped**: ibid., pp. 130, 131 and 135.

41 **upon a cow**: ibid, p. 291.

43 **reign of terror**: 'The Grammar Schools of England and Wales,' *The Church of England Quarterly Review* 9 (1840), p. 159.

44 **good while after**: cited in Alan Stewart, *Close Readers: Humanism and Sodomy in Early Modern England* (Princeton, 1997), p. 97.

44 **are not agreed**: cited in Lynn Enterline, *Shakespeare's Schoolroom: Rhetoric, Discipline, Emotion* (Philadelphia, 2012), p. 49.

44 **to boys' buttocks**: Thomas Nashe, *Summer's Last Will and Testament*, in Stanley Wells (ed.), *Thomas Nashe* (London, 1964), p. 127.

45 **presented by children; juice**: John Marston, *What You Will*, 2.2.86–87, 68 (I am grateful to Janet Clare for letting me see the lineation in her edition of the play, which will appear in the forthcoming Oxford *Complete Works of John Marston*).

45 **secret parts**: cited in Alan Stewart, 'Boys' buttocks revisited: James VI and the myth of the sovereign schoolmaster', in Tom Betteridge (ed.), *Sodomy in Early Modern Europe* (Manchester, 2002), pp. 131–47, p. 131.

51 **third university**: George Buc, *The Third University of England* (London, 1631); William Harrison refers to the Inns of Court and Chancery as 'the third [university] in London' in his *The Description of England* (1577) (ed. by Georges Edelen, Washington, D.C., 1968, 1994), p. 65.

54 **serviture**: mentioned in a letter by John Dowdall in 1693, cited in Bart van Es, '"Johannes fac Totum"? Shakespeare's First Contact with the Acting Companies', *Shakespeare Quarterly* 61.4 (2010), pp. 551–77, p. 559.

55 **miserably wrecked**: Joseph Hale, *Quo Vadis?* (London, 1617), sig. B3r.

55   **with our feathers**: [Robert Greene?], *Greene's Groats-Worth of Wit, Bought with a Million of Repentance* (London, 1592), sig. F1v.

56   **was in pain**: cited in Christopher Matusiak, 'Was Shakespeare "not a company keeper"? William Beeston and MS Aubrey 8, fol. 45v', *Shakespeare Quarterly* 68.4 (2017), pp. 351–73, p. 354.

57   **between them**: John Aubrey, *Aubrey's Brief Lives* (ed. by Oliver Lawson Dick, London, 1949, 2016), p. 21.

58   **without a mother**: John Berkenhead, 'On the happy collection of Mr Fletcher's works, never before printed', cited in Jeffrey Masten, *Textual Intercourse: Collaboration, Authorship, and Sexualities in Renaissance Drama* (Cambridge, 1997), p. 136.

58   **second best bed**: cited in Germaine Greer, *Shakespeare's Wife* (London, 2007), p. 316.

60   **with one another**: cited in Sasha Handley, *Sleep in Early Modern England* (New Haven, 2016), p. 176.

61   **cheeks are glazed**: John Marston, 'Satire 3', in *The Metamorphosis of Pygmalion's Image, and Certain Satires* (London, 1598), sig. D7v.

62   **sin against nature**: John Florio, *Queen Anna's New World of Words* (1611), cited in Bray, *Homosexuality in Renaissance England*, p. 53.

62   **mankind or beast**: 'An Act for the Punishment of the Vice of Buggery', cited in Kenneth Borris (ed.), *Same-Sex Desire in the English Renaissance: A Sourcebook of Texts, 1470–1650* (New York, 2004), p. 87.

62   **preposterous amor**: John Bale, *The Acts of the English Votaries* (1560), cited in ibid., p. 25.

62–63   **detestable and abominable; not to be named**: Edward Coke, *The Third Part of the Institutes of England* (1644), cited in ibid., p. 97.

63   **horrible vice; that nature abhorreth**: Antonio de Corro, *A Theological Dialogue Wherein the Epistle to the Romans is Expounded* (1575), cited in ibid., p. 23.

63   *res in re*: Coke, *Institutes*, cited ibid., p. 97.

63   **wickedness of life**: cited in E. R. C. Brinkworth, *Shakespeare and the Bawdy Court of Stratford* (Chichester, 1972), p. 13.

64   **burn [. . .] in love**: Ovid, *Metamorphoses*, p. 299.

65   **infant king**: Virgil, 'Pastoral IV', trans. John Dryden (1697) in *The Works of Virgil* (London, 1903), pp. 460–1.

66   **thy soul possessed**: Virgil, 'Pastoral II,' in ibid., pp. 451–54.

66   **ill-formed friendship**: Erasmus, *On the Method of Study* (1512), cited in Andrew Wallace, *Virgil's Schoolboys: The Poetics of Pedagogy in Renaissance England* (Oxford, 2010), pp. 111–12.

67   **saviour Christ's Alexis**: cited in Arthur Freeman, *Thomas Kyd: Facts and Problems* (Oxford, 1967), pp. 181–83.

67   **sinners of Sodoma**: Richard Baines, 'A Note Containing the Opinion of Christopher Marly Concerning his Damnable Judgement of Religion, and Scorn of God's Word' [1593?], in Marie H. Loughlin (ed.), *Same-Sex Desire in Early Modern England, 1550–1735. An Anthology of Literary Texts and Contexts* (Manchester, 2014), p. 316.

67   **never sought for**: *Plutarch's Lives of the Noble Grecians and Romans*, trans. Thomas North (1579), (facsimile, Stratford-upon-Avon, 1928), 8 vols, 2, pp. 107–13.

67   **love of boys**: Plutarch, *Moralia*, trans. Edwin L. Minar, F. H. Sandbach and W. C. Helmbold (Loeb Classical Library, Cambridge, MA, 1961), pp. 311–25.

68   **treatise of Plutarch**: *The philosophy commonly called The Morals, written by the learned philosopher Plutarch of Chaeronea*, trans. Philemon Holland (1603), cited in Bruce Smith, *Homosexual Desire in Shakespeare's England: A Cultural Poetics* (Chicago, 1991, 1994), p. 40.

69   **unlawful fleshliness**: Edmund Spenser, *The Shorter Poems* (ed. by Richard A. McCabe, London, 1999), pp. 38–39.

70   **waves of enjoyment**: Lucian, 'Erotes', in *Works*, trans. M. D. McLeod (Loeb Classical Library, London, 1967), pp. 150–235.

71   **happy and blissful**: translation slightly adapted from Bette Talvacchia, *Taking Positions: On the Erotic in Renaissance Culture* (Princeton, 1999), p. 201.

71   **a Roman work**: Johannes de Witt in the 'Adversaria' of Aernout van Buchell, fols. 131v–132v, Utrecht University special collections online (https://www.uu.nl/en/special-collections/collections/manuscripts/buchelius-booth/adversaria-by-aernout-van-buchell, accessed 30 October 2023).

86   **ever and ever**: Gabriel Harvey, *An Advertisement for Pap-Hatchet and Martin Mar-Prelate* (1589), cited in Reavley Gair, *The Children of Paul's: The Story of a Theatre Company, 1553–1608* (Cambridge, 1982), p. 109.

86   **player-like**: John Marston, *Antonio's Revenge* (1602), 1.5, cited in Andrew Gurr, *The Shakespearean Stage 1574–1642* (Cambridge, 1970, 1980), p. 95.

86   **over-doing**: George Chapman, *The Widow's Tears* (1605), 4.1, cited in ibid., p. 96.

86–87   **churches in England**: Claudius Holyband (Claude Desainliens), *The French Schoolmaster* (1573), cited in Gair, *Children of Paul's*, pp. 35–36.

88–89   **idolatrous heathen poets**: Anon., *The Children of the Chapel Stript and Whipt* (1569), cited in Shen Lin, 'How Old Were the Children of Paul's?', *Theatre Notebook* 45 (1991), pp. 121–31, pp. 123–24.

89   **to inordinate lust**: Stephen Gosson, *The School of Abuse* (1579), cited in Joseph Lenz, 'Base Trade: Theater as Prostitution,' *ELH* 60.4 (1993), pp. 833–55, p. 833.

89   **sodomites, or worse**: Philip Stubbes, *The Anatomy of Abuses* (1583), cited in Jonathan Goldberg, *Sodometries: Renaissance Texts, Modern Sexualities* (Stanford, CA, 1992; New York, 2010), p. 118.

94   **loving woman's part**: Mary Wroth, *The Countess of Montgomery's Urania* (1621), cited in Smith, *Homosexual Desire*, p. 149.

94   **very facial expression**: Henry Jackson, letter of September 1610, Corpus Christi College, Oxford, MS 304, fols. 83v and 84r. Translation by Dana F. Sutton, Shakespeare Documented, Folger Shakespeare Library (https://shakespearedocumented.folger.edu/resource/document/excerpts-henry-jacksons-letter-recording-performance-othello-oxford, accessed 30 October 2023).

95   **strained [themselves]**: Michel de Montaigne, 'Of the force of imagination', in *The Essays of Montaigne. Done into English by John Florio* (1603), cited in Patricia Parker, 'Gender Ideology, Gender Change: The Case of Marie Germain', *Critical Inquiry* 19.2 (1993), pp. 337–64, p. 342.

103   **the masculine gender**: cited in Michael Shapiro, *Gender in Play on the Shakespearean Stage: Boy Heroines and Female Pages* (Ann Arbor, MI, 1996), p. 23.

104   **to abuse them**: William Prynne, *Histrio-mastix* (London, 1633), sigs. Ee2r–v.

104   **ravish a man**: Thomas Middleton, *Father Hubburd's Tales, or The Ant and the Nightingale* (London, 1604), sig. D1r.

104   **of the boys**: Thomas Dekker, *The Gull's Horn-book* (1609) (ed. by E.D. Pendry, Cambridge, MA, 1968), p. 99.

104   **the ladies, claps**: Thomas Killigrew, *The Parson's Wedding* (1672), cited in Thomas A. King, *The Gendering of Men, 1600–1750. Vol 1: The English Phallus* (Madison, WI, 2004), p. 94.

105   **beautiful boys**: John Rainolds, *Th'Overthrow of Stage Plays* (1599), cited in Mary Bly, *Queer Virgins and Virgin Queans on the Early Modern Stage* (Oxford, 2000), p. 77.

105   **in a hot-house**: John Marston, *What You Will*, 3.3.24–25, 39–41.

106   **lewd and dissolute**: Henry Clifton's complaint, 15 December 1601, Star Chamber Proceedings, Elizabeth, Bundle C 46, 39, printed in Irwin

Smith, *Shakespeare's Blackfriars Playhouse: Its History and its Design* (London, 1966), p. 485.

107 **well-singing children**: Nathaniel Giles's commission to impress children, July 1597, Patent Rolls, 39 Elizabeth, part 9, membrane 7, dorso, printed in ibid., p. 482.

107 **mercenary player**: Clifton complaint, pp. 485–86.

114 **boys were fools**: Baines, 'Note', in Loughlin (ed.), *Same-Sex Desire*, p. 316.

115 **reckoning**: Charles Nicholl, *The Reckoning: The Murder of Christopher Marlowe* (London, 1992, 2002).

118 **Juno's unrelenting hate**: Virgil, *Aeneid*, trans. John Dryden (1697), in *The Works of Virgil* (London, 1903), p. 1.

121 **with perpetual felicity**: cited in Alan Stewart, *The Cradle King: A Life of James VI and I* (London, 2003), p. 51.

122 **most amorous manner**: ibid.

122 **inward affection; and kiss him**: cited in ibid., p. 53.

123 **ravening fowl; ESME STEWART DWIKE**: [James Stuart], *The Essays of a Prentice in the Divine Art of Poesy* (Edinburgh, 1584), sigs. H3r and G3r.

125 **in the brothel**: cited in Katherine B. Crawford, 'Love, Sodomy, and Scandal: Controlling the Sexual Reputation of Henry III', *Journal of the History of Sexuality* 12 (2003), pp. 513–42, p. 524.

125 **deceitful Ganymedes**: ibid., p. 526.

125 **his noble seed**: cited in Gary Ferguson, *Queer Re(Readings) in the French Renaissance: Homosexuality, Gender, Culture* (Aldershot, 2008), p. 134.

126 **ever I saw**: cited in Alan Stewart, 'Edouard et Gaverston: New Ways of Looking at an English History Play', in Kirk Melnikoff (ed.), *Edward II: A Critical Reader* (London, 2017), pp. 97–117.

129 **be once perceived; disordered manners; voluptuous pleasure**: The Holinshed Project (1587 edition): Volume 6, pp. 341 and 318 (https://english.nsms.ox.ac.uk/Holinshed/toc.php?edition=1587, accessed 31 October 2023).

131 **incestuous shameless Ganymede**: Michael Drayton, *England's Heroical Epistles* (London, 1597, 1598), sigs. D2v–D3r. He also told the story in *The Legend of Piers Gaveston* (1593–4) and *Mortimeriados. The Lamentable Cruel Wars of Edward the Second and the Barons* (1596).

131 **bewitching**: Elizabeth Cary [Falkland], *The History of the Life, Reign and Death of Edward II* (London, 1680), sigs. F1r–v and C1r.

136 **inordinate desires**: The Holinshed Project (1577 edition): Volume 4, p. 1098 (https://english.nsms.ox.ac.uk/Holinshed/texts.php?text1=1577_5321, accessed 31 October 2023).

144   **plagues are plays:** sermon delivered by Thomas White, 3 November 1577, cited in Gair, *The Children of Paul's*, p. 5.

145   **all but toys**: Thomas Nashe, *Summer's Last Will*, in Wells (ed.), *Thomas Nashe*, p. 129.

146   **heathenical pamphlets**: Philip Stubbes, *The Anatomy of Abuses* (1583), cited in Ian Frederick Moulton, *Before Pornography: Erotic Writing in Early Modern England* (Oxford, 2000), p. 83.

147   **pleasant fables:** Thomas Peend, *The Pleasant Fable of Hermaphroditus and Salmacis* (London, 1565), in Sophie Chiari (ed.), *Renaissance Tales of Desire* (Newcastle-upon-Tyne, 2012).

147   **delectable discourses**: 'Scylla's Metamorphosis: interlaced with the unfortunate love of Glaucus; whereunto is annexed the delectable discourse of the discontented satire; with sundry other most absolute poems and sonnets', Thomas Lodge, *Scylla's Metamorphosis* (London, 1589), title page.

148   **instead of pleading**: Hall, *Quo Vadis?*, sigs. B2v–B3r.

148   **variety of learning:** James Orchard Halliwell (ed.), *The Autobiography and Correspondence of Sir Simonds D'Ewes, Bart., During the Reigns of James I and Charles I*, 2 vols (London, 1845), 1, p. 147.

148   **by his companion**: Thomas Wroth, 'Advice to a Templar', Folger Shakespeare Library, Washington D.C., MS V.a.575, fol. 1v (translation of Latin tag: '*Noscitur ex socio, qui non cognoscitur ex se*').

148   **device of friendship**: Desmond Bland (ed.), *Gesta Grayorum, or the History of the High and Mighty Prince Henry of Purpoole Anno Domini 1594* (Liverpool, 1968), p. 35.

149   **the Augustine nuns**: in a manuscript collection compiled *c.*1603, British Library Additional MS 22601, fols. 43v–48v.

149   **these several lines**: cited in Moulton, *Before Pornography*, p. 47.

150   **pleasant and delectable**: Ovid, *Metamorphoses*, p. 3.

152   **Court and Chancery**: Lodge, *Scylla's Metamorphosis*, sig. Aor.

154   **breasts of girls**: Ovid, *Metamorphoses*, p. 299.

154   **prodigious lusts**: ibid., p. 11.

157   **wanton Adonis**: cited in *Shakespeare's* Poems, ed. by Katherine Duncan-Jones and H. R. Woudhuysen (London, 2007), p. 6.

157   *Venus and Adonis*: cited in Katherine Duncan-Jones, 'Much Ado with Red and White: The Earliest Readers of Shakespeare's *Venus and Adonis* (1593)', *The Review of English Studies* 44.176 (1993), pp. 479–501, p. 490.

158   **sweet Master Shakespeare**: Anon., *Return from Parnassus, Part 1*, cited in ibid., p. 498.

158 **wanton pamphlets; marrow-bone pies**: Thomas Middleton, *A Mad World, My Masters* (ed. by Peter Saccio), 1.2.47–48, in Gary Taylor and John Lavagnino (eds), *Thomas Middleton: The Collected Works* (Oxford, 2007).

161 *Henrico Comiti Southamtoniae*: John Clapham, *Narcissus. Siue amoris iuuenilis et præcipue philautiæ breuis at que moralis descripto* (London, 1591), sig. A3r.

165 **lovers of poets**: cited in G. P. V. Akrigg, *Shakespeare and the Earl of Southampton* (London, 1968), p. 37.

165 **plays every day**: cited in Lara M. Crowley, 'Was Southampton a Poet? A Verse Letter to Queen Elizabeth,' *English Literary Renaissance* 41.1 (2011), pp. 111–45, p. 130.

165 **name in Arts**: cited in ibid., p. 124.

166 **play wantonly**: cited in Duncan-Jones, 'Much Ado with Red and White', p. 485.

167 **wiser**: cited in *Shakespeare's Poems*, p. 44.

173 **Night of Errors**: Bland (ed.), *Gesta Grayorum*, p. 32.

174 **goddess chaste**: Sonnet V, Samuel Daniel, *Delia. Containing certain sonnets, with the complaint of Rosamond* (London, 1592), sig. B3r.

175 **wit cannot endite**: Sonnet III, Edmund Spenser, *Amoretti and Epithalamion* (London, 1595), sig. A3r.

176 **private friends**: Francis Meres, *Palladis Tamia: Wit's Treasury* (London, 1598), sig. Oo2r.

177 **glass of divinity**: Amour 23, Michael Drayton, *Idea's Mirror: Amours in Quatorzains* (London, 1594), sig. D4r.

177 **thy sacred eyes**: Amour 2, in ibid., sig. B1v.

186 **throat most wickedly**: *Salopian Shreds and Patches* (1885), cited in Andrew Worrall, 'Biographical Introduction: Barnfield's Feast of "all Varietie"', in Kenneth Borris and George Klawitter (eds), *The Affectionate Shepherd: Celebrating Richard Barnfield* (Selinsgrove, 2001), pp. 25–40, p. 28.

197 **Chettle praised 'Daphnis'**: Henry Chettle, *Piers Plainness Seven Years Prenticeship* (London, 1595), sig. I2r.

201 **private friends, etc**: Meres, *Palladis Tamia*, sigs. Oo1v–2r.

203 **Master Richard Barnfield**: ibid., sig. Oo4v.

203–4 **Fame die never**: unlineated verse in *Poems in Diverse Humours* (1598), in Klawitter (ed.), *Poems*, p. 171.

206 **a male object**: the view of the editor and critic George Steevens (1736–1800), cited in Pequigney, *Such Is My Love*, p. 30.

213 **fluency and grace**: A. H. Bullen, Introduction, in *An English Garner: Some Longer Elizabethan Poems* (London, 1903), pp. xiv–xv.

216   **it's just Roman**: I've adapted this phrasing from Anne Lake Prescott, 'Barnfield's Spenser: "Great Collin" and the Art of Denial' in Borris and Klawitter (eds), *The Affectionate Shepherd*, pp. 85–98, p. 92.

219   **hath appointed it**: cited in Bernard Capp, *The Ties That Bind: Siblings, Family, and Society in Early Modern England* (Oxford, 2018), p. 6.

219   **your younger brother**: *The Elder Brother*, 3.4.33–34, in Fredson Bowers (ed.) *The Dramatic Works in the Beaumont and Fletcher Canon*, vol. 9 (Cambridge, 1994).

221   **was not happy**: Bullen, *An English Garner*, p. xiv.

221   **any personal feelings**: cited in Worrall, 'Biographical Introduction,' p. 27.

221   **injurious and ungodly**: cited in Capp, *The Ties That Bind*, p. 7.

223   **and universally proscribed**: [Edward Vernon Utterson (ed.)?], *Cynthia* (Beldornie, Isle of Wight, 1841), p. 45.

224   **wretched infidel stuff**: cited in Katherine Duncan-Jones (ed.), *Shakespeare's Sonnets* (London, 1997), p. 69.

228   **satires or epigrams**: cited in Adam Hansen, 'Writing, London, and the Bishops' Ban of 1599', *The London Journal*, 43.2, pp. 102–19, p. 103.

229   **and flat heresy**: cited in ibid., p. 105.

229   **in Love's luxury**: Marston, *Metamorphosis of Pygmalion's Image*, sig. B7r.

231   **issue, and posterity**: Grant of arms to John Shakespeare, 20 October 1596, Shakespeare Documented (https://shakespearedocu-mented.folger.edu/resource/document/grant-arms-john-shake-speare-draft-1, accessed 4 November 2023).

232   **minion and conceit**: cited in Stewart, *Cradle King*, p. 257.

232   **mimics and catamites**: cited in Bray, *Homosexuality in Renaissance England*, p. 55.

233   **never to forgive**: cited in Smith, *Homosexual Desire*, p. 14.

234   **[man] in England**: cited in Stewart, *Cradle King*, p. 265.

234   **to the contrary**: cited in ibid., p. 266.

234   **advancing the beautiful**: 'promovere pulchros', Isaac Casauban [inaccurately ascribed], *Corona Regia* (Leuven [?], 1615), sig. D9v.

235   **as the people**: cited in Stewart, *Cradle King*, pp. 278–79.

235   **hanged for sodomy**: cited in Lisa Jardine and Alan Stewart, *Hostage to Fortune: The Troubled Life of Francis Bacon* (London, 1998), p. 465.

Index

Credit: Sarah M. Lee

Will Tosh is head of research at Shakespeare's Globe, London. He is a scholar of early modern literature and culture, a dramaturg for Renaissance classics and new plays, and a historical adviser for television and radio. He is the author of two previous books, and he appears regularly in the media to discuss Shakespeare and his world. He lives in London.